THE STORIES

WE LIVE BY

THE STORIES

WE LIVE BY

Personal Myths and the Making of the Self

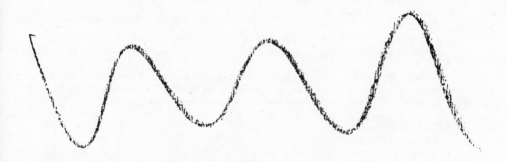

Dan P. McAdams, Ph.D.

THE GUILFORD PRESS   new york and london

For my mother

Grateful acknowledgment is made to the following for permission to quote from their work:
Ruth Krauss, "A Hole Is to Dig: A First Book of First Definitions." Copyright © 1952 by Ruth Krauss, renewed 1989 by HarperCollins. Reprinted with permission of HarperCollins.

James Fowler, *Stages of Faith* (Harper & Row, 1981). Reprinted with permission of HarperCollins.

Karen Horney, *The Adolescent Diaries of Karen Horney* (Basic Books, 1980). Reprinted with permission of HarperCollins.

The Guilford Press
A Division of Guilford Publications, Inc.
72 Spring Street, New York, NY 10012

Printed in the United States of America

This book is printed on acid-free paper

Last digit is print number. 9 8 7 6 5 4 3 2

Library of Congress Cataloging-in-Publication Data

McAdams, Dan P.
    The stories we live by: personal myths and the making of the self
/ Dan P. McAdams.
        p.   cm.
    Originally published: New York: William Morrow & Company, 1993.
    Includes bibliographical references and index.
    ISBN 1-57230-188-0 (pbk. : alk. paper)
    1. Self psychology.   2. Identity (Psychology)   3. Psychology —
Biographical methods.   I. Title
[BF697.M164   1996]
155.2'5—dc21   96-49264
                                                          CIP

Preface (1997)

What do we know when we know a person? What do we know when we think we know ourselves? These are simple but profound questions which most people have wondered about in one way or another, perhaps in the context of their most important relationships, or perhaps in thinking about who they are and what makes their lives make sense. These are also key questions for personality psychologists, like myself, who collect and interpret data on persons and generate meaningful scientific theory about the significance of human lives.

The central idea of this book is a disarmingly simple one: in the modern world in which we all live, *identity is a life story.* A life story is a personal myth that an individual begins working on in late adolescence and young adulthood in order to provide his or her life with unity or purpose and in order to articulate a meaningful niche in the psychosocial world. The emphasis in this book is on *how the story develops,* from birth to old age. I offer a lifespan developmental theory of how modern people create identities through narrative, beginning with the origins of narrative tone in infancy and ending with the midlife and older adult's efforts to craft a satisfying ending for the life story by establishing a generative legacy of the self. The theory I present stems from scientific personality research that I have done and from my reading of a voluminous research and theoretical literature produced by many others in different disciplines.

So, what do we know when we know a person? To begin with, we know something about a person's "traits." Virtually anybody who knows my wife will ascribe to her traits such as "intense," "conscientious," and "warm." As they get to know her better, they might make more nuanced and personalized kinds of statements about her: "She loves classical music but hates opera"; and "She dominates lawyers in the courtroom but turns to mush when our 10-year-old makes her most impetuous demands." But trait attributions and conditional statements can only go so far in describing who my wife is. To know her well, you would need to know her *identity*—that is, you would need to know what it is about her life that provides her with meaning, unity, and purpose. And what provides my wife's life with meaning, unity, and purpose is indeed what provides most modern lives with these qualities. It is a story. To know my wife well, you have to know her life story.

The publication of this paperback version of *The Stories We Live By* by The Guilford Press is a recognition of both the positive response this book has received, and the current influence of the "narrative approach" in psychology and other branches of the social sciences and humanities. In recent years, stories of the self, as described in this book, have become the focus of research in areas as diverse as attachment and critical theory. Even romantic love has been viewed as a story co-authored by lovers.

Amidst all this contemporary scholarship, the distinctive contribution of this book is its focus on the structural details of the life story as they develop over time. As we will see, a life story includes many different features and aspects, including a distinctive narrative tone, personal imagery, thematic lines, ideological settings, pivotal scenes, conflicting protagonists, and an anticipation of the ending to come. Each of these features has its own developmental logic; each arises in salience at a particular point in the human life cycle; and each is fully contextualized in the time, place, and ethos of a given individual's life.

I believe that the major psychosocial challenge facing all of us as modern adults is to make something *good* of our lives in our own time, place, and ethos. To do so, we seek to render our lives into meaningful stories that contribute in generative ways to the stories created by our children, our friends, our neighbors, and even our fellow citizens of the world. To a large extent, the good life is justified by the good story. And the good life story is one of the most important gifts we can ever offer each other.

C O N T E N T S

9

Life and Myth

If you want to know me, then you must know my story, for my story defines who I am. And if *I* want to know *myself*, to gain insight into the meaning of my own life, then I, too, must come to know my own story. I must come to see in all its particulars the narrative of the self—the personal myth—that I have tacitly, even unconsciously, composed over the course of my years. It is a story I continue to revise, and tell to myself (and sometimes to others) as I go on living.

We are all tellers of tales. We each seek to provide our scattered and often confusing experiences with a sense of coherence by arranging the episodes of our lives into stories. This is not the stuff of delusion or self-deception. We are not telling ourselves lies. Rather, through our personal myths, each of us discovers what is true and what is meaningful in life. In order to live well, with unity and purpose, we compose a heroic narrative of the self that illustrates essential truths about ourselves. Enduring human truths still reside primarily in myth, as they have done for centuries.

This book presents a new theory of human identity. The theory is built around the idea that each of us comes to know who he or she is by creating a heroic story of the self. I aim to explore and explain how each of us constructs, consciously and unconsciously, a personal myth. Your myth is unique to you; more than anything else it is what makes you unique. It is not my purpose here to show you how your myth is like somebody else's. I do not believe that we learn much about ourselves by discovering that we are of a certain "type." Instead, each of us must try to comprehend the specific nature of our unique life course and personal journey if we are to know who we are and how our own life may be made most meaningful.

What is a personal myth? First and foremost, it is a special kind of story that each of us naturally constructs to bring together the different parts of ourselves and our lives into a purposeful and convincing whole. Like all stories, the personal myth has a beginning, middle, and end, defined according to the development of plot and character. We attempt, with our story, to make a compelling aesthetic statement. A personal myth is an act of imagination that is a patterned integration of our remembered past, perceived present, and anticipated future. As both author and reader, we come to appreciate our own myth for its beauty and its psychosocial truth.

Though we may act out parts of our personal myth in daily life, the story is inside of us. It is made and remade in the secrecy of our own minds, both conscious and unconscious, and for our own psychological discovery and enjoyment. In moments of great intimacy, we may share important episodes with another person.[1] And in moments of great insight, parts of the story may become suddenly conscious, or motifs we had believed to be trivial may suddenly appear to be self-defining phenomena.

A few popular psychology books written in recent years have argued that the ancient Greek myths provide a set of universal instructions for human living.[2] The authors encourage us to embark upon an intensive psychological journey through which we may perceive and understand the particular gods and goddesses that reside within us. The search for the mythic "hero within," one especially rhapsodic author claims, "takes us eventually to the promised land, where we can be genuinely prosperous, loving, and happy."[3] These popular books, based mostly on clinical anecdote rather than scientific research and theory, present simplified and romanticized portraits of personality types.

I believe that human lives are much too complex for a typological approach, and too socially inflected to support any argument that says the truth resides solely within. I do not believe that there are gods and goddesses within you, waiting to be recognized. We do not discover ourselves in myth; we *make ourselves* through myth. Truth is constructed in the midst of our loving and hating; our tasting, smelling, and feeling; our daily appointments and weekend lovemaking; in the conversations we have with those to whom we are closest; and with the stranger we meet on the bus. Stories from antiquity provide some raw materials for personal mythmaking, but not necessarily more than the television sitcoms we watch in prime time. Our sources are wildly varied, and our possibilities, vast.

The development of personal myth may be traced from infancy to old age. In Chapter 1, I provide a context for my developmental view of personal myths by considering the meaning of stories in human lives. In Chapter 2, I begin with infancy and early childhood. Even before we consciously know what a story is, we are gathering material for the self-defining story we will someday compose. From the early bond of attachment formed with our parents, our first year of life leaves a legacy of optimism or pessimism that will influence the narrative tone we later adopt as adults. A second legacy of our earliest years may be the distinctive emotionally charged imagery we employ in our personal myth, whose roots lie in the fantasy play of preschoolers. The central themes of power and love run as motivational currents through our personal myth in adulthood, and as we see in Chapter 3 their sources may be followed back to the stories we hear, learn, and create in elementary school. In adolescence, we create an ideological setting for our personal myth to situate our story in a context of what we believe to be true and good. Adolescence heralds the beginning of mythmaking proper in the human life cycle, as teenagers begin to see their lives in storied, historical terms (Chapter 4).

Chapters 5 and 6 explore the fashioning and refinement of main characters in personal myth, a process we begin in early adulthood. Main characters work to personify our basic desires for power and for love. These main characters, or internalized "imagoes," may assume such prototypical guises as the warrior, the sage, the lover, the caregiver, the humanist, the healer, and the survivor, among others. The kind of main characters we script into our self-defining stories help determine the quality of our overall identity. Discontent and malaise in our early adult years may often signal problems in the scripting of our characters. As we see in Chapter 7, such problems may also bear on issues of human faith and the quest for meaning.

Chapter 8 considers how personal mythmaking may become more integrative in our middle-adult years and beyond as we seek to bring opposing parts of our story together into a vitalizing and harmonious whole. We also become concerned at mid-life with the anticipated ending of the life story and the new beginnings that we may be able to generate in our work lives, in family, and in community. Effective parenting, teaching and mentoring, long-term friendships, occupational commitments and achievements, creative contributions in the arts and sciences, volunteer work—all of these activities and a host of others, some grand and some humble, can be part of what I call in Chapter 9 the "generativity script" of personal myths. The generativity script links the individual personal myth to the collective stories and myths of society as a whole and to the enterprise of promoting and improving human life and welfare from one generation to the next.

In the book's final chapter, I encourage you, the reader, to begin the exploration of your own personal myth. The last chapter briefly considers ways in which you may identify, live, and change your myth.

The personal myth continues to develop and change through most of our adult years. But some of us, in the last years of our lives, will suspend the making of myth and begin to take final stock of what we have made. The psychologist Erik Erikson describes this last stage in the human life cycle as a time in which we confront the issue of "ego integrity vs. despair."[4] As I see it, to find integrity in life is to look back upon one's personal myth and determine that, for all its shortcomings and limitations, it is good. The perspective is that of the creator looking back upon the fruits of his or her creation and gracefully accepting what has been made. If the creator rejects the creation, the creator experiences despair. The identity is not worth accepting, and it is too late to create a new one.

I suspect that most of us will look back on the creation of our personal myths with a mixture of acceptance and rejection. Until we reach those postmythic days, however, we wait in suspense for the time when each of us must adopt the role of literary critic, and offer the definitive analysis and review of the identity each of us has labored to write and live.

This book is based on scientific research and theory. The "data" have been collected from real people, living and describing real lives. For the most part, these are relatively "normal" people who are not involved in long-term psychotherapy, or hospitalized for psychiatric illness. Over the past thirteen years, I have undertaken a series of psychological research projects while teaching at Saint Olaf College, Loyola University of Chicago, and most recently, Northwestern University. Reports of some of the research have appeared in scientific journal articles and in chapters of professional books written for psychologists and other social scientists.[5] The origins of this book's central argument can be traced to the first chapters of my professional book *Power, Intimacy, and the Life Story*, published in 1985.[6]

Aspects of the research have been supported by numerous small grants from Loyola University of Chicago as well as a sabbatical leave from that university during the winter and spring of 1988. A 1980 grant from the American Lutheran Church supported a study of students' religious-belief systems, described briefly herein. The collection and analysis of new data and the final preparation of the manuscript were made possible by a major grant from The Spencer Foundation, received in the summer of 1990, and by a grant from Northwestern University.

Numerous friends and colleagues have contributed in different ways to the making of this book. My sincerest appreciation goes to the graduate students whom I taught and with whom I worked at Loyola University of Chicago during the years 1986–1989. Among these students were Rachel Albrecht, Ed de St. Aubin, Barry Hoffman, Denise Lensky, Tom Nestor, Julie Oxenberg, Dinesh Sharma, and Donna Van de Water. I would also like to thank Katinka Matson for her unflagging support and Maria Guarnaschelli for her infectious enthusiasm and wise guidance as I labored to write this book. Other people who have been most helpful and encouraging in recent years include Becky Blank, Marcus Boggs, Rodney Day, Bob Emmons, David Feinstein, Bob Hogan, George Howard, Jane Loevinger, Gina Logan, David McClelland, Richard Ochberg, Karen Rambo, Mac Runyan, Janet Shlaes, Abby Stewart, Carol Anne Stowe, David Winter, and most of all, my wife, Rebecca Pallmeyer.

PART I

Making Lives into Stories

This is what fools people: a man is always a teller of tales, he lives surrounded by his stories and the stories of others, he sees everything that happens to him through them; and he tries to live his life as if he were telling a story.

—*Jean-Paul Sartre*

God made man because he loves stories.
—*Elie Wiesel*

CHAPTER 1

The Meaning of Stories

At the age of thirty-five, Margaret Sands made a two-thousand-mile pilgrimage across the country with her teenage daughter in order to break into an abandoned chapel and "rip the place apart."[1] The two of them scaled a Cyclone fence surrounding a former Catholic boarding school for girls. Margaret's daughter pried open a window, squeezed through it, and ran around to the back of the building to open a door and let her mother inside. Twenty-five years had passed since Margaret left the school. Everything looked smaller to her now, but the smell was a familiar one she had always associated with primitive loathing and fear.

Margaret brazenly pushed her way to a place no women had been allowed—behind the altar. She kicked the walls and punched the pulpit and the pews. She made blasphemous gestures to the cross and the icons. With her car keys, she carved out two rough inscriptions on the chapel's great wooden doors: "I hate nuns" and "They beat children." Then, she calmly told her daughter, "We can leave now."

After visiting relatives and old friends, Margaret drove back to Chicago having accomplished a mission of extraordinary personal significance. What for others might be an act of petty vandalism was for her a sacred ritual grounded in a personal myth—a tragic and heroic story of "a wasted life," in Margaret's words, but one that affirms hope, progress, and the promise of triumph in the face of a neglecting and abusive world.

I heard this story because Margaret volunteered to participate in a social-science research study in the fall of 1986. I ask people to tell me the stories of their lives because I believe their verbal accounts hold the outlines of internalized personal myths. I know that not everything people tell me is important, and that some of what they say may function merely to make them "look good" in my eyes. I also know that there is much that will remain untold, no matter how successful our interview and how intimate our rapport.[2] But an individual does not suddenly invent a personal myth in the course of an interview. The myth is there all along, inside the mind. It is a psychological structure that evolves slowly over time, infusing life with unity and purpose. An interview can elicit aspects of that myth, offering me hints concerning the truth already in place in the mind of the teller.

Margaret's interview is filled with accounts of the dramatic events in her life. Amid the many poignant and frightening scenes, the numerous villains, and one or two heroines, I listen closely for the self-defining myth—the kernel of the narrative that I believe most clearly characterizes her identity as an adult. The myth itself is embedded in the complicated series of accounts. It is the *central* story behind the various episodes she tells me.

She begins her interview with the same kind of solemn resolve I imagine it took to walk up to the altar and defy her Catholic past. "I was born on July 21, 1941, in San Diego, California, and at age forty-five, I do not believe very strongly in my foundation as a human being." Margaret tells a story about foundations, weak and strong, the hidden and indispensable support structures that lie at the base of human lives.

According to her personal myth, childhood failed to provide Margaret with a foundation steadfast enough to sustain her growth and assure her happiness. At the very end of her two-hour interview, Margaret concludes, "You can't tamper with a foundation and have expectations about being a fulfilled human being." Still, she seeks to undo some of the damage wrought on her own life by giving her daughter what she never had. If she cannot repair the fissures within her own soul, she can at least provide a strong enough foundation to enable her child—a child she once almost gave away—to have a chance to become stable, happy, and fulfilled in her own life. Margaret's suffering and Margaret's gift are inextricably linked in her personal myth. *Because* she hurts so much, she tries to shield her daughter from the same pain.

"The setting was set for stress before I was born," Margaret remarks. Her mother was a beautiful, brilliant, and hopelessly naive writer and actress when she married a heavy-drinking opera singer nineteen years her senior. She was upper-middle-class and "half Jewish." He was Protestant and had been married once before. Her parents strongly opposed the marriage, but she found the man dashing and sophisticated. The two planned to achieve stardom in Hollywood.

Margaret remembers little from the first four years of her life, but knows her parents divorced when she was four and a half years of age. At that time, Margaret's mother decided to take up a new career in real estate, and on the advice of a local priest, sent her daughter to an elite Catholic boarding school. Thus began a chapter of life Margaret calls "The Institutionalization of a Human Being—Age Five to Ten," the five horrendous years that destroyed her foundation. While she received a good academic education, Margaret reports that she was regularly beaten, abused, and humiliated by the nuns. During these years, her mother also suffered from serious illnesses, including recurrent respiratory problems. "She had a hole in her lungs; her foundation was also not very good," Margaret remarks. Because of her illness, she was rarely able to visit her daughter. "I was imprisoned for five years; I was abandoned and left with pathetic old women; those years have haunted me ever since."

Margaret remembers with crystal clarity the day she was released from boarding school. Her mother's health had improved, and they journeyed back to Chicago to live with Margaret's grandparents. To Margaret's horror, her mother passed up the good local schools in the heavily Jewish neighborhood where they now lived and sent Margaret to another boarding school. Margaret describes the second school as a "dumping ground for street people and incorrigible youth. . . . I was abused by the other kids. They stole my record collection. They stole all my things." After a year and a half, she ran away from the new school. She ended up in downtown Chicago at a Walgreens drugstore. She ate a bowl of chili at the lunch counter before calling her mother on the pay phone and threatening to never come home again if not released from the boarding school at once. "I blackmailed her," Margaret says, at the age of twelve. This was the first major showdown in Margaret's life, and she prevailed.

Margaret expresses considerable anger and bitterness about men and women in authority during her childhood years, including neglectful neighbors, hypocritical teachers, and the abusive nuns. She substitutes pity for conscious rage, however, when considering her own mother. She sees her mother as a hapless victim, whose fragile health and weakened will composed *her* own faulty foundation. While the nuns abused her and the children stole her belongings, Margaret seemed to be headed for the same helpless fate. But adolescence and young adulthood herald an emerging assertive self, a "hell-raiser," as Margaret describes it. Unlike her mother, "I'll give it all. Whatever I do, I know I will always leave a mark."

If the drugstore phone call was the first concrete indication of Margaret's defiant self, her confrontation with an adoption agency marks a second and even more significant victory. Unmarried, twenty-one years old, and pregnant, Margaret was pressured by family and friends to give her baby up for adoption. Once the baby was born, she agreed to house the baby in a private agency for two weeks, after which time she would sign the adoption papers. But when the time came, she could not sign them. The agency officials furiously tried to convince her to go through with the plan, but Margaret would not give in. She screamed at the authorities to give her baby back to her. They cursed her and tried to humiliate her, but finally had to relent. Again Margaret prevailed. "This determined an awful lot of the rest of my life," she says.

That life has revolved around relationships with her daughter and her ailing mother. She has been a caregiver for both of them. Margaret has never married, though she and her daughter's father for a time claimed to be married in order "to keep up appearances." She has been sexually involved with a few men and at least one woman in the intervening years, but she has carried on these "affairs" in secret as a way of keeping them from occupying center stage in her personal myth. Relationships based on long-term sexual and intimate commitments require a firm personal foundation. Margaret will never have this, she insists. The only commitment she can possibly sustain, therefore, is to her daughter—the commitment to care and foundation building that defines her adult strivings.

In 1970, "my mother died in my arms," she says, after suffering a sudden heart attack at home. Sixteen years later, Margaret still cries when she speaks of her mother. Her daughter graduated from high school and moved out on her own a few years ago, planning to pursue a career in one of the helping professions (as a nurse or social worker, for example). Margaret feels that she is still working to provide her daughter with the firm foundation she never had.

Professionally, Margaret has worked as a magazine editor, office manager, and sales representative. Her political interests were galvanized by the women's movement in the 1970s, and she did a great deal of volunteer work for various women's organizations during that time. While she now fears that her future seems too hazy, she would eventually like to make a substantive contribution in the area of "women's health." This would probably require her to return to college and obtain, at minimum, a bachelor's degree. Most American women, even one possessing the extraordinary determination Margaret displays, would not find it feasible to retool for a new career in their late forties. It is difficult to predict precisely what Margaret's next move will be within the narrative framework she has established for her life.

The psychological tests we administered to Margaret suggest that she consciously regards herself as a nontraditional woman who has defied the cultural stereotypes of femininity in order to make a strong mark on her world. On a measure of "sex roles," she describes herself as especially "independent," "aggressive," and "individualistic," adjectives typically associated with cultural stereotypes of masculinity.[3] On a more subtle measure of psychological motivations, however, Margaret reveals an extremely strong *need for intimacy*—a desire to engage others in warm, close, and sharing interaction. Women typically score somewhat higher than men on intimacy motivation, but even by women's standards Margaret's score is very high.[4] Her score on the *need for power* is surprisingly low, suggesting that for all her conscious insistence she is aggressive and individualistic, she is not strongly driven by concerns for individual power in her life.

Margaret has provided her life with unity and purpose by creating a tragic personal myth about her struggles to undo a horrible past through assertive action and gentle caring. The story contains many setbacks and failures, but at least she seems to recognize two significant achievements. First, she has provided her daughter with the foundation she never had. Second, she has taken her symbolic revenge on the nuns. Desecrating the chapel may have been the first important step in recasting her personal myth in self-fulfilling terms. But we can see that more mythmaking needs to be done.

From the standpoint of her own psychosocial development, we might suggest that Margaret devote her considerable creative energies to the enterprise of rebuilding her identity, to take into account the fact that she has helped build another's identity—her daughter's. Now that her daughter has moved away, Margaret may find that she has time in her life to repair her own foundation, this time from a position of relative strength. Her story shows that she can persevere. She is not the fragile innocent her mother was. She is a hardened survivor who has transcended her circumstances.

Margaret needs to reformulate the narrative of her life so that the story better recognizes her heroic achievements. This might enable her to reach a reconciliation with her past, and propel her forward with energy and direction toward a future she would be proud to create. I believe that hers will always be a tragic myth. But it may become a myth that will inspire others and, indeed, inspire Margaret herself, to find deeper satisfaction than she ever could have imagined possible that lonely afternoon at the Walgreens lunch counter, when she was poised to take control of her life for the very first time at the age of twelve.

What Is a Story?

My six-year-old daughter knows what a story is. She is not, of course, able to give me a formal definition that would satisfy an academic, but she knows a story when she hears one. When I read to her two different unfamiliar passages, five minutes in length, one a folktale about a boy with magical powers, and the other a set of instructions for a children's game, she has no trouble identifying the first as a story. The second—also written to be interesting and entertaining to children—she says, is "something else," and "not as much a story." In six years she has already developed a sense of *story grammar*.[5]

She expects, as we all learn to expect, that a story will have certain consistent features. First we know that a story has a *setting* of some kind, which we normally discover early on. " 'Twas the night before Christmas, when all through the house . . ." immediately locates us in a time and place, preparing us for a Yuletide story. "Once upon a time in a faraway place" tells us the most important thing about the setting is that it is out of the ordinary. Not all stories develop their settings—while some evoke vivid associations of particular times or places, others move briskly through the where and when to get to the main action. Where the setting is ambiguous, a story may seem confusing or disconcerting. Samuel Beckett exploits this effect in *Waiting for Godot*. The setting for this story is a blasted landscape beside a road and a single tree. Such a setting could be anywhere, and casual references to the Eiffel Tower and some prior catastrophe lead us to the jarring conclusion that the location may be in a devastated Europe. But Beckett's provision of such a limited context within which to place events is unusual. His play violates some of our assumptions about the structure of stories in a way my six-year-old (and I suspect many of us) may not fully expect or appreciate.

A second expectation is that a story will have human or humanlike *characters*. At the beginning of a story, until something happens, a character exists in a kind of equilibrium. Before anything happens, we will often learn certain basic things about the character, such as what he or she looks like, how old he or she is, and so on. Eventually, there is an *initiating event*. In a well-known fairy tale, the mother sends Little Red Riding-Hood off to take care of her grandmother, and the action of the story begins. The initiating event motivates the character to make the *attempt*, the effort to attain a certain goal. The character intends to reach the goal smoothly, but inevitably a Big Bad Wolf (or his equivalent) is waiting along the path.

When Little Red Riding-Hood meets the wolf, the "plot thickens." In terms of story grammar, we see that the attempt leads to the *consequence*. The wolf is the consequence of Little Red Riding-Hood's attempt to carry the cakes to her grandmother. Her *reaction* is to divulge the location of the grandmother's cottage. Now the grandmother is also in danger, and our expectations for the story extend forward to future episodes in which the two main characters will face each other down. Little Red Riding-Hood intends to carry the cakes, but the wolf intends to eat her. Their differing intentions will necessarily bring them into conflict.

Each episode of a story may be seen as a sequence of the elements I have just described. An initiating event leads to an attempt. The consequence gives rise to a reaction. One episode follows another, each containing the same structural sequence.[6] Episodes build, and the story takes form.

Within this basic structure, there are by now innumerable literary devices and conventions to enhance a story's mounting tension, and enrich the ways in which different episodes relate to each other. For example, an author may use flashbacks to inform us halfway through a story that our middle-aged hero was abandoned by his parents shortly after birth. Through the use of shifting perspectives, an author may relate the same events through the competing points of view of different protagonists or observers. Trivial early events may foreshadow momentous later ones.

As tension builds across the many episodes of a story, we experience a desire for an eventual resolution. Aristotle proposed that the tension increases to a climax, a high or turning point in the drama. What follows soon afterward is the solution of the plot, called the *denouement*.

In Little Red Riding-Hood, tension mounts as we move through the woods to Grandmother's house, where the wolf, in Granny's nightgown, awaits the girl. The first-time listener feels suspense and curiosity—two indispensable emotions in a good story.[7] The wolf eats the girl and falls asleep. A woodsman arrives, and chops open the wolf's stomach to rescue the little girl and her grandmother. Following this climactic event is the denouement. Amazingly, the wolf is still sleeping. The woodsman fills the wolf's empty gut with boulders. When he wakes, the wolf falls down dead from the weight. Little Red Riding-Hood returns home, and with her return the story ends. The ending brings us back to the place of the beginning, but Little Red Riding-Hood has changed—as have we.

If you pay close attention to the kinds of things you hear and say in a normal day, you may be surprised to learn how much of your experience involves stories. Watching television, we observe an endless series of stories in a multitude of forms. Situation comedies from *I Love Lucy* to *Roseanne* are structured as relatively simple stories with well-defined settings, initiating events, attempts, consequences, and reactions. The comic climax is followed by a rapid denouement. After a commercial break, a brief upbeat conclusion brings the story "home" again.

Serials like *All My Children* and *L.A. Law* consist of a series of overlapping and intersecting stories. The writers of these shows do not want to resolve everything in the course of a single episode. They hope to keep viewers interested over a series of shows by extending plots, and sustaining their tensions, from one week to the next. Even game shows and nightly news reports are structured, to a certain extent, like stories.[8] We watch an episode of a game show to see who, in the end, will win. Many news items are presented as ministories, each with a setting, characters, and plot. Less obviously, the anchormen and anchorwomen, the sportscaster, and the weather expert take us on a narrative journey and then return us home "safe and sound" with upbeat human-interest stories or lighthearted commentaries at the very end of the newscast. They hope to leave us smiling, resolved, and more likely than before to return to the program again.

Beyond our TV viewing, we encounter all kinds of stories in everyday social activities. We tell them to friends, acquaintances, and strangers. We hear them at the office, in classrooms, at home, while shopping, playing, eating, and drinking. We dream stories, or at least we make sense of dreams by casting them in a narrative form. We confer upon the world and our conduct in it a storied quality.

The Narrating Mind

Human beings are storytellers by nature. In many guises, as folktale, legend, myth, epic, history, motion picture and television program, the story appears in every known human culture. The story is a natural package for organizing many different kinds of information. Storytelling appears to be a fundamental way of expressing ourselves and our world to others.

Think of the last time you tried to explain something really important about yourself to another person. Chances are you accomplished this task by telling a story. Or think of an especially intimate conversation from your past. I suspect that what made the conversation good was the kind of stories that were told and the manner in which the stories were received. Indeed, much of what passes for everyday conversation among people is storytelling of one form or another. This appears to be so pervasively true that many scholars have suggested that the human mind is first and foremost a vehicle for storytelling.[9] We are born with a narrating mind, they argue.

Imagine our ancient ancestors at day's end, in that ambiguous interlude between the victories and defeats of the daylight and the unseen dangers and deep sleep of the dark. Home from the hunt, or resting at the end of a day's foraging for food, providing for the young, and preserving the tribe, our primordial forebears sit down together and take stock. Before night falls, they tell stories of the day. They pass the time by making sense of past time. They tell of their experiences to entertain and enlighten one another and, perhaps, on occasion, just to stay awake. E. M. Forster, the novelist and essayist, once speculated:

> Prehistoric man listened to stories, if one may judge by the shape of his skull. The primitive audience was an audience of shock-heads, gaping round the campfire, fatigued with contending against the mammoth or the woolly rhinoceros, and only kept awake by suspense. What would happen next?[10]

Stories told at day's end create a shared history, linking people in time and event as actors, tellers, and audience. The unfolding drama of life is revealed more by the telling than by the actual events told. Stories are not merely "chronicles," like a secretary's minutes of a meeting, written to report exactly what transpired and at what time. Stories are less about facts and more about meanings. In the subjective and embellished telling of the past, the past is constructed—history is made. History is judged to be true or false not solely with respect to its adherence to empirical fact. Rather, it is judged with respect to such narrative criteria as "believability" and "coherence." There is a narrative truth in life that seems quite removed from logic, science, and empirical demonstration. It is the truth of a "good story." In the words of one writer, this is a form of truth with which our ancient ancestors were intimately familiar:

> No one in the world knew what truth was till someone had told a story. It was not there in the moment of lightning or the cry of the beast, but in the story of those things afterwards, making them part of human life. Our distant savage ancestor gloried as he told—or acted out or danced—the story of the great kill in the dark forest, and that story entered the life of the tribe and by it the tribe came to know itself. On such a day against the beast we fought and won, and here we live to tell the tale. A tale much embellished but truthful even so, for truth is not simply what happened but how we felt about it when it was happening, and how we feel about it now.[11]

The psychologist Jerome Bruner has argued that human beings understand the world in two very different ways.[12] The first he calls the "paradigmatic mode" of thought. In the paradigmatic mode, we seek to comprehend our experience in terms of tightly reasoned analyses, logical proof, and empirical observation. In the second, "narrative mode" of thought, we are concerned with human wants, needs and goals. This is the mode of stories, wherein we deal with "the vicissitudes of human intention" organized in time.

Masters of the paradigmatic mode try to "say no more than they mean."[13] Examples are scientists or logicians seeking to determine cause-and-effect relationships in order to explain events and help predict and control reality. Their explanations are constructed in such a way as to block the triggering of presuppositions. Theoretical constructs do not encourage differences of opinion; instead, a theory proposes an unambiguous objective truth. Such a theory can be tested, and either supported or disproven. Vague formulations are of little use to paradigmatic thinkers, as there is no rigorous method available to test the relative truth of a vague idea. Much of our educational training reinforces the paradigmatic mode.

For all of its power and precision, however, the paradigmatic mode is a strangely humbler form of thought than story making. It is not able to make much sense of human desire, goals, and social conduct. Human events are often ambiguous, and resistant to paradigmatic efforts to understand them. By contrast, good poets and novelists are masters of the narrative mode. Their stories are especially effective when, in Bruner's words, they "mean more than they can say."[14] A good story triggers presuppositions. We have all had the experience of comparing with a friend what we "got out" of a good movie, play or novel, only to learn that the two of us have read or understood the same story in very different ways. This is part of the fun and value of stories, for they give us differing ideas and opinions around which to have conversations and arguments. Good stories *give birth* to many different meanings, generating "children" of meaning in their own image.

In the narrative mode of thought, we seek to explain events in terms of *human actors striving to do things over time.* I might attempt to explain a friend's unusual behavior in terms of what I think he wants in life and why he has been unable to get it. My account may go back in time to frustrations he experienced three years ago with his wife. To understand him, I say, you must know the story I am going to tell. Similarly, we must hear the story of a troubled childhood to understand why one thirty-five-year-old law-abiding woman drove two thousand miles to desecrate an abandoned chapel.

Human experience is storied because of the way most of us comprehend such human actions as being organized in time. Indeed, our characteristic perspective on time may be most responsible for our fascination with, and aptitude for, stories. The philosopher Paul Ricoeur writes that "time becomes human time to the extent it is organized after the manner of narrative; narrative in turn is meaningful to the extent it portrays the features of temporal existence."[15] What Ricoeur means is that human beings tend to comprehend time in terms of stories. As time passes, events happen. But events do not happen randomly—actions lead to counteractions; attempts, to consequences. For many of us, time seems to move forward, and through its forward trajectory human beings change, grow, give birth, die, and so on. There is development and growth as well as death and decay.

When we comprehend our actions over time, we see what we do in terms of a story. We see obstacles confronted, and intentions realized and frustrated over time. As we move forward from yesterday to today to tomorrow, we move through tensions building to climaxes, climaxes giving way to denouements, and tensions building again as we continue to move and change. Human time is a storied affair.

Stories That Heal

We are drawn to stories for many reasons. Stories entertain us, make us laugh and cry, keep us in suspense until we learn how things will turn out. Stories instruct. We learn how to act and live through stories; we learn about different people, settings, and ideas.[16] Aesop's fables and the parables of Jesus suggest lessons—some simple and some profound—about good and bad behavior, moral and immoral ways of conducting our lives, dilemmas concerning what is right and what is wrong. Stories help us organize our thoughts, providing a narrative for human intentions and interpersonal events that is readily remembered and told. In some instances, stories may also mend us when we are broken, heal us when we are sick, and even move us toward psychological fulfillment and maturity.

The psychoanalyst Bruno Bettelheim wrote eloquently about the psychological power of children's fairy stories.[17] Bettelheim believed such tales as "Jack and the Beanstalk" and "Cinderella" help children work through internal conflicts and crises. When a four-year-old girl listens to the story of Cinderella, Bettelheim suggests, she may unconsciously identify with the heroine's frustration and sadness and her eventual triumph. Similarly, a child may identify with a male hero like Jack, who faces the menacing giant but eventually outwits him and escapes much the richer and wiser. The protagonists of these stories are unassuming children, like the listeners. Their deeply felt fears and concerns match closely the unconscious fears lurking in the hearts of children.

In Bettelheim's view, the fairy tale speaks softly and subtly to the child, promoting psychological growth and adaptation. The fairy tale encourages the child to face the world with confidence and hope. Cinderella and Jack live happily ever after. Wicked stepsisters and ogres are punished in the end. Things have a way of working out, even when they look terrifying.

As adults, we may identify just as strongly with the protagonist of a story, experiencing episodes vicariously and emerging from a narrative encounter happier, better adjusted, more enlightened, or improved in some way. In his best-selling book *When Bad Things Happen to Good People*, Rabbi Harold Kushner tells many true stories

the culture of a particular group of people. Such stories may be deemed sacred, and we reserve for them the term *myth*. In religious societies myths are believed to *embody* primordial characteristics of reality, and thus are distinguished from legends or other less sacred forms of stories. Traditional myths concern transcendent beings, such as gods, spirits, and larger-than-life nobles and heroes like Oedipus.[24]

Myths incorporate archetypal symbols that remain viable today if our imaginations are active enough to make us conscious of, and curious about, our origins and our destiny.[25] Myths capture a given society's basic psychological, sociological, cosmological, and meta-physical truths. A society's myths reflect the most important concerns of a people. By giving narrative form to a diverse collection of elements, they help to preserve the society's integrity and assure its continuity and health.[26]

What myths traditionally have done on the level of culture, a personal myth can accomplish for a human being.[27] A personal myth delineates an identity, illuminating the values of an individual life. The personal myth is not a legend or fairy tale, but a sacred story that embodies personal truth.

To say that a personal myth is "sacred" is to suggest that a personal myth deals with those ultimate questions that preoccupy theologians and philosophers. Many social commentators argue that Americans and Europeans live in a demythologized world; many of us no longer believe in an orderly universe governed by a just God. In the midst of this existential nothingness, we are challenged to create our own meanings, discover our own truths, and fashion the personal myths that will serve to sanctify our lives.

Despite the demythologized world Margaret Sands faces, she never gives up in her struggle to find unity and purpose in her life. She must wrench meaning out of the many difficult years of her past and her uncertain prospects for the future. Bitterly rejecting all organized religion, Margaret calls herself a "flaming agnostic." Yet she often prays to her dead mother and grandmother. The two occupy a sacred space in Margaret's life, as central figures in her personal myth. Her epic pilgrimage to the California chapel was a sacred ritual for her; by cursing the church she was able to affirm her own goodness and the sanctity of her own life. She is becoming able to express, in deed and word, what she believes to be true, good, and beautiful, and to vilify what is, for her, evil and profane.

Fashioning a personal myth is not an exercise in narcissistic delusion, or a paranoid attempt to establish oneself as God. Instead, defining the self through myth may be seen as an ongoing act of psychological and social *responsibility*. Because our world can no longer tell us who we are and how we should live, we must figure it out on our own. The making of a personal myth is a psychosocial quest. As mature adults we are all challenged to structure our needs for power and for love, and to fashion a myth within the social and historical context to which we are ethically and interpersonally beholden.

How Does the Myth Develop?

Even as infants, we gather material for our personal myths. The gathering occurs spontaneously and unconsciously, for the most part, as influences of all kinds come to shape our expectations about life and myth. Before children even know what a story is, they find themselves engaged in experiences that will have an impact on the stories they will someday encounter and construct.

In their first relationships of love and trust, infants develop unconscious attitudes about hope and despair. Babies learn the first unconscious lessons about how the world works and how human beings can be expected to behave. An infant's relationship with mother and father is likely to influence the long-term development of a myth's narrative tone. Every personal myth has a pervasive narrative tone, ranging from hopeless pessimism to boundless optimism. For Margaret Sands, the general tone is pessimistic, as she seeks meaning and purpose within a narrative couched in insecurity and framed in tragic terms.

Preschool children collect the central images that someday will animate their personal myths. Arresting images make stories memorable to children of this age. The plots of many stories may be too hard to grasp *in toto*, but preschoolers remember the images. Four-year-olds make sense of their experience in terms of the emotionally charged symbols and images they collect—representations, for instance, of home and school, mommy and daddy, God and the devil,

Snow White and the Wicked Witch of the West. While much of this early imagery passes into oblivion as children grow up, some significant images and representations survive into adulthood and are incorporated into the personal myth. We catch a glimpse of self-defining imagery in Margaret Sands's return to the chapel. The religious icons and symbols from her childhood are invested with deep feelings of loathing and regret.

As children begin formal schooling, they develop increasingly logical and systematic thought, and they come to appreciate stories as thematically organized wholes. They recognize that story characters are striving to reach certain goals over a period of time. From stories, as well as from other sources, school-age children begin to establish their own motivational patterns. Goals and desires are consolidated into stable dispositions centered on the needs for power and love. These patterns of desire will ultimately be reflected thematically in their personal myths. Motivated by a strong desire for intimacy, Margaret has constructed a personal myth that underscores caregiving and helping others. Yet she is still quite ambivalent about establishing long-term intimate relationships with friends or lovers.

We first become self-conscious mythmakers in our late-adolescent years, when we confront head-on the problem of identity in human lives. The adolescent begins by consciously and unconsciously working through an ideological setting for the myth—a backdrop of fundamental beliefs that situates the story within a particular ethical and religious location. Therefore, the transition from adolescence to young adulthood is an especially significant phase in the development of human identity. A fundamental challenge of mythmaking in adolescence and young adulthood is to formulate personally meaningful answers to ideological questions so that one's identity can be built on a stable foundation. People tend to establish the ideological setting in late adolescence and very early adulthood, and for most the setting remains relatively intact and constant for the rest of their years. Margaret's hardheaded agnosticism provides an ideological setting for her personal myth. It remains today an unquestioned backdrop for the plot of her story.

Young adults in their twenties and thirties concentrate their mythmaking energies on the creation and refinement of main characters. Our myths and our lives are generally too complex to be populated by a single main character. Myths draw their characters from an individual's imagoes, which are internalized complexes of actual or imagined personas. Many personal myths contain more than one dominant imago, as central protagonists within the self interact and sometimes conflict in the making of identity. We see a vivid example of this in the narrative tension between Margaret the caregiver and Margaret the hell-raising rebel. Indeed, the richest and most dynamic personal myths are populated by a number of conflicting and elaborate imagoes. Integrating and making peace among conflicting imagoes in one's personal myth is a hallmark of mature identity in the middle-adult years.

All good stories require a satisfying ending. As we move into and through our middle-adult years, we become increasingly preoccupied with our own myth's denouement. Yet all of us are profoundly ambivalent about the sense of an ending. Few of us are eager to die. Mature identity requires that we leave a legacy that will, in some sense, survive us. Many individuals, at this stage in their lives, refashion their myths to ensure that something of personal importance is passed on. As we see in Margaret's story, a child may come to represent the transmission of something good within the self into the next generation.

As the great mythologist Joseph Campbell has written, "It has always been the prime function of mythology and rite to supply the symbols that carry the human spirit forward, in counteraction to those other constant human fantasies that tend to tie it back."[28] Like the religious and cosmic myths that humankind has created across the ages, a personal myth can carry forward something about humankind that is worth preserving and improving. The stories we create influence the stories of other people, those stories give rise to still others, and soon we find meaning and connection within a web of story making and story living. Through our personal myths, we help to create the world we live in, at the same time that it is creating us.

CHAPTER 2

Narrative Tone
and Imagery

On the first day of my class in developmental psychology, I ask my students to imagine that they are each one day old and that they have been asked by a national magazine to tell a story about their first day of life outside the womb. The exercise urges them to think playfully about what a newborn's experience might be like. It is designed to reveal some of the students' implicit assumptions about human development. I get some pretty amazing accounts. I have had newborn babies still attached to their umbilical cords gaze directly across a crowded room and immediately recognize their fathers, aunts, and distant cousins. (What all these people are doing in the delivery room is beyond me.) Other infants in my class are more primitive. They look out on the world and see nothing but a buzzing and blooming confusion. Or they may see nothing at all, so wrapped up are they in their own private worlds of fantasy and sleep.

Of course, my assignment asks the students to hurry things up. We all know that newborns cannot speak and tell stories. By the time human beings are ready to do these things, they have completely forgotten what the first day of life was like. In fact, the human being seems to be the least hurried of all animal species when it comes to development. At the end of the first day of life, newborn chicks are able to follow a mother hen all around the barnyard. It takes us a year or two before we develop comparable motor skills. But we go much further in our development than do chicks. A chick will never be interviewed by a national magazine to tell his life story, even as a mature adult. It is not until age five or six that a human being has a relatively clear sense of what a story is. It is not until late adolescence or young adulthood that a human being typically begins to think of his or her own life in storied, mythic terms. Before adolescence, we have no life story. We have no identity.

But this does not mean that we construct our identity in adolescence from nothing. Instead, we have been "collecting material" for the story since Day One, even though we don't remember Day One. The years of infancy and childhood provide us with some of the most important raw material for our identities. The first two years of life leave us with an unconscious legacy that especially affects the narrative tone of our story. It is a legacy about hope and trust and about how the world works and how stories are supposed to turn out. And in the next four years of our lives, the unconscious collects a wealth of imagery that we will later make use of to embody the narrative pattern.

Attachment

During the first year of life, the infant develops a bond of love with the mother and other caregivers. Developmental psychologists call this bond *attachment*.[1] Babies are not "attached" in any meaningful sense at birth. This means that they have not yet developed a special relationship of trust and security with the mother, or with anybody else, at that point. Furthermore, there is nothing magical about the first few minutes out of the womb. No immediate "bonding" is taking place at this time, at least not from the infant's point of view.[2] Instead, attachment develops gradually during the first year, passing through predictable stages and sequences. By the time the infant is one year of age, he or she has generally established at least one attachment bond, typically with mother or another primary caregiver. According to some theorists, the establishment of this bond is the single greatest accomplishment of the first year of life.[3] It is a psychosocial landmark around which all subsequent development is oriented.

We begin to see signs of the developing attachment bond around two months of age. At this time, infants begin to make eye contact with other people and show endearing smiles in the presence of others. At first, they are likely to be highly promiscuous in their social overtures. When Uncle Dwight comes to town to see his four-month-old niece for the first time, she may greet him with the warm smile and fascinated stare of a lover. When he comes back to visit again five months later, she may recoil in fear. It is neither his new beard nor his new girlfriend that scares her off. It is rather that she has grown up a lot in the short interim. At nine months of age, she is much choosier about who gets the smiles, the gazes, and the coos. Uncle Dwight is a stranger to her. Most infants develop "stranger anxiety" in the second half of the first year of life. It is normal, and Uncle Dwight should not be insulted. His niece is saving her loving advances for a select few—those familiar persons with whom she feels security and trust.

Child psychiatrist John Bowlby describes attachment as a "goal-corrected system."[4] The system is composed of a number of attachment behaviors. These include smiling, eye contact, crying, following, clinging, and sucking. Each of these behaviors develops according to its own schedule during the first few months of life. Thus babies are able to cry and to suck from the first day onward, but they do not show social smiles until a couple of months later, and they do not begin to crawl and follow people until even later in the first year. In the second half of the first year of life, these various behaviors get organized. They all become part of the attachment system. The formation and development of the system is an instinctive part of human nature.

The system is organized around two goals, one short-term and one long-term. The short-term goal is to assure that the baby and the caregiver remain in close physical proximity. Therefore, each attachment behavior functions according to this goal. Babies will smile or make eye contact in order to warm up an interaction with another person and beckon that person to come closer. They will follow the caregiver to remain close. They may cry as a way of signaling distress, which works to bring the caregiver close again in order to relieve the distress. The various attachment behaviors work together, teaming up with or compensating for each other, in a complex and dynamic synthesis.

The long-term goal of attachment is the survival of the infant. If human babies and mothers were not predisposed to become attached, then babies would not survive. The human infant is so dependent and helpless for so long that some kind of system like attachment must be part of human nature, or else we would all die at very early ages, long before we were able to reproduce and pass our genes down to the next generation. The argument is most compelling when one considers the way of life that human beings have pursued during most of our stay on earth. Paleontologists and anthropologists speculate that for over 95 percent of our evolutionary history human beings lived as hunters and gatherers, moving across the savanna or through the forest in small groups. We survived and flourished through individual cunning and social cooperation. Attachment has traditionally functioned, therefore, to protect infants from predators and other dangers.

By their first birthday, virtually all babies in all human societies are attached. But they are not attached in the same way. A growing body of research suggests that the quality of attachment bonds ranges widely.[5] In studies in which psychologists observe how babies behave when they are briefly separated from their mothers in a laboratory setting, they have identified four different kinds of attachment bonds, sometimes referred to as A, B, C, and D.

The most favored is secure attachment. Babies who manifest this pattern of attachment with their mothers are sometimes called "B-babies." Securely attached infants at age one will, like most one-year-olds of any kind, protest vigorously when separated from their mothers. But when mother comes back from a three- or four-minute separation, she is greeted warmly and with enthusiasm. These infants seem to use their mothers as "secure bases" from which to explore the world. When mother is with them, they move around their environments with great ease and confidence, checking back with mom, with a glance or a smile, to make sure that everything is still okay. For B-babies, mother appears to provide a sense of basic trust. Mother makes the world trustworthy.

Three forms of insecure attachment have been identified. A-babies show an "avoidant" pattern of attachment. They tend not to explore the world as vigorously and confidently as do B-babies when mother is available as a base. If mother leaves for a short period and then returns, A-babies may ignore her or rebuff her overtures when she tries to reunite with them. It is as if they were saying, "You left me—OK, I'll leave you!" C-babies show a different pattern of insecurity, called a "resistant" or "ambivalent" pattern. When mother returns after a brief separation, the C-baby may approach her in a friendly manner but then angrily resist being picked up. C-babies are noted for their angry reactions to the caregiver upon her return, though they will also show passive responses reminiscent of A-babies. Finally, D-babies show seriously disturbed and "disorganized" patterns of attachment, characteristic of infants who have suffered repeated physical abuse. These unfortunate babies appear to be confused and disoriented in the presence of mother. Mother is generally unable to calm them down when they are distressed. They do little exploring in her presence.

Research suggests that a majority of one-year-old infants exhibit secure attachment. Approximately two thirds of the babies in studies of middle-class families are classified as B-babies. A-babies and C-babies make up most of the others, composing around 25–30 percent in the samples studied. Thankfully, the D pattern appears to be relatively rare, though we cannot be sure because D-babies were identified in research for the first time only a few years ago.[6] Most of the research has studied first-born babies with their mothers. Most babies, however, develop more than one important attachment bond in the first year. Bonds to fathers, other family members, and baby-sitters may be extremely important in the infant's early development, but scientific research has not explored these relationships in much depth as yet.

There is a great deal of interest in what factors may produce different patterns of attachment. It appears that the quality of interaction between caregivers and the infant in the first few months of life may play an important role. In this regard, one study has shown that mothers of securely attached infants tend to hold their babies more carefully and tenderly and for longer periods of time during early infancy than do mothers of insecurely attached infants.[7] Other studies have suggested that maternal sensitivity may be a consistent predictor of attachment.[8] Observations of mothers and babies at home and in the laboratory during the infant's first three months suggest that mothers of infants who are later classified as securely attached respond more frequently to crying, show more affection when holding the baby, are more likely to acknowledge the baby with a smile or conversation when entering the baby's room, and are better at feeding the baby because of their attention to the baby's signals, compared with mothers of babies later deemed insecurely attached.

Psychologists do not yet know how differences in mother-infant attachment influence the development of personality through adulthood. So far, research on attachment has followed children only through elementary school. These studies, however, suggest that secure attachment at age one is associated with a number of positive outcomes in later childhood. For instance, children who are securely attached at age one tend to show somewhat more pretend play and exploratory behavior at age two than do their peers who are insecurely attached.[9] In nursery school and kindergarten, children securely attached at age one are rated by their teachers as more socially competent, by their peers as more popular, and by observers as showing more dominance and initiative. Therefore, infants who experience a basic trust in their first relationship in life appear to behave in more autonomous and masterful ways in childhood. Secure attachment in infancy may promote the development of a confident and cohesive childhood self.

The Self

Long before adolescence raises doubts about the "real me" behind the many roles I play, each of us knows certainly that the "me" exists in space and time as a causal, continuous, and independent agent. Even as a young child, I know that when I do something it is I who am doing it, that I can cause things to happen in the world, and that I am separate from others who have their own sense of self. If I didn't know these things, life would be next to impossible. Imagine feeling that it isn't you who is moving your arms and legs when you ride a bicycle or drive a car but it is "somebody else." Imagine that when you go to bed this evening, you are not sure that the "you" who will wake up in the morning will be "you." People do experience these kinds of distortions in the self sometimes, in certain altered states of consciousness or perhaps under enormous stress or peculiar circumstances. They are also familiar symptoms of psychoses like schizophrenia. But for most of us, most of the time there exists a basic sense of self that goes unquestioned and assumed.

The search for unity and purpose in life during the adolescent and adult years—the quest to develop one's own personal myth—does not call into question this most fundamental sense of self. Indeed, before a person can develop an identity, he or she must have a basic sense of self to begin with. We must know certainly that we exist as persons with some control and autonomy in the world before we can begin the long process of determining who we are.

Our basic sense of self is consolidated in the first two or three years of life. Many scholars believe that this sense of self takes characteristic form in the context of the developing attachment bond between caregiver and infant.[10] Psychiatrist Daniel Stern suggests that at around eight or nine months of age the infant begins to develop a sense of "subjective self." At this time, the quality of play between mother and infant is likely to change in important ways. Infants begin to share their subjective feeling states with the caregiver. And they seem to expect the caregiver to do the same with them. This is all done without words. For example, the baby may become very excited when he reaches for a toy, and express this excitement with an exuberant "aaaah!" Then he will look at mother to see how she will react. Mother may respond by scrunching up her shoulders and performing a shimmy with her upper body. The shimmy lasts about as long as the baby's "aaaah!" and is equally excited, joyful, and intense. The mother's dance mirrors the baby's "aaaah!" The form is the same for both, even though one is movement and the other is sound.

When mothers and babies respond to each other like this, they are sharing what is inside them at the moment and attempting to match up or attune their emotional states. With subtle artistry, they are adjusting their reactions to each other and affirming each other's experience. In a preverbal way, they are "saying" to each other, "I know what you are going through. I'm experiencing the same thing!" Stern calls this "affective attunement."[11] Through affective attunement, the infant comes to understand better his own and other people's inner states. At a basic preverbal level, he understands that people have separate experiences that they may share with one another and that in the sharing we come to know and to care for each other.

The psychoanalytic theorist Heinz Kohut describes a similar process in the development of the self, using the term "mirroring."[12] In the first year of life, Kohut maintains, the mother's most important role in promoting the development of a cohesive sense of self is to mirror the child's "grandiosity." This means that she must confirm and admire the child's strength, health, greatness, and specialness. She must reflect back and celebrate the child's budding agency and power. The infant needs to experience himself as the apple of his mother's eye. At a basic unconscious level, he needs to believe that mother affirms the goodness and integrity of his own subjective experience. She can be trusted to be there and to applaud, sharing the excitement and the joy that the infant feels in a world made secure and trustworthy by her presence.

Many psychiatric disorders of the self—such as pathological narcissism and fragmentation—may have their origins in faulty mirroring during the first few years of life. These disorders can be extremely severe. In some of them, the individual is unable to develop meaningful relationships with any other people because he or she is devoid of an inner confidence in any inherent personal wholeness, goodness, or vitality. Other less dramatic manifestations are apparent in people who repeatedly suffer from low self-esteem.

Through affective attunement and mirroring, the infant consolidates a sense of subjective self. In the second and third years of life, the child's sense of self expands further. Children come to recognize themselves in mirrors and begin to develop an image of their own face and body.[13] With the advent of language, they begin to apply verbal labels to themselves and others, developing a "verbal self." The verbal self is built upon the subjective self, but does not replace it. For the two-year-old, the verbal self is limited to simple expressions such as one's own name and the color of one's hair. Through childhood, the verbal self becomes more refined and articulated as the child comes to describe him or herself in more and more sophisticated ways. In his descriptions of himself, a three-year-old may say that his name is Jason and he likes to watch *Sesame Street*. A six-year-old may describe herself as a "nice girl" and "best friends with Jennifer." A ten-year-old may know that he is "smart in school," is "a good second baseman but a weak hitter," and tends to "argue with my brother about who should clean up the room on Saturday mornings." Eventually, the verbal self will come to encompass a personal myth.

Narrative Tone

As infants, we are not yet storytellers. But as we experience our first human relationship in attachment and develop a basic sense of self, we are also learning our first lessons about stories. The first two years of life leave us with a set of unconscious and nonverbal "attitudes" about self, other, and world, and about how the three relate to each other. Before we understand what a story is, we have seen how human beings interact with each other and how they try to do things over time. We have experienced our own intentions. We have tried to do things in the world, and we have witnessed the results of our strivings.

The most fundamental relationship between the personal myths we fashion in adulthood and the first two years of our lives may be expressed in what I call narrative tone. While some life stories exude optimism and hope, others are couched in the language of mistrust and resignation. Erik Erikson writes that the enduring legacy of infancy is hope. The infant who experiences the secure and trusting attachment bond with the caregiver moves through childhood and beyond with faith in the goodness of the world and hope for the future. Hope is "the enduring belief in the attainability of fervent wishes."[14] The infant emerges from the first two years of life with an unconscious, pervasive, and "enduring belief" concerning the extent to which wishes, intentions, desires, and dreams are "attainable." Secure attachment reinforces an optimistic narrative tone. It strengthens the unconscious belief that when people try to do things they will ultimately succeed. It proclaims that the world is trustworthy, that it is predictable, knowable, and good. Insecure attachment creates a less hopeful tone. A pessimistic narrative suggests that human beings do not get what they wish for, that human intentions are repeatedly foiled over time. From a more pessimistic perspective, the world is capricious and unpredictable, narratives take unforeseen turns, and stories are bound to have unhappy endings.

Narrative tone is perhaps the most pervasive feature of a personal myth in adulthood. It is a feature of the myth that I begin to see revealed very early on when I interview people and ask them to tell me the stories of their lives. Indeed, we begin to detect it in the very first sentence of Margaret Sands's interview. Narrative tone is conveyed both in the content of the story and in the manner in which it is told. An optimistic story can be optimistic because good things happen, or because, even though bad things happen, the person remains hopeful that things will improve. Similarly, a pessimistic story can be pessimistic because of the series of misfortunes and bad events, or because good things are given a negative cast.

Narrative tone speaks to the author's underlying faith in the possibilities of human intention and behavior. It reflects the extent to which a person dares to believe that the world can be good and that one's place can be more or less secure within it. This belief is prerational, prelogical. People are often not conscious of the childhood origins of their characteristic worldview because it is so familiar a part of their experience. This is not to say that the belief, the faith, cannot be altered. Major life events and developmental change may certainly have an impact on the extent to which we adopt a relatively hopeful or hopeless perspective on life. But the first and, for many of us, the most formative influence on narrative tone seems to be the early developmental course through which we establish a relatively secure or insecure attachment relationship.

Psychologists and common sense tell us that we are generally better off adopting a positive narrative tone than a negative one in creating stories to make sense of our lives. Much has been written in the last thirty years about "the power of positive thinking."[15] It is commonly held that positive thinking can help people recover from illnesses, endure personal hardship, and triumph over a host of other adversities. Though many of these claims are exaggerated, scientific research suggests that some of these popular ideas may indeed be true. Recent research has shown that "dispositional optimism"—"a generalized expectancy that good, as opposed to bad, outcomes will generally occur"—has positive effects on coping with illness.[16] Optimists are more likely than pessimists to take positive steps in their thinking and behavior to confront stress and challenge in life. Apparently, expectations that things will work out well in the end support positive and life-affirming strategies for coping during difficult times.

In her recent book entitled *Positive Illusions,* social psychologist Shelley Taylor garners an impressive body of research and theory to suggest that human beings tend to see their own lives in more positive terms than an objective appraisal would warrant.[17] Many of us repeatedly deceive ourselves into thinking that we are better off than we "really" are, says Taylor. We tend to live by "positive illusions." These illusions tend to work well for us, as long as they are not too extreme. When we believe that life is relatively good and that we are in control of our fate, we tend to cope better with adversity and meet challenges with confidence and hope.

Taylor has examined positive illusions in women who have undergone surgery for breast cancer.[18] Based on intensive interviews of these women and their family members, Taylor concludes that healthy adjustment to threatening life events, like cancer, involves three interrelated themes: the search for meaning, gaining a sense of mastery, and self-enhancement. The search for meaning involves the need to understand why a crisis occurred and what its impact has been. To derive personal meaning from a bad event, one must construct a personal story to make sense of the event. Breast cancer is a complicated disease with many possible causes, most of which remain largely unknown. Physicians find it virtually impossible to pinpoint the exact cause of the cancer in any particular individual. Taylor's research shows that most women eventually develop a story about the origins of their own disease. Many attribute the illness to stress, hereditary factors, or poor diet. Some point to a particular carcinogen to which they may have been exposed. Some suggest a particular event or accident—one of Taylor's subjects believed her breast cancer resulted from being hit by a flying Frisbee! In virtually every case, these women have no real means of knowing why the cancer occurred. They simply reflect the human yearning to make sense of subjective experience through narrative rather than empirical fact.

According to Taylor, successful adaptation to threatening life events involves gaining a feeling of mastery over the event in order to manage it. Again, optimistic illusions prevail: Nobody can be sure a change in life-style will stave off cancer, though such changes may help alter the odds. But by formulating personal stories about the past (cause of illness) and future (mastering the illness), these women were able to assimilate the cancer into their own personal myths. Furthermore, some of the women were able to bolster their self-esteem, further enhancing their ability to cope with the disease, by concentrating on positive images. Some of these also had an illusory quality. A favorite method for accomplishing self-enhancement was to compare oneself to other cancer patients who seemed to be doing poorly. Through downward comparisons like these, a patient might sustain the hopeful belief that she was indeed doing better than most others in similar situations.

We see, therefore, that narrative tone may be applied to many different kinds of stories in life—from narrative explanations of one's disease to the larger personal myths that people create to provide their entire lives with unity and purpose. Some psychologists believe that human beings bias their stories about themselves in a positive direction and that the bias is beneficial.[19] The evidence for this seems most convincing in studies like Taylor's, in which the stories people construct can be readily compared to objective reality. When it comes to personal myths, however, it is a bit more difficult to determine objective reality. Personal myths may indeed be subject to certain positive biases. Nonetheless, tremendous differences in narrative tone can be observed. We draw on the entire spectrum of comic and tragic narrative possibilities in making sense of our own lives.

Mythic Forms

Each of us creates a personal myth that in all its details is like no other story in the world. The different forms our story may take are many. But they may not be limitless. Despite the diversity, there are a finite number of basic story forms that people tend to adopt in creating personal myths. Literary scholars have found useful the discrimination between four very general forms—*comedy, romance, tragedy,* and *irony.*[20] These forms provide a useful scheme for approaching personal myths as well. They help us to understand a myth's overall narrative tone. In simple terms, comedy and romance provide an optimistic narrative tone, while tragedy and irony suggest a pessimistic tone.

Comedy is generally associated with the season of spring. Like spring, it brings the sense that the world is starting afresh and that things will work out. Comic plots, whether or not they are funny, concern how people find happiness and stability in life by minimizing obstacles and constraints. The hero or heroine is typically an ordinary person who seeks the pure and simple pleasures of life. He or she often struggles to get together with others in warm and loving relationships. Comedies often celebrate domestic love. Comic stories typically end in union, as with the proverbial wedding in Shakespearean comedy or in fairy tales such as "Cinderella" and "Sleeping Beauty." The central message of comedy seems to be this: We are each given the opportunity to achieve happiness and to avoid pain and guilt in life. We each have the opportunity to seek a happy ending for the life stories we live and tell.

The romance is just as optimistic. But while comedy affirms the joy of domestic life and love, romance celebrates the excitement of adventure and conquest. The season is summer; the pursuit is hot and passionate. Stories of a hero's exploits, from Homer's *Odyssey* to the modern *Raiders of the Lost Ark,* are the stuff of which romance is made. In this kind of story, the protagonist embarks on a perilous journey, overcomes great obstacles, and triumphs in the end. Other characters in the story either support or oppose the protagonist's quest. The central issue of a romantic myth involves how to move onward from one adventure to the next, with the ultimate goal of emerging victorious and enlightened. Unlike comedy, the romantic hero or heroine is viewed in exalted terms, as somebody who is bolder, wiser, or more virtuous than most everybody else. The message is this: We embark on a long and difficult journey in life in which circumstances constantly change and new challenges continually arise. We must keep changing and moving if we are to win in the end. But we are confident that we will win.

In marked contrast to comedy and romance, tragedy suggests a pessimistic narrative tone. The season is fall—a time of decline and movement toward death. Tragic stories concern gods and heroes dying, falling from grace, sacrificing themselves, and accepting isolation. In the classic tragedy, the hero finds himself or herself separated in some fundamental way from the natural order of things. This separation makes for an imbalance in nature, which is righted only by the tragic hero's downfall. Like Oedipus in the great Greek myth, the tragic hero may be supremely proud, passionate, and of soaring mind; yet these extraordinary attributes are exactly what make for imbalance and eventual ruin. In personal myths, the central tragic issue is avoiding or minimizing the absurdities of life, which threaten to overwhelm even the greatest human beings. As in romance, the hero is exalted, but in this instance as an extraordinary victim and not an adventurous hero. The message: We are confronted by inescapable absurdities in which we find that pain and pleasure, sadness and happiness, are always mixed. Beware. The world is not to be trusted. The best intentions will lead to ruin.

Finally, there is irony, whose season is winter. Included in this category are stories of the triumph of chaos. An ironic myth attempts to sort out the shifting ambiguities and complexities in human existence. The ironic protagonist may assume many forms. One favorite is the successful "rogue" or "fool" who employs satire to expose absurdities and hypocrisy in social convention. Another is the "antihero" of some modern novels, whose world appears to be devoid of opportunities for comedy, romance, or tragic heroism, but instead manifests itself as a puzzle whose solution is forever withheld. In personal myths, irony records failed attempts to solve the mysteries of life. Thus, the narrative tone is pessimistic, and negative emotions such as confusion and sadness predominate. As in comedy, the protagonist is rather common, and not exalted. The message: We encounter ambiguities in life that are larger than we are and that are, for the most part, beyond our comprehension. We must do the best we can.

Each of us draws on every form in constructing our personal myths. No single life story is pure tragedy or pure comedy. Rather, there are narrative mixtures. Each mixture is unique. Most mixtures, nonetheless, emphasize one or two of the forms and minimize the others. Optimistic personal myths tend to adopt comic and romantic formats. Pessimistic narratives prefer tragic and ironic tones. Psychologists do not know exactly why some choose optimistic and others pessimistic forms. It is tempting, of course, to say that narrative tone is determined by the events of a life. If, in general, good things happen to us, then our myth is comic or romantic, and if not, then tragic or ironic. But there is no simple correspondence between narrative tone and life history.

Personal myths involve an imaginative reconstruction of the past in light of an envisioned future. They are subjective creations—illusions, in a sense, whether they be positive or negative. One of the virtues an individual derives from studying his or her myth is in making conscious a personal predilection for viewing the world, which may previously have seemed part of the nature of the world and not of the self.

In infancy we do not yet understand the world in storied, mythic terms. Yet an unconscious attitude about the nature of stories is taking form. In our earliest experiences of attachment and the differentiation of the self, we are developing a fundamental sense of how the world works and what we can expect from human intentions enacted over time. Secure attachment may nudge us in the direction of comedy and romance; insecure attachment, in the direction of tragedy and irony. Our attitudes about story and the vicissitudes of human intention develop further through childhood, incorporating a wide range of experiences. By the time each of us reaches adolescence and adulthood, we are ready to create stories of a certain quality or type. By the time we think seriously about the meaning of our own lives, we may already be predisposed to create that meaning through the filtering glass of tragedy, comedy, irony, or romance.

Imagery and Myth

A turning point in my older daughter's life was the day she saw *Snow White and the Seven Dwarfs*. She was three years old. *Snow White* had just been rereleased and was playing at a local cinema. I was apprehensive about taking Ruth to see her first full-length movie. Would she be able to sit through it? The show promised to be at least an hour and a half in length, and I worried she would get bored. What if she had to use the bathroom? I certainly could not escort her into the ladies' room, and I was not keen on taking her in with the men. Probably we would have to go home. I parked the car very near the theater exit, and I chose two seats on the aisle so that we could make a quick getaway. We sat down, and I waited nervously for the movie to begin.

Almost two hours later, Ruth was still riveted to the screen. Her eyes hungrily took in the ending credits as they rolled by, though I knew she couldn't read them. She had not moved a muscle since the curtain rose. I must admit that I, too, loved the movie, enchanted by the music and the dazzling animation. But Ruth had seemed mesmerized.

For two years after that, my family lived with Snow White and the seven dwarfs. All seven of the little men rode with us every day in the car to nursery school—Grumpy, Happy, Doc, Bashful, Sleepy, Sneezy, and Dopey. The Wicked Queen, the Peddler Woman (who is the Queen in disguise), the Queen's Huntsman, and the Handsome Prince frequently joined us for dinner. When Ruth first met a classmate named William, she told him that she lived in a little cottage tucked far away in the woods. William insisted she was crazy. He had seen our house, and he knew there were no woods in Chicago. William didn't want to ride to school every day with such a silly girl. He announced his preference to make the trip alone in the future—in his red flying car.

Later, William and Ruth became friends. When William would come to our house for lunch, Ruth might pretend that she was the Wicked Queen and William, the Queen's Huntsman. Together, they might terrorize her little sister, Amanda, who was but one year old and cast in the pitiful role of Snow White. They stole her stuffed animals and threatened to lock her up; they hid poison apples under her pillow. On other days, though, Ruth herself might be Snow White, organizing regular birthday parties for Grumpy, her favorite dwarf, taping pink crepe paper all over the dining room, and making birthday cakes out of sugar, pepper, water, and oregano.

My daughter was obsessed with the story of Snow White. Yet it was not so much the integrated, full-length story—from beginning to end—that fascinated her. Rather, it was the various pieces of the story, easily divorced from their narrative context, that she brought into her daily fantasy life. One day she might be the Wicked Queen. The next day she might be Bashful. Her identification with each of these characters would be temporary and idiosyncratic. One time, in the role of Grumpy she rescued three of the "Little Ponies" stranded on a cliff. In the movie version of "Snow White," Grumpy never rescues anybody. And there are no ponies in the story—Ruth found them in a popular television show.

The preschool child's world of make-believe is inconsistent, magical, and fluid. It is populated by a rich and ever-expanding repertoire of images. It is the images in stories—not the stories themselves—that children appropriate. Ruth knows the whole story of Snow White, but it is not the whole story that captures her imagination, for it is too big and complex, too systematic and progressive for a child of her age to make use of in her play. Instead, Ruth dwells on the images of dwarfs, queens, and innocent little girls, reworking them daily into her own fantastical plots.

This is how preschool children play and, to a certain extent, how they think. They appropriate images from their culture to suit their immediate personal wishes and desires. They make the image do what they want it to do, even in ways that seem strange and illogical to adults. Snow White can be dead one minute and alive the next. She can do things that are completely unrelated to her original identity in the fairy tale. She can fly through the air on a broom or become invisible like a ghost. She can accompany the Scarecrow, the Tin Man, and the Cowardly Lion to the Land of Oz, or to heaven, or to a nearby grocery store to buy grapefruit to be squeezed on the head of the Wicked Witch of the West, so that the Wicked Witch will melt away as she does in the movie.

The personal myth that an adult constructs is not a fairy tale. But like a fairy tale (and like virtually any kind of story one can imagine) every personal myth contains and expresses a characteristic set of images. One stockbroker's personal myth is saturated with the imagery of mounting acceleration: Life moves faster and faster each day, people race to reach the top, but they never get there. A mother tells a life story filled with the verdant imagery of lush gardens, children blooming like flowers, lives reaching fruition in accord with nature's ways. Throughout our preschool years, we are unwittingly busy collecting and stockpiling images. By the time we reach young adulthood, we have accumulated a veritable treasure trove of personalized symbols and fantasized objects. As adults, we draw creatively upon the imagery in fashioning our personal myths. Like my daughter Ruth, adults make the images do what they want them to do. Therefore, in order to understand our own myths we must explore the unique way in which each of us employs imagery to make sense of who we are.

Where Imagery Starts:
The Child's World of Make-believe

A three-year-old understands the world through images, and each image has its own personally meaningful definition. Ruth Krauss captures this sense beautifully in her nursery poem "A Hole Is to Dig: A First Book of First Definitions":

Mashed potatoes are to give everybody enough
A face is so you can make faces

A face is something to have on the front of your head
Dogs are to kiss people
Hands are to hold
A hand is to hold up when you want your turn
A hole is to dig

The ground is to make a garden
Grass is to cut
Grass is to have on the ground with dirt under it and clover in it
Maybe you could hide things in a hole
A party is to say how-do-you-do and shake hands
A party is to make little children happy
Arms are to hug with
Toes are to wiggle
Ears are to wiggle
Mud is to jump in and slide in and yell doodleedoodleedoo
Anh-h-h! Doodleedoodleedoo-oo!
A castle is to build in the sand
A hole is to sit in
A dream is to look at the night and see things
Snow is to roll in

Buttons are to keep people warm
The world is so you have something to stand on
The sun is to tell you when it's every day
When you make your bed you get a star
Little stones are for little children to gather up and put in little piles
Oo! A rock is when you trip on it you should have watched where you were going
Children are to love

A brother is to help you
A principal is to take out splinters

A mountain is to go to the top
A mountain is to go to the bottom
A lap is so you don't get crumbs on the floor
A mustache is to wear on Halloween
A hat is to wear on a train
Toes are to dance on
Eyebrows are to go over your eyes
A sea shell is to hear the sea
A wave is to wave bye-bye
Big shells are to put little shells in
A hole is to plant a flower
A watch is to hear it tick
Dishes are to do
Cats are so you can have kittens

Mice are to eat your cheese

Noses are to rub
A nose is to blow
A match is to blow
A whistle is to make people jump
Rugs are so you don't get splinters in you
Hunh! Rugs are so dogs have napkins
A floor is so you don't fall in the hole your house is in
A hole is for a mouse to live in
A door is to open
A door is to shut
A hole is to look through
Steps are to sit on
A hole is when you step in it you go down
Hands are to make things
Hands are to eat with
A tablespoon is to eat a table with
A package is to look inside
The sun is so it can be a great day

A book is to look at[21]

Children see the world in terms of what it can do and mean for them. A face is so you can make faces. A principal is to take out splinters. After years of studying how children make sense of their own experience, the eminent Swiss psychologist Jean Piaget concluded that the preschooler functions within a *preoperational* stage of cognitive development. In the preoperational stage, thinking is commonly and strikingly egocentric in nature.[22] The "ego" or self is placed at the center of all. The child's interpretation of reality is thoroughly subjective and driven by his or her own preferences, needs, wishes, and momentary moods. There is little attempt made to see the world from another person's point of view.[23] Why is the sky blue? you may ask. A three-year-old may answer, "Because blue is my favorite color."

From the viewpoint of the three-year-old, the world is yet to be comprehended in a systematic and logical manner, as a complex realm within which cause-and-effect relationships may be discovered over time. The three-year-old does not categorize and classify experience according to agreed-upon standards and systems. She does not seek to be consistent in her reasoning from one situation to the next. Indeed, the rules of thought seem to change with each new situation as the child's subjective orientation and state change. In this sense, preoperational thinking is episodic. Associations between episodes often defy rational logic. In the poem, the child says, "The sun is to tell you when it's every day." The very next line seems to digress: "When you make your bed you get a star." But there is a strong association between the two lines, even though the second doesn't seem to have anything to do with the overall "rule" of the poem—that is, defining things.

The central image in the poem is, of course, the hole. We learn that a hole is to dig, that one may dig holes to plant a garden or a flower, that maybe one can hide things in a hole, that a hole is to sit in, that a hole is to look through, etc. These are one young child's understanding of the image of a hole. Holes are a big deal for children, like "splinters." Children have strong feelings about these things. Imagery connects thoughts and feelings in personally meaningful ways.

The sharp line drawn by most adults between fantasy and reality is blurred in the mind of the three-year-old. "A dream is to look at the night and see things," the poem tells us. For an adult, this is a false definition, for it suggests that the waking stargazer and the sleeping dreamer are engaged in the same activity. The very nature of reality is a problem for the young child, as Piaget suggested years ago. Yet in thinking about our own children and others, the child's confusion between the real and the imagined does not usually bother us too much. Nor did it bother Piaget, who found in the child's world of make-believe a fertile terrain for the making of meaning. We are likely to encourage the child's egocentric and idiosyncratic engagement of the world through image and the imagination. Many parents promote fantasy and make-believe, with the correct conviction that in so doing they are enriching the child's play and promoting psychological growth and development.[24]

The predominant mode of play in the preschool years is what psychologists call symbolic play.[25] Symbolic play is driven by the child's idiosyncratic use of symbols and images in episodes of make-believe. Such play has been called "behavior in the simulative mode."[26] The behavior simulates real world events, but the simulation is "buffered from its consequences."[27] Amanda may eat the "poison apple" that her sister hid under her pillow, but she will not die, because in play the real-world consequences do not ensue. Play is not for keeps. Snow White may eat the poison apple, but instead of dying, or even fainting away as if she were dead, she may fight a duel with an enemy, because in play my daughter has decided that that is what Snow White should indeed do, in the very next episode. Even within the play sequence, operating fully in the simulative mode, Snow White may be buffered from the consequences of her actions. If my daughter decides that Snow White is not going to die, then she won't die, no matter how many poison apples she eats. This kind of play does not play by "the rules."

Play becomes more rule-governed as children grow older. The games of later elementary school are less episodic and egocentric than the younger child's world of make-believe. Behavior still operates in the simulative mode, in that games are not supposed to be "for keeps," either. But games are organized by rules, goals, and themes. Baseball does not work well if the players change the rules with every move. If you strike out, you must leave the batter's box, even if you were pretending to be Snow White, or Wade Boggs. Games require that players adopt an objective, third-person perspective, that they agree upon a common understanding of reality. Episodes are organized within a meaningful, goal-directed sequence. As we grow up, play becomes more complex, organized, and regularized. It becomes divorced from one's private symbolism. The private image of the moment gives way to the public sequence of structured events.

Where Imagery Comes From: The Role of Culture

Like our very identities, imagery is both discovered and made. To a certain extent, children, as well as adults, make their own images. But the nature of the making is strongly dependent on the available raw materials, and the raw materials are to be discovered in and through culture. Each culture provides its members with a vast but finite catalog of images. Every person is exposed to and draws upon parts of the catalog in a unique way. Therefore, every member of a culture is unique in some way, at least as far as his or her personal imagery is concerned. Still, differences between cultures can be considered, for even in their uniqueness members of one culture share common imagery and may, as a group, differ in important ways from members of a different culture. Thus, my daughter Ruth would approach her play differently were she born in rural France in A.D. 800; her behavior would reflect the family and society that shaped her world. And Amanda would have undoubtedly developed a different image of "home" had she been raised on an Israeli kibbutz.

Social scientists often point to the family unit as the major vehicle for cultural transmission in childhood. The process is sometimes called socialization. Imagery, too, is conveyed within the family. Through their actions and words, parents expose children to a wide assortment of images and symbols. Much of this exposure may take place unconsciously. Children unknowingly "incorporate," or take into themselves, such images of their parents as the good mother, the frustrating mother, the seductive mother, the strong father, the threatening father, the helpless father, the witch, the goddess, the ogre, and so on. Young children may unconsciously appropriate these images into their fantasies and play, and the images may also be lodged in the unconscious realms of the mind.[28] Functioning as what some psychologists call "internalized objects," these emotionally charged images may become parts of the self, continuing to exert an unconscious influence on behavior and experience through one's adult years.[29] An adult's personal myth will often be suffused with the unconscious imagery of early childhood, established in the complex family dynamics of the first three or four years of life.

While the family is a major source of lasting images that are laden with strong emotions, other important sources of imagery in culture must also be recognized. Among the more important sources for many children and adults is religion. Recently, psychologists have begun to examine the development of religious faith in children and adults. Psychologist James Fowler suggests that faith is a human universal and that it can be understood as developing in stages.[30] Regardless of a child's or a family's religious background, Fowler maintains, virtually all people come to comprehend the world with respect to "ultimate concerns," developing implicit understandings of what is ultimately good and true and what their relation to an ultimate cosmos is.

According to Fowler's research, preschool children are likely to exhibit the stage of intuitive-projective faith. Children in the intuitive-projective stage "combine fragments of stories and images given by their cultures into their own clusters of significant associations dealing with God and the sacred."[31] Fowler illustrates the stage with an interview of Freddy, who was six years old and was being raised in a Catholic family at the time. Here follows an excerpt from Fowler's interview:

Interviewer (I): What happens to you when you die?
Freddy (F): I don't know. Never been up in heaven before, only when I was a baby.
I: When you were a baby you were up in heaven?
F: Yeah.
I: How do you know that?
F: Well, 'cause I felt the cold.
I: It's cold in heaven?
F: Yeah, no, I think it's warm, real warm.
I: Where is heaven?
F: Uh, high, high, high up in the sky.
I: What's it look like?
F: Uh, high mountains, so I know about heaven.
I: Who's in heaven?
F: God.

I: Just God? Is he by himself?

F: No.

I: Who else is there?

F: There's, there's the shepherds—the shepherd man—I mean the wise men that are dead.

I: Is there anyone else in heaven?

F: Baby—no, not baby Jesus.

I: No?

F: 'Ca—yeah, baby Jesus is God.

I: He is?

F: Yeah.

I: Okay. Is anybody else in heaven?

F: There's Mary. Saint Joe—that's all I know.

I: So heaven is where people go when they die?

F: Your spirit goes up.

I: Oh, your spirit. What is your spirit?

F: It's something that helps you—helps you—helps you do everything.

I: Yeah, where is it?

F: In your body.

I: Inside you?

F: Yeah.

I: And what does it help you do?

F: Helps you do lots of things.

I: Like what?

F: I don't know. Maybe—maybe walking. Maybe seeing around and stuff. That's all I know.

I: All right. Can you tell me what God looks like?

F: He has a light shirt on, he has brown hair, he had brown eyelashes.

I: When you do something bad, does God know?

F: Yes. He spreads all around the world in one day.

I: He does? How does he do that?

F: He does 'cause he's smart.

I: He's smart? How does he get all around the world in one day?

F: Uh—he can split or he can be like God.

I: He can split into lots of things?

F: Yeah.

I: Can he do anything he wants?

F: Yeah.

I: There's not anything he can't do?

F: He can do things, things that are good, not bad. God never tells a lie in his life.

We can see that Freddy has been exposed to a large set of symbols and stories, from which he has composed his own images of the nature of an ultimate environment. His approach is delightfully eclectic and impressionistic. As does my daughter with Snow White, Freddy makes God do what he (Freddy) wants. God is able to split up into pieces or stay in his original form, depending on how much ground he has to cover at a given time. He wears a light shirt and has brown eyelashes. Freddy's images of God and heaven reflect the magical and fluid quality of preoperational thought. Fowler points out that many children from nonreligious homes show similar patterns of appropriating imagery to describe an ultimate environment, though their sources of image and symbol may be more limited. He interviewed Sally, a four-and-a-half-year-old girl whose parents have made intentional efforts to avoid exposing her to religious symbols:

Sally (S): Sometimes I believe in God, but my mother and father never believed in God.

Interviewer (I): Why do you believe in God?

S: Because on those shows they believe in God, like on *Leave It to Beaver* and Davey [the Lutheran Church in America's animated cartoon series, *Davey and Goliath*], you know that? Especially on Davey; there's a lot of that. Saturday morning we wake up kind of early and we watch Davey. And like today I watched *Beaver* and *Father Knows Best*, but they don't have much about God.

I: Is God real to you?

S: Ummm—yeah. . . . sometimes I think it's real.

I: What does God look like?

S: He doesn't look like anything. He's all around you.

Sally has picked up religious images and symbols from her environment, even though her parents reject traditional religious perspectives. Such images are not likely to attract a great deal of emotional energy in Sally's life without further religious socialization. Thus, while she may become familiar with some of the more salient images of the dominant religions in contemporary American society—Christianity and Judaism—these images will probably not become central constituents of the imagery she develops as an adult to define who she is. Of course we cannot predict exactly what will happen in this regard. Sally may develop a personal myth that draws heavily on such imagery, but in order to do so she would have to immerse herself in a particular religious tradition.

For some adults, religious imagery serves as a powerful force in personal mythmaking. Judeo-Christian religious traditions contain a wealth of compelling images that are repeatedly imported, with strong emotional associations, into personal myths. Among these images are the garden, the forbidden fruit, the cunning serpent, the flood, parting of the sea, manna from heaven, the land of milk and honey, the burning bush, the cloud of fire, the wilderness, the shepherd, the devil, the covenant, the baby Jesus, the wise men, the lamb, the bread and the wine, the cross, the resurrection, the disciple, the martyr, the messiah, the six-pointed star. These kinds of images contain powerful meanings for some people. Such images are also reinforced and articulated in religious ritual, religious rhetoric, and prayer.

Sally alerts us to another profound source of imagery in culture, for virtually all of the religious imagery to which she has been exposed comes from television. It is difficult to overestimate the power of television in particular, and the media in general, as sources of imagery in American society, and in many other societies as well. In many ways, television is ideally suited to convey images. Many television shows follow an episodic format through which quick scenes are set and little vignettes are quickly played out. This maximizes the number and diversity of images that can be conveyed. Television commercials have mastered this format. Many of the most successful commercials do not directly feature a product or service at all. Rather, they create, in a few seconds, a series of positive images to which it is hoped the viewer will associate the product. McDonald's becomes a clean and happy place where families go to talk and to smile. Coors beer relates to rugged terrain and "natural" men. Luxury sports cars are sold with images of speed, grace, and elegance.

While many bemoan the pervasive influence of television in American culture, few believe that there is much that anybody can do to decrease its influence in the near future. Virtually all of American society has become videocentric. As I write this, I have on my desk this morning's *New York Times*, which contains a feature article identifying President and Mrs. Bush's favorite television shows and movies.

Given its pervasive influence, it is difficult to reach a simple conclusion concerning the value of television's impact upon the making of personal images, especially among young children. Television is certainly responsible for some of the most repugnant images children will find anywhere. Of course, children will strive to make the images do what they want them to do. But destructive and violent images or desperate images of grasping materialism are sometimes difficult to transform into something benevolent and bright, even in the vivid imagination of the four-year-old.[34] Yet television also brings us Big Bird and lovable Grover from *Sesame Street*. Shows like *Mr. Rogers' Neighborhood* suggest extremely constructive roles for adults. Even such characters as the Teenage Mutant Ninja Turtles are infused with certain redeeming features, though not enough of them in the eyes of many parents.

Jean-Paul Sartre defined an image as a synthesis of feeling, knowledge, and inner sensation, captured in an episode in time.[35] The mind of the preschooler seems especially open to this kind of synthesis. Children are not in a position to determine the quality of the imagery to which they are exposed. Yet the quality of the imagery has as much long-term influence on the quality of their lives and identities as narrative tone receives from infancy. We begin to generate and collect the images for our personal myths in early childhood. They are the raw material out of which personal myth is to be made. Thus, imagery, along with narrative tone, is childhood's essential contribution to adult identity. In this way, our prerational past will inevitably return, for better or worse, to shape our understanding of who we are and how we fit into the adult world.

CHAPTER 3

Theme and Ideological Setting

A s we move in stories from tone and image to theme and ideology, we proceed developmentally from infancy and early childhood to late childhood and adolescence. A story theme is a recurrent pattern of human intention. It is the level of story concerned with what the characters in the narrative want and how they pursue their objectives over time. It is at the level of theme that elementary-school children most clearly apprehend the meaning of stories.

Ideology is a systematic body of values and beliefs. In adolescence, ideology takes on an unprecedented importance. The adolescent formulates an ideological setting to provide a backdrop of belief and value upon which the plot of his or her particular life story can unfold.

The Emergence of Motivational Themes in Childhood

In elementary school (ages six–twelve), children begin to see clearly how human behavior—in stories and in life—is organized by internal intentions played out over time. They recognize, for the first time, that different people and different characters have consistent desires that energize and direct their behavior. Elementary-school children begin to understand their own behavior in similar terms, as goal-directed, motivated, and purposeful. As their insight into human behavior and experience increases, their own internal wants and desires become organized into stable motivational dispositions.

Power and love are the two great themes of myth and story. Protagonists and antagonists are striving, in one way or another, to do one or both of two basic things: (1) to assert themselves in powerful ways, and (2) to merge themselves with others in bonds of love, friendship, and intimacy. Desires for power and love provide gods and goddesses, heroes and heroines, kings and queens, curious little boys and brave little girls alike with energy, direction, and purpose. They move the plot forward; they make the action meaningful. If we were unfamiliar with the human experiences of power and love, we would be unable to understand most of the stories we see and hear. We would not know why characters do what they do.

Power and love are the two great themes of stories because they correspond to the two central psychological motivations in human life. Characters in stories are trying to accomplish what we are all trying to accomplish in our lives. They desire, as we do, to expand, preserve, and enhance the self as a powerful and autonomous agent in the world, and to relate, merge, and surrender the self to other selves within a loving and intimate community.

As children move through elementary school, their thinking takes on a systematic quality, attaining the level of cognitive development called concrete operations.[1] The older child understands the consistent relationships between and among objects and concepts in the world. He or she comes to realize that concrete reality functions according to certain fundamental principles and systems—principles such as "gravity" and "the conservation of matter," and systems such as "arithmetic." If you dropped a lead weight and it began to float upward, a four-year old might be amused. A ten-year-old, however, might be shocked, or disoriented, or suspicious. The ten-year-old knows how the world must work, and this particular event violates assumptions that he knows to be true.

The older child is able to comprehend motivations for characters' actions in richer and more sophisticated terms than he or she could accomplish as a preschooler. Characters are now seen as relatively consistent actors who are motivated by internal desires and anticipated goals. In stories, older children want to know what the characters want. They realize that what the characters want determines, to a large extent, what they will do. The Wicked Witch of the West becomes more than a mere "image"—black, scary, flying, accompanied by menacing flying monkeys. She is also Dorothy's nemesis, who needs the ruby slippers, who intends to defy Glinda and the Munchkins, who wants desperately to keep the heroine and her companions from accomplishing their own intentions, and reaching the Land of Oz.

When the child moves from the cognitive stage of preoperations to that of concrete operations, thinking becomes governed by rules. The fantastical fancies of the four-year-old become somewhat tempered and constrained as the older child comes to understand the limitations imposed by logic and reality. The four-year-old freely appropriates story images to make them do what he or she wants them to do. If the child wants it to be this way, Snow White can take on a foe in a sword fight, and win. The older child, however, sees inconsistencies and limitations here. This is not the kind of thing that Snow White would want to do. It is not true to her character because her motives tend to run much more in the direction of gentle communion than bold engagement. Narrative action must conform to theme. Given Snow White's desires, there are certain things that it simply does not make sense for her to do.

What Do We Want?

One of the oldest questions in human psychology is the question of motivation. To motivate is to set into motion, to get things moving in a particular direction. What forces within the person set human behavior into motion? What are the internal "springs" of human action? They are usually seen as forces within the person that energize, direct, and select behavior over time. A person's motives are like internal engines that move the person to act in characteristic ways.

Over the last three thousand years, philosophers, poets, scientists, psychologists, and other observers of human nature have proposed many different theories of human motivation.[2] Some have argued that human behavior is energized, directed, and selected by one grand motive. For instance, Aristotle suggested that all living organisms are motivated to realize their own inherent destiny.[3] More than two thousand years later, psychologists such as Carl Rogers and Carl Jung have asserted similarly that the single inherent tendency in healthy human living is toward *self-actualization*.[4] Though they disagree on many of the specifics, Aristotle, Rogers, and Jung are in general agreement that a single basic spring to human action can be invoked to explain why people act the way they do.

On the other end of the spectrum, we have viewpoints proposing a host of different motives, all of which are instrumental in providing human behavior with its characteristic energy and direction. According to this view, human behavior is extremely complex; no single motive can explain it all. Rather, many different motives exist, though some motives may be "better" or more "mature" than others. In the *Republic*, Plato put forth three basic human motives, each corresponding to a distinct portion of the mind. These are (1) the appetites, which are determined by basic bodily wants and needs; (2) courage and fortitude, which motivate people to do heroic acts; and (3) reason, which motivates people to strive for "the Good."[5] More than two thousand years later, in 1890, William James—the father of American psychology—contended that three is by no means enough. He proposed a long list of human instincts or impulses, including motives of fear, sympathy, sociability, play, acquisitiveness, modesty, nurturance, and love.[6]

Occupying a middle position is a third group of theorists who conceive of human motivation in terms of two fundamental motives, one in conflict or tension with the other. The ancient Greek philosopher Empedocles argued that two grand forces—"love" and "strife"—rule the universe. Love unites all things; strife separates. The clouds in the sky, the animals in the forest, the people in the city, come together through love and separate, sometimes violently, through strife. History, too, is ruled by the two masters, as periods of unity are followed by epochs of discord. After love brings things together, strife gradually sorts things out again until all is broken and divided. Then love again begins to reunite and heal. A person's life is similarly ruled.[7]

Many modern theories of human motivation seem to approach from different angles Empedocles' dialectic. For instance, Sigmund Freud proposed in 1920 that human thought and behavior are governed by two sets of instinctual tendencies, in conflict with each other.[8] In Freud's view, the "life instincts" motivate human beings to seek each other out in sexual, pleasurable, and loving unions. The "death instincts" propel human beings toward masterful and destructive sorts of behavior, through aggression and bold displays of personal power. In Freud's view, the life and death instincts operate unconsciously. We are propelled to act in ways that are both loving and powerful by internal forces over which we have little control and about which we consciously know very little.

Since Freud, a significant number of psychologists have put forth theories of human motivation that pit two general tendencies against each other. The first tendency appears to include the overlapping strivings for power, autonomy, independence, status, and experiences rich in the emotion of excitement. The second tendency subsumes the overlapping strivings for love, intimacy, interdependence, acceptance, and interpersonal experiences suffused with the emotion of joy.[9] This motivational duality in human existence is probably best described by the psychologist David Bakan, who distinguishes between *agency* and *communion*.[10] According to Bakan, agency and communion are the two "fundamental modalities in the existence of living forms," organizing a great variety of human wants, needs, desires, and goals.[11] Agency refers to the individual's striving to separate from others, to master the environment, to assert, protect, and expand the self. The aim is to become a powerful and autonomous "agent," a force to be reckoned with. By contrast, communion refers to the individual's striving to lose his or her own individuality by merging with others, participating in something that is larger than the self, and relating to other selves in warm, close, intimate, and loving ways. Bakan's position proves to be an especially valuable one in comprehending the basic motivational themes expressed in both personal myths and human lives.

Research indicates that the desires for power and achievement constitute two highly agentic motives (see Appendix 1). Psychological tests have been developed to measure the relative strengths of these motives in different people's personality profiles. People high in power motivation show a strong and consistent preference for experiences of feeling strong and having impact on the environment, compared with people low in power motivation. They tend to be highly conscious of prestige and status in life; they are likely to take bold risks; they are drawn to positions of high leadership and influence; they tend to be quite dominant in social groups; they perceive their own friendships in powerful, agentic terms; and, among men, they tend to experience difficulties in romantic love relationships, such as dating and marriage. People high in achievement motivation show a strong and consistent preference for experiences of feeling competent and doing better in the performance of tasks compared with people low in achievement motivation. They tend to be very efficient and levelheaded in their career pursuits; they are likely to take prudent and moderate risks; they tend to plan carefully for the future; they are innovative; and they derive great satisfaction from their work, in general preferring work to leisure.

Power and achievement motivation are the two faces of human agency. They both share an emphasis on the active assertion of the self over and against the surrounding environment. A person can establish him or herself as a forceful agent in the world through having impact or through doing better. In both cases, the person acts to consolidate his or her own individuality—separating the self from the surrounding environment by mastering that environment and making it do what the person wants it to do.

While our desires for power and achievement may motivate us to assert ourselves in effective and influential ways and to control, even master, our environments, our longings for close and warm relationships with other human beings pull us in a different direction, to the private life of intimate interpersonal communion. Indeed, for some of us, the desire for love and intimacy is even grander and more compelling than our wishes for success, fame, and influence. As the novelist E. M. Forster wrote, "It is the private life that holds out the mirror to infinity; personal intercourse, and that alone, that ever hints at a personality beyond our daily vision."[12]

Human communion, research indicates, involves overlapping desires for intimacy and love (see Appendix 1). Through love and intimacy, each of us is able to relate to others in warm, close, and supportive ways. Some people seem to be more communal in their life motivations than are others. They may show markedly high levels of intimacy motivation, revealed in the ways they act and speak with their friends and in social groups, how they are seen and judged by others who know them, what they think about and how they feel over the course of a normal day, and how they understand their relationships with important people in their lives. Intimacy and love are not precisely the same experiences. But both are born of communion and remain part of an extended family of human experiences, all tied together for their emphasis on human ties.

Motive and Theme: Late Childhood

Motives help to organize our behavior, providing energy and direction for various things we do. Motives help to shape our identities by emphasizing particular themes in the personal myth. But motives are not the same thing as themes. A motive exists within a person's personality. It is an internal disposition that begins to take form in the elementary-school years. A theme exists in the story. It is a cluster of narrative content having to do with what characters in the story recurrently want or intend.

It is in the years of elementary school that an individual's real life motives begin to take form. Agentic motives for power and achievement and communal motives such as the intimacy motive begin to govern desires, goals, and actions. As the child comes to see human behaviors as being purposeful and organized, his or her own behavior becomes correspondingly more purposeful and organized, too. The child's developing interpretation of behavior parallels personality development at this time.

Different ten-year-olds may be compared and contrasted in terms of the relative strengths and qualities of their different agentic and communal motives. It makes sense to speak of these children as "having" particular motives at this time, because we can see that their behavior is recurrently energized and directed by clusters of desires and goals. By contrast, a four-year-old's behavior is not motivationally well organized. The four-year-old certainly has desires and wants, but these have not as yet been integrated within his personality into stable motivational dispositions. In a sense, the personality of a four-year-old is structured to know what it wants in the short run but not in the long run, over time. The older child acts according to long-term intentions that have become organized into consistent preferences and wants for particular qualities of human experience.

Children in elementary school have motives, but they do not as yet have identities. In other words, their recurrent wants and desires have coalesced to form stable motives, but the motives have not as yet been translated into central themes in their own personal myths. Still, motives help to determine what children do and how they do it. For example, the interpersonal behavior of fourth and sixth graders appears to be strongly associated with their relative standing on intimacy motivation. Michael Losoff, Rebecca Pallmeyer, and I conducted a study in which we determined intimacy-motive scores from imaginative fantasies told by fourth and sixth graders and then correlated these scores with various indices of behavior.[13] We found that children high in intimacy motivation tended to have more stable and enduring relationships with their "best friends," to know more about their best friends' personal lives, to be rated by their teachers as especially "affectionate" and "sincere," and to be seen by their classmates as relatively friendly kids who make very few enemies, compared with children scoring lower in intimacy motivation. What is interesting and important is that intimacy-motive scores of children were unrelated to intelligence test scores and school grades. In other words, the extent to which you desire warm and close relationships in grade school seems to have nothing to do with how smart you are.

By at least fourth grade, characteristic levels of particular social motives can be assessed in children's personalities. It is important to note, however, that once formed in childhood, a person's motives are not set in stone. Motives may change and develop over time. Therefore, such personality dispositions as the power motive and the intimacy motive are only moderately and relatively stable over time. This means that they are not likely to change in any significant way from, say, one day or one week to the next. But over the course of the life span, they may indeed change as a function of life experience. Thus, an adolescent boy who is high in power motivation may find that his power needs are less strong when he reaches the age of thirty. A twenty-five-year-old woman may have a very strong need for intimacy, which may decrease markedly by the time she reaches age forty-five.[14] Various motives may ebb and flow over the life span, in ways that are unique for each person. When such ebbing and flowing occurs in the adult years, identity may change in corresponding ways. If a man's power motivation increases markedly from early adulthood to mid-life, we would expect that his evolving personal myth would reflect the change. We would expect a greater preponderance of agentic themes in his myth at mid-life than we would have seen when he was a younger man.

Our favorite stories usually contain those motifs and themes to which we are most strongly attracted as children. These will often reflect those organized desires, conscious or not, that are our strongest motives. The motives themselves will probably be organized according to the two great motivational categories in human life— agency and communion. Theme is an aspect of myth with which we are already familiar by the time we face the identity challenges of adolescence and young adulthood. Thus, by the time we begin to compose our personal myth, we are predisposed to create our identities along certain thematic lines.

I Don't Know Who I Am Anymore: Adolescence

There is a great temptation among adults to romanticize adolescence, to make it seem more wonderful or more dreadful than it really was for us, or than it really is for adolescents today. Some psychologists have fallen into this trap by overemphasizing, on the one hand, the creative genius and potential for growth and fulfillment in adolescence or, on the other, the tumultuous crises, the mood swings, and the general craziness of the teenage years. Indeed, there remains a vigorous debate among psychologists today concerning the extent to which adolescence is a period of "storm and stress" on the one hand or relatively peaceful continuity on the other.[15] Therefore, we should be somewhat cautious in our consideration of adolescence and the extent to which adolescents experience significant concerns about identity. I believe the most sensible conclusion to reach is this: Because of certain biological, cognitive, and social changes that do seem to occur in the adolescent years, the stage is psychosocially set for the emergence of identity as a new problem in life at this time. The problem emerges in different ways for different adolescents, and it emerges at different rates and intensities. Not everyone experiences an identity crisis. Yet most are challenged, in one way or another, to begin the search for a new self.

Identity begins to become a problem in life when a person first notices incongruities between who he or she was at one time and who he or she is now. The incongruities may be experienced on the level of the body. Kindergartners know that as they get older they get bigger. They realize that their bodies are slowly changing over time. In general, this realization does not bother them too much, for the change is expected and quantitative and, for the most part, bigger is "better." But puberty may bring relatively sudden changes that are qualitative as well as quantitative, for both adolescent boys and girls. The changes may or may not be expected, but they are nonetheless unprecedented in the life span. The girl develops breasts and pubic hair, and begins menstruating. The boy's penis and scrotum grow, facial hair appears, the voice deepens, and so on. We all remember these changes. They don't need to be traumatic to stimulate our wonderment about what is going on.

Puberty ushers in sexual longings and desires that we have not consciously known before, at least not with the overt intensity and pervasiveness that we come to experience in the adolescent years. This, too, is unprecedented in the human life span. No matter how sophisticated we are as thirteen-year-olds, no matter how "ready" we are for being a teenager, no matter how many television shows and movies we have watched portraying sexual relationships, the feelings are new to us, and they reinforce the fact that some important change has taken place. Relationships with our peers change, too, as a result of puberty's force. Our social world becomes eroticized; relationships with certain people now seem to be newly charged with excitement and anticipation.

It is in part our own adolescent sexual awakening that world mythologies have symbolized when a young hero—a Jason, an Aeneas, a Buddha—journeys across a threshold to enter a dangerous and seductive land.[16] Some psychoanalysts maintain that the awakening is actually a reawakening from sexuality's long slumber following the young child's resolution of the Oedipus complex. Indeed, some argue that the adolescent's newfound sexual feelings may be redirected to the parents, as teenagers come to experience a second Oedipus complex.[17] In world mythologies, the young hero sometimes experiences a sense of "nostalgic beauty" in the early stages of his journey.[18] Such episodes symbolize the sexual longing he has known before, unconsciously, as a child.

Biological and sexual changes are only part of the picture. Certain changes in thinking may be equally influential. Jean Piaget argued that in adolescence many people enter the cognitive stage of *formal operations*.[19] According to Piaget, at this time in the life cycle we are first able to think about the world and about ourselves in highly abstract terms. In formal operations, one is able to reason about what is and what might be in terms of verbally stated and logically deduced hypotheses. Before adolescence, argues Piaget, we simply cannot do this. Therefore, the eight-year-old skillfully classifies and categorizes the world with wonderful accuracy and aplomb but is cognitively bound to the concrete world of *what is* rather than the abstract world of *what might be*.

Ask a bright fourth grader to recite the capitals of the fifty states and you should not be surprised if he or she rattles them off with 100 percent precision. However, if you ask that same prodigy to speculate as to what the capitals might be if there were only ten states, he or she is likely to have more trouble. The child may find the proposition inherently ridiculous, because the United States is in fact made up of fifty states. He or she may also find it extremely difficult to devise a systematic plan for determining what the criteria of a capital should be in this hypothetical scenario. The elementary-school child is a slave to concrete facts: Reality is everything. Once the adolescent encounters formal operations, in contrast, reality is understood as a *subset* of what might be. The real is one manifestation of the possible, and viable and internally consistent alternative realities can also be imagined.

The formal operations stage of cognitive development promotes a serious questioning of reality. The adolescent may look at the realities of the present and the past and contrast them with hypothetical possibilities concerning what might have been (the past) and what might yet be (the future). How might I have been different if I had been born a girl instead of a boy? What if I had lived during the time of the Civil War instead of now? How might I be different from what I am now? What if I were a Hindu? What might happen if I were to believe that there was no God? What might happen if I were to join the army? Adolescents begin to take seriously the possibilities of alternative lives and systems of living. In some cases, they explore new and previously unthinkable ways of experiencing the world, and question things learned in childhood that now seem "old." This introspective and abstract orientation may result in the formulation of "hypothetical ideals"—the ideal family, religion, society, life.[20] Adolescent idealism depends on the advent of formal operational thinking.

The new mental skills may also put stringent demands on a person's life and behavior. The person is now likely to ponder inconsistencies in his or her own life, especially with respect to the different roles or selves adopted in daily behavior and experience. The adolescent boy sees that he swaggers with pride and bravado when in the company of his buddies but shudders meekly when he talks to a girl. The adolescent girl sees that she is conforming and placid in the classroom but rebellious at home. At church, she is polite and deferential; with her girlfriends, spontaneous and warm; with her siblings, haughty and arrogant. The adolescent begins to understand that one must be many different things to many different people. And this realization is troubling, for it suggests that one is not being one's "real self" in certain situations. The eight-year-old does not worry about the extent to which her behaviors do or do not reflect who she really is. The adolescent, by contrast, knows that what you do may not reflect who you are, that there is a disparity in everyday life between the me that you see and the real me inside. The disparity may be so striking as to summon up questions that have never been asked before: Who is the real me? Who am I?

In order to know who I am, I must also know who I am not. The point of departure in personal mythmaking is the dawning realization that I am not what I was. I am not a child anymore. Now that I have a past, I must leave it behind. I must accept the call of identity in order to find my own truth—a truth that will surely be different from what I knew as a child. The adolescent takes leave of the frameworks and certainties of the past and searches for new answers to new questions in life. Particular authority figures may come to represent the past, and they, like the past, may come to be rejected. A mother may be seen as being out of touch with the times. A father may now be criticized for failing to be strong, responsible, manly, or loving enough. Such criticism may be deserved in some instances. In others, the criticism seems to be a necessary but temporary step in the making of myth. Certain authority figures are made into negative identities.[21] At the time they are created, they personify what an individual doesn't want to become. They are the first villains and fools in the adolescent's new story.

While there are villains, there are also kings and queens. These may also be people in authority, even parents. The adolescent does not have to "rebel" from the family in order to begin the process of forming an identity. The departure from the past may be more subtle, more complex. Parents, teachers, ministers, and friends may help to shepherd the adolescent through difficult passages in life. They may provide invaluable advice about decisions concerning school, work, and love. In world mythologies, the young hero frequently receives critical help from wise benefactors—sages, goddesses, and supernatural aides. Without their help, the hero's journey is probably doomed. We should not be misled, therefore, into thinking that mythmaking is a solitary quest. There are indeed dangers to face, and risks that we all must take, and take alone. But the adolescent's search for identity is initiated and played out in a social context. We come to know who we are through relationships and in social settings. To depart from the past is not to leave the world behind. It is rather to move from one world to another.

As we begin our mythmaking in adolescence, we learn that our peers, too, are asking the same kinds of questions. Such questioning may be encouraged by people we know, and even by societal institutions. In American middle-class society, principals, school counselors, teachers, and parents all expect adolescents to struggle with their identities. Compulsory schooling ends at age sixteen, and young people face choices about what roles they should write for themselves in the adult world—whether they should go to college, enter the military, begin a trade, marry and start a family. In the best of circumstances, society welcomes and provides guidance for the adolescent's departure. To leave home psychologically is to leave childhood and begin the journey toward maturity and responsible citizenship in a social world. It is in the best interests of society, then, that the adolescent's break from the past be understood as necessary and good.

Developmental psychologist David Elkind may have discovered some of our initial attempts at mythmaking—some "first drafts" of our life stories—in his investigations of the diaries and letters teenagers write.[22] Elkind argues that adolescents often construct *personal fables* in their fantasies, and convey them to others and to themselves in their diaries and correspondence. These stories often affirm the teenager's perceived uniqueness: "Nobody has ever done what I have done; nobody has ever seen what I have seen; nobody can truly understand me; I am unique and beyond your comprehension." They may celebrate the self's greatness, as when the young person spins fantasies about becoming the greatest scientist the world has ever known, writing the great American novel, or changing the world in one glorious sweep.

The personal fable may look like a delusion of grandeur, but in its proper developmental place it is normal and even healthy. Once the young person is able to entertain hypothetical propositions, a Pandora's box of possible life courses opens up. Scenarios that bear little or no relation to reality spring forth. It is as if the adolescent doesn't know what to do with the wonderful new mental powers he has. Personal fables are the exuberant outpourings of a (big) kid in a cognitive candy store. With time and experience, these unrealistic fables of self will fade. But they represent an important move in the development of the self. The personal fable is a very rough draft of an integrative and self-defining life story. It can be edited, rewritten, reworked, and made more realistic as the young person becomes more knowledgeable about the opportunities and limitations of defining the self in his or her particular society. As we formulate more mature life stories in adulthood, we realize that our identities begin and must ultimately remain woven into a historical and social fabric.

The Ideological Setting

Ideology is an aspect of identity that becomes a central issue in human lives during our teenage years. At about the same time in my life when I begin to entertain alternative possibilities for the self, I begin to address basic questions about what is right and what is true. Erik Erikson writes:

We will call what young people in their teens and early twenties look for in religion and other dogmatic systems *ideology*. At the most it is a militant system with uniformed members and uniform goals; at the least, it is a "way of life," or what the Germans call, *Weltanschaung*, a world view which is consonant with existing theory, available knowledge, and common sense, and yet is significantly more: an utopian outlook, a cosmic mood, or a doctrinal logic, all shared as self-evident beyond any need for demonstration.[23]

The adolescent mind is an ideological mind. Writes Erikson, "It is the ideological outlook of society that speaks most clearly to the adolescent who is eager to be affirmed by his peers and is ready to be confirmed by rituals, creeds, and programs."[24] The emergence of formal operations thinking paves the way for the philosophical musings of adolescence. Of course, not every adolescent spends a great deal of time considering philosophical questions. But many do spend time doing this, as research done by myself and by other psychologists amply shows.[25] More important, it is not until adolescence that the mental skills become available for considering ideological questions with any degree of sophistication.

Ideology concerns questions of goodness and truth. In order to know who I am, I must first decide what I believe to be true and good, false and evil about the world in which I live. To understand myself fully, I must come to believe that the universe works in a certain way, and that certain things about the world, about society, about God, about the ultimate reality of life, are true. Identity is built upon ideology.[26]

A person's ideology functions as a "setting" for identity. It locates the personal myth within a particular ethical, religious, and epistemological "time and place." It provides a context for the story. The action in Nathaniel Hawthorne's novel *The Scarlet Letter* would make little sense if it were removed from the context of a Puritan town in Colonial America. Hawthorne's tragic story about a young woman condemned by her fellows for adultery would be a very different story indeed if it were transferred to present-day San Francisco. Similarly, Margaret Sands's act of vandalism seems senseless outside the ideological context of her militant agnosticism and her negative experiences with the Catholic Church.

Included within our ideological settings may be our beliefs about religion and spirituality, morality and ethics, politics, and even aesthetics. What is good? What is true? What is beautiful? How does the world work? How should the world work? What does life mean? How do human beings relate to each other? How should human beings relate to each other? These are all ideological questions over which philosophers, theologians, and poets have puzzled for centuries. They are questions that confront each of us, even if we do not spend a lot of time thinking about them every day.

Existential philosophers say that each of us is "thrown" into the world at birth at a particular point in time and space, with certain inborn capabilities and limitations, and our personal challenge is to make something meaningful out of our lives. The condition of our "thrownness" determines many aspects of our lives. If I am thrown into the world of the American South in the early 1800s as a black boy born of slaves, the chances are good that I will become a slave. If I am thrown into a contemporary rural Indian village as a woman, I am likely to follow the Hindu precepts for feminine identity, marrying at an appropriate age and remaining forever deferential to my husband. By contrast, if I am thrown as a male into a wealthy and white American family in the early 1950s, my prospects are much different. Thrownness is the "luck of the draw"—completely arbitrary and beyond anybody's control.[27] Our personal ideologies derive in large part from our attempts to figure out just where we have been thrown.

The problem of identity and ideology may be a modern problem, most characteristic of middle-class Westerners living in industrial societies. In more agrarian and traditional societies and at earlier points in history, the problem of finding or creating the self in late adolescence and young adulthood—a self grounded in self-generated truths—may not have been so crucial. In societies in which sons are expected to grow up to do what their fathers do and daughters expected to follow in the footsteps of their mothers, identity is conferred upon the young person by a social structure. In such a context, ideology and occupation are received from established authorities, exploration of alternatives is minimal, and commitment to the status quo is a *fait accompli*.

Even among the intellectuals of Western societies, the notion that a person should find or create a unique self may be a relatively recent idea. In his book *Identity: Cultural Change and the Struggle for Self,* social psychologist Roy Baumeister (1986) examines the forces that first led Westerners to report that they were experiencing identity crises. As Baumeister views it, evidence of identity exploration may be gleaned from reports of two different kinds of problems in human living. The first is the problem of continuity over time. Identity becomes a problem when the person begins to wonder, "Am I the same today as I was three years ago?" "Will I be the same ten years from now?" The second is the problem of differentiation. Identity confronts the person with the task of determining how he or she is different from other people—others who, on the surface at least, seem quite similar to the self.

Baumeister concludes that identity was not a major problem in Western societies before 1800. Medieval society in Europe operated on the basis of lineage, gender, home, and social class. A person's identity was assigned to him or her according to those external criteria. Certain strains of individualism emerged during the medieval era, including Christianity's emphasis on individual judgment and on individual participation in Church ritual. The Protestant Reformation split the ideological consensus of Europe and made religious belief a serious identity problem for many educated people. The rise of capitalism opened up economic opportunities and created an upwardly mobile middle class. Many people of the seventeenth and eighteenth centuries therefore confronted significant choices in their religious beliefs—whether to follow Rome or Geneva, for instance—and enjoyed the prospect of enhancing material well-being through entrepreneurial activity in the marketplace.

As Europe entered what has been termed the Romantic era in the last decade of the 1700s, the Christian Church's power was rapidly waning, and many Europeans were questioning the legitimacy of long-established political systems, as happened in the French Revolution. Men and women of the Romantic era substituted creativity, passion, and cultivation of the inner self for Christianity as models for identity formation and personal ideology. The Romantics also became increasingly dissatisfied with the relationship of the individual to society. This dissatisfaction was expressed as a concern for individual freedom, and it eventually gave birth to various Utopian movements in the nineteenth century. In general, after 1800 a societal consensus about basic truths and ultimate values had been lost. The person had now to fashion his or her own ideology as a foundation for identity.

In the twentieth century, the concern for identity has grown stronger as Westerners face a proliferation of occupational and ideological choices. In addition, many social critics have lamented a growing alienation among twentieth-century adults who, more than ever before, have lost faith in authoritative institutions. In the Romantic literature of the nineteenth century, individual heroes struggled valiantly against societal constraints. In much of twentieth-century literature, by contrast, the individual feels overwhelmed, even helpless, and more concerned than ever with differentiating from others.[28] It has become almost trite to say that we Americans and other members of industrialized democracies live in a "postmodern" world, that our world is forever changing, and that it is difficult for us to keep up. Still, such statements are instructive, for they alert us to the peculiar characteristics of contemporary life that work to render identity what one scholar has called "the spiritual problem of our time."[29]

As an aspect of identity, then, ideology is a central problem in contemporary life. In order to fashion a self-defining personal myth, each of us must also come to some implicit conclusions about the meaning of the world, so that our identities may be anchored by ideological truths. Furthermore, like identity, ideology is something with which we wrestle in a social context. The social environment in which we live and mature shapes the development of our basic beliefs and values. We come to understandings about truth, beauty, and goodness through conversations with friends and family, in classrooms, playgrounds, and workplaces. Very few of us go off to the mountains for three years to figure it all out by ourselves. Instead, we consolidate the ideological settings for our personal myths through the enterprise of living with and among people.

The emergence of ideology in adolescence may mark a curious transition in the human life cycle with respect to how the individual uses story to construct the self. The child's evolving understanding of stories impacts on how he or she gathers together resources for the making of identity in later years. The stories that children repeatedly hear, see, make, and love influence the kinds of tones, images, and themes they will eventually incorporate in the creation of their own personal myths in their adult years. When we come to adolescence, however, the role of stories becomes somewhat confusing, because stories do not satisfy the ideological demands of the adolescent mind. Fairy tales, legends, myths, and all sorts of other stories are not always clear about what the person should believe to be right and to be true about life and about the world.

From the standpoint of the adolescent who is looking for an ideology in which to believe, stories may contain much that may seem superfluous—concrete details, conflicting motives, complicated plots, contradictory messages. This may all be irrelevant in the eyes of the person who wants a single logical and coherent system of belief. And stories may contain precious little that can easily be taken out of the concrete narrative and extended, in an abstract manner, to all of life. Adolescents begin to see that stories have different, even conflicting, messages about what is right and true. While Christ's parable of the prodigal son urges the person to accept lovingly even the most flagrant sinner, the story of Noah and the flood shows that sinners should be destroyed. How does one reconcile these inconsistencies?

More satisfying than stories to the adolescent mind may be theories and creeds and other systematic explications. Religious creeds, for example, tell the "believer" what is true for every concrete situation and for all time. They provide a coherent system of belief and value upon which the adolescent can stake his or her ideological claims. Listen to the sweeping and unambiguous language of the Apostles' Creed, memorized by many Christians when they are "confirmed" as teenagers in the Catholic Church and in many Protestant denominations:

I believe in God, the Father almighty,
　　　creator of heaven and earth.

I believe in Jesus Christ, his only Son, our Lord.
　　　He was conceived by the power of the Holy Spirit
　　　　　and born of the virgin Mary.
　　　He suffered under Pontius Pilate,
　　　　　was crucified, died, and was buried.

85

He descended into hell.
On the third day he rose again.
He ascended into heaven,
    and is seated at the right hand of the Father.
He will come again to judge the living and the dead.

I believe in the Holy Spirit,
    the holy Catholic Church,
    the communion of saints,
    the forgiveness of sins,
    the resurrection of the body,
    and the life everlasting. Amen.[30]

The Apostles' Creed is not a story. Rather, it is a list of what every individual who abides by this religious orientation is supposed to believe to be true. Within it are briefly enumerated such Christian doctrines as the creation of the world, the virgin birth, the forgiveness of sins, the resurrection of Christ, and the Trinity. Many Christian denominations teach teenagers various rationales for each of these doctrines. The doctrines are explained point by point through careful analyses of scriptural references that are sometimes called "proof texts." Like the proofs that high-school students learn in their geometry classes, these pedagogical exercises draw on the adolescent's newfound ability to engage in abstract formal thinking. They also provide a reasonable rationale for beliefs and values—a rationale that the adolescent mind appears to be especially primed to accept.

The ideological setting for an individual's life story may develop further through one's adult years. While some psychological research suggests that late adolescence and young adulthood are particularly formative periods in the life span for ideology,[31] a few adults do make important changes in their belief systems in later years. Nonetheless, many, if not most, people reach a kind of steady state with respect to ideology in late adolescence or early adulthood. With the consolidation of an ideological setting, therefore, we are able to ground our identities on a base of perceived truth.

What Is Good? What Is True?

Each ideological setting, like each personal myth, is unique in some way. Yet it is possible to detect some common types. There would appear to be two principal ways to comprehend and categorize ideological settings. The first is to focus on content, and the second is to examine structure. Content refers generally to what a person believes to be right and true, whereas structure refers to how those beliefs are organized. Although content and structure influence each other, the ideas still provide a useful perspective from which to approach the complicated topic of personal ideology.

Agency and communion are the two superordinate content themes in narrative. These same themes appear to characterize fundamental beliefs and values in ideological settings.

Consider for a moment an ideological setting centered on the content theme of agency. Such a belief system would value the autonomy and well-being of the individual over everything else. Individual rights are emphasized over social responsibilities. Individual freedom is dearly prized. Human beings are viewed as powerful and autonomous agents in the world who inevitably conflict with each other or intrude on each other's personal space. Therefore, laws and norms are required in order to deal fairly with clashing agents, with competing individual interests. As John Stuart Mill wrote in his famous essay, *On Liberty,* one's rights as an individual extend only so far that they do not interfere with another's rights.[32]

In a world of autonomous agents, good behavior benefits all individuals. But it benefits them as individuals, not necessarily as parts of a larger whole. Good behavior promotes individual development, growth, fulfillment, advancement, well-being, freedom, etc. Bad behavior, by contrast, undermines or threatens the good of the individual. Because each has his or her own subjective view of the world, people need to abide by general and abstract principles of justice that transcend personal loyalties and biases and provide for the universal good. Without these principles, an agentic world deteriorates into chaos, with each individual bent on maximizing his or her own gain at the expense of all others. A proper ideology in an agentic world, therefore, is one that emphasizes general principles of ethics—like the Ten Commandments or the Golden Rule.

A highly communal ideological setting offers a sharp contrast. A communal ideology would value the group and interpersonal relationships most highly. Social responsibilities become more important than individual freedoms and rights. While it is certainly important to be fair in a communal context, it is more important to care for others, and to be connected to others in bonds of friendship or kinship. From the perspective of communion, people are seen as potentially interdependent organisms linked to each other through particular commitments and responsibilities. While laws governing individual behavior cannot be ignored, from a communal perspective, most of social life takes place outside the agentic domain of competing individuals. The complex problem of living peacefully and productively among particular people is therefore the focus of law and morality.

From a communal point of view, the goodness of a particular action can only be evaluated by taking into consideration its ramifications in a social context. Abstract principles of justice and universal imperatives may not be very relevant because they do not speak to specific situations. What is good and what is true depend on who is involved and what is at stake.

The psychologist Carol Gilligan has written eloquently of the distinction between agentic and communal ideologies in her influential book *In a Different Voice: Psychological Theory and Women's Development.*[33] Gilligan contends that we may hear two contrasting "voices" when we listen to people talk about what is right and true in their lives. According to Gilligan, men are more likely to frame their understandings of moral issues in terms of individual rights, abstract principles of fairness and justice, and the value of the autonomous individual. This is in keeping, says Gilligan, with the general masculine view that human growth and fulfillment mean increasing individuation and self-sufficiency over time. By contrast, women are more likely to center their discussions of moral issues on communal care and responsibilities. From a more feminine perspective, human growth and fulfillment are couched in terms of meaningful connections to others and commitments to the world. According to Gilligan, women's "different voice" has traditionally been devalued in our male-dominated world. In ideology, and perhaps in identity as well, the agentic has been elevated at the expense of the communal.

Gilligan's claims are controversial. To date, systematic psychological research has not provided definitive support for Gilligan's claim that men and women differ significantly with respect to these two ideological voices.[34] Nonetheless, there is a growing recognition of the utility of employing Gilligan's distinction in examining the beliefs and values of both men and women. It appears that some men have highly agentic and some highly communal ideological perspectives, and that the same may be said for women. Whether or not men tend toward the agentic and women toward the communal with respect to fundamental values and beliefs, however, we still do not know.

While we may comprehend the content of an ideological setting from the standpoint of agency and communion, we may examine the structure of ideology by asking the question, How complex is a person's belief system? A complex system is highly differentiated and integrated.[35] This means that a complex system has many parts or distinctions (and so, is differentiated) and that the many parts are connected to each other in many ways (and so, is integrated). A simple system is one in which few distinctions are made, and few connections are discerned.

Developmental psychologists have shown that as children mature and enter adolescence and then adulthood, their belief systems become more complex. With respect to beliefs about moral action,[36] justice,[37] interpersonal responsibility,[38] politics,[39] and religious faith,[40] the child's simplistic and stereotypical patterns of reasoning usually give way to more sophisticated and subtle patterns in later years. Early on, children see moral, legal, interpersonal, political, and religious issues from a very concrete and self-centered point of view—what is good is good for me alone; a friend is a person who is nice to me; political leaders are either all good or all bad. In middle stages, children and adolescents adopt a more complex social perspective as they come to realize that individual needs and viewpoints must be balanced against those of groups and society as a whole. At the highest stages, people adopt internalized principles and standards that take into consideration competing points of view at different levels of analysis. With respect to personal ideology, the most mature perspectives are often the hard-won results of ideological struggle and a prolonged journey in which values and beliefs are repeatedly challenged, tested, and transformed.

By the time a person has moved through adolescence and entered young adulthood, he or she has experienced a good deal of growth and development with respect to ideological setting. It is likely that beliefs and values that were once rather simplistic and egocentric have become articulated in more mature ways, in a more sophisticated ideological framework that sees shades of gray and subtleties in the determination of what is good and what is true. Nonetheless, people differ dramatically with respect to just how complex and mature their ideological settings appear at the end of adolescence. Developmental psychologists have documented important individual differences in how adolescents and young adults understand moral, ethical, religious, and political issues, ranging from perspectives reminiscent of childhood (described as especially "low" stages in moral development, faith development, etc.) to impressively differentiated and integrated perspectives (higher stages) that are viewed by psychologists as particularly mature, advanced, and enlightened. Research also suggests that these individual differences remain relatively stable through the adult years.[41] In other words, the kind of ideological setting we establish in adolescence—its structure and its content—will probably stay with us through our adult years, with, in most cases, but minor changes and variations.

Sometime during late adolescence or young adulthood, therefore, most of us reach a point when we feel fairly confident about what we believe to be right and true. In adolescence, we are temporarily drawn away from stories toward more abstract and logical systems. Stories for a time fail to provide reliable and valid ideological answers. But after the consolidation of an ideological setting in late adolescence or young adulthood, we are ready to return to story, this time from the standpoint of the story maker—the adult charged with authoring his or her own personal myth.

CHAPTER 4

Becoming
the Mythmaker

Life becomes mythic in our teenage years. The formation and reformation of identity remains thereafter the central psychosocial task of the adult years. From adolescence onward we face this task of creating an integrative life story through which we are able to understand who we are and how we fit into the adult world. As our views of ourselves and our worlds change over time, we revise the story. Making life into myth is what adulthood is all about. Erik Erikson tells us:

> To be adult means among other things to see one's own life in continuous perspective, both in retrospect and prospect. By accepting some definition as to who he is, usually on the basis of a function in an economy, a place in the sequence of generations, and a status in the structure of society, the adult is able to selectively reconstruct his past in such a way that, step for step, it seems to have planned him, or better, he seems to have planned it. In this sense, psychologically we do choose our parents, our family history, and the history of our kings, heroes, and gods. By making them our own, we maneuver ourselves into the inner position of proprietors, of creators.[1]

By "selectively reconstructing our past," as Erikson puts it, we attain the status of "creator." We create a self that is whole and purposeful because it is embedded in a coherent and meaningful story. None of us is in a position to choose his or her own parents, or the circumstances of infancy and childhood. But maturity demands the acceptance and meaningful organization of past events. As adults, we impose a mythic plan on our lives where no plan existed before. We create myth so that our lives, and the lives of others, will make sense. Through myth we determine who we are, who we were, and who we may become in the future.

As the older adolescent or young adult begins to fashion a personal myth, he or she may move through a process of *psychosocial moratorium.*[2] Young people in moratorium actively explore new alternatives in life. They experiment with new and different attitudes about God, sex, politics, and life-style. They try on new roles and relationships. They buck the conventions of their childhoods by constructing new frameworks for understanding themselves and their worlds. They become creative historians as they experiment with different ways of making sense of their early years, their relationships with their parents, and even their ethnic, religious, and class roots.

Through exploration, the young person gets a better sense of what resources for building identity exist in his or her environment. These resources include social networks that are supportive of such a personal search, available job and educational opportunities, relationships in which mature love and intimacy may be experienced, and sundry cultural systems, life-styles, and ways of being. Modern American society offers middle-class and upper-class people a rich variety of resources for the making of identity. Working-class and poor persons are given fewer options. Women are offered somewhat different resources than are men. A person must do the best he or she can with whatever is at hand. There are no purely "self-made" men or women. In life, as in myth, we can never transcend our resources.

In the ideal course for identity formation, society encourages psychosocial moratorium and provides the young person with safe havens and settings for experimentation. Moratorium works best when we do not play it "for keeps." The young person should feel that it is safe to try on new roles without undue long-term risk. If he wants to be a Buddhist this week, he should be able to do so without having to commit himself to spending twenty years in Tibet. While

92

society does not wish to encourage all forms of exploration, a certain degree of societal tolerance and acceptance is necessary if a young person is to grow and flourish in moratorium. Some educators have argued eloquently that a strong liberal arts curriculum in college can enhance the development of identity by encouraging young people to think critically about their own assumptions in life, and by promoting their explorations of alternative ways of acting, feeling, and believing.[3] The college years provide one of the most effective environments our society has discovered for nurturing psychosocial moratorium.

Over half of the adults interviewed in my studies of personal myth have attended college, and of these approximately two thirds report that their college experiences encouraged them to question some aspect of their lives that they had previously not thought to question. Some talk of explorations in religious belief. A young man raised in a conservative Catholic family meets students from other religious traditions at the university and comes to doubt the "universal truths" of his own faith. A woman from a family in which no religious traditions are observed finds intriguing the issues raised in a theology course and joins an ecumenical campus church so that she may explore her own spirituality in depth. Other people talk of rethinking occupational goals and concerns. A sophomore headed toward a career in medicine finds he has a gift for writing fiction and is encouraged by a professor to pursue a career in the arts. A woman whose parents have urged her to become a nurse gets the highest grades in her chemistry classes and begins to consider graduate school in the sciences. Many people also talk of experiments in life-style. A young man quits dating women as he candidly confronts his own homosexuality, and becomes involved in the campus gay community. A young woman moves out of the dormitory to live with her boyfriend—an act unthinkable for her only a year before. A wealthy white suburbanite becomes close friends with a group of foreign students from a developing country. He moves out of his parents' home and into a very humble apartment with his friends. He begins to question the value of a materialistic life-style, and wonders if his privileged status as a wealthy American hasn't indirectly contributed to the exploitation of other societies.

Ideally, the explorations of moratorium lead to adult commitments. The most important commitments are ideological, occupational, and interpersonal. After exploring alternative systems of belief and value, the young adult has a clearer sense of personal ideology, with personalized religious, ethical, and political viewpoints. He or she is ready to assume a place in the world of work, and to make long-term commitments of friendship and love.

In contemporary American society, psychosocial moratorium does not necessarily lead to universal truth. The adolescent or young adult is not likely to learn that there is a single appropriate way to lead a life. Instead, a young person discovers that there may be many viable religious perspectives. There may be many different kinds of occupations that lead to success and fulfillment. There may even be several people in the world with whom to share life happily in marriage. The pervasive relativism of adult life in contemporary America makes it difficult for thoughtful people to believe that there is a single right and a single wrong answer for most of life's difficult questions, including questions of identity. Amid the relativism, however, the young person must still act. He or she must make a commitment to a truth that is right for a particular time. An individual's choices must be measured and informed, certainly, but he or she must also be ready to leap out of moratorium on faith. We can never know for certain how things will work out in the long run. But we must be committed to trying our hardest to make them work.

There is a tension in identity commitment. It is the tension between the individual's needs and proclivities on the one hand and the demands of society on the other. In healthy identity development, the individual must negotiate skillfully between wild rebellion and blind conformity. Commitment should enable a person to create a personalized niche, but one within society. One cannot make sound commitments if one rejects everything that society has to offer. Alienation and anomie run counter to healthy identity development. Similarly, one cannot make sound commitments by selling out to the status quo and passively accepting whatever it is that society hands out. One should not explore identity conscientiously only to settle for the most conventional clichés in self-definition. Rather, one must find a place in a complex social world. Identity is something of a collaboration between the person and the social world. The two are together responsible for the life story.

Identity commitments are made both to the future and the past. Part of the exploration we undertake in moratorium involves exploring who we once were. In world mythologies, the young hero on his journey may find that strange forces, odd persons, and new adventures seem oddly intimate and familiar, as if they have been known all along. So it is in identity development. Everything is not completely new in moratorium. Some of what we encounter may indeed be quite old, though it may show itself in a new and unexpected guise. Therefore, when we make ideological, occupational, and interpersonal commitments in life, we recapture and reformulate essential aspects of our own past. Healthy identity affirms both change and continuity.

Not all identity commitments are forever. Once a person has completed a phase of moratorium and made commitments to value, work, and family, the exploration is not ended. Identity is not fully "achieved" in young adulthood.[4] Flux and change are likely to occur again, especially in the realms of work and relationships. The adult life span does not take a smooth, consistent course. Nor does it develop through a series of constantly repeating cycles, stages, phases, or seasons.[5] Instead, there are likely to be periods of relative stability in which commitments are lived out, interspersed with periods of relative change, in which the person may go through another moratorium. We should expect alternating and irregular phases of exploration and commitment, with each life progressing along a unique course. During periods of exploration, the person is likely to be revising in significant ways the self-defining myth. During periods of commitment, the myth remains relatively stable.

The Arc of an Adult Life

Unlike the well-known stage theory of identity put forth by Erik Erikson, I do not see identity formation as confined to late adolescence and young adulthood. I believe that what Erikson views as subsequent developmental stages—"intimacy" and "generativity"— are best understood as identity concerns. Once an individual realizes that he or she is responsible for defining the self, the issue of self-definition remains a preoccupation through most of the adult years. Identity may eventually recede as a central issue, but only in old age, or that period of time that Erikson has demarcated as the final stage of psychosocial development, the stage concerned with "ego integrity vs. despair."

Contrary to Erikson,[6] and Freud before him (who contended that early childhood experience strongly determines adult personality), a significant number of psychologists and sociologists today believe that adult lives are relatively malleable and that significant change in psychological functioning may be observed after one's twenty-first birthday. To a certain extent, this belief is grounded in Western assumptions about the autonomous individual. As members of the same societal and historical milieu, Western psychologists tend to espouse many of the same values held dear by middle- and upper-middle-class Western society at large. We would like to believe that each of us, even in our mature years, may control and create our own lives in a personally meaningful way. We hope that each individual may follow his or her unique pathway.

In the last twenty years, psychologists and psychiatrists such as Daniel Levinson,[7] George Vaillant,[8] Roger Gould,[9] and David Gutmann[10] have theorized about adult development in terms of a predictable series of challenges or seasons in life. Before them, Carl Jung,[11] Else Frenkel-Brunswik,[12] Robert Havighurst,[13] Robert White,[14] and Bernice Neugarten[15] provided influential frameworks for charting an individual's developing identity in the adult years. These theorists do not agree on every point, and strong arguments against all of their positions can be formulated.[16] One major limitation of most of these approaches is that they tend to rely too much on the narrative accounts provided by white, professional men who have grown up in relative prosperity in post–World War II America. Some recent research has focused on women,[17] but minority adults and adults situated at the lower end of the socioeconomic continuum have not received very much attention. Little cross-cultural research has been conducted. And we know even less about the contours of adult development from earlier points in American history.

Any psychological study of adult development must therefore begin with some important qualifications. Concepts such as "maturity" and "healthy development" are shaped by cultural assumptions that we rarely call into question. Most of us, as middle- or upper-middle-class citizens of a Western democracy, tend to believe that mature adults should shoulder some responsibility for their own lives, work as well as play, assume productive roles in society, strive for psychological autonomy and financial independence, prepare their children for the challenges of modern life, and so on. As a society, we tend to value freedom, autonomy, mastery, and responsible commitment among adults. Our beliefs concerning how people should and do shape their lives in their twenties and thirties are guided by these values. Views of adult development are likely to be very different in other societies, however. Western models of healthy adult development are not likely to work very well in explaining the development of fundamentalist Islamic women, or men living in rural Afghanistan. Very few, if any, psychological theories can, in good faith, make cross-cultural claims.[18]

Keeping these important limitations in mind, we may perceive a generalized sketch emerging from many writings on the topic of early adult development. The sketch is an idealized composite that may not apply in its particulars to any specific adult life. There are many exceptions to every generalization, and each individual life is not likely to be as orderly and well arranged as the sketch suggests. Still, the sketch is useful as a chart of what many of us have come to expect we will confront in the third and fourth decades of our lives.

We enter adulthood in our twenties. According to Daniel Levinson, it is in this decade that our efforts are centered on the task of "Getting into the Adult World." From the perspective of Robert Havighurst, the person in his or her twenties must assume initial adult roles in the realms of family, work, and civic responsibility. Most men and many women enter the world of full-time employment during this period. The more fortunate and generally more educated young adults step into their first positions on various career ladders, hoping to rise to higher echelons in the years to come. By the time they reach their thirtieth birthdays, the vast majority of adults have moved out of their parents' residences and established lives of relative independence, often marrying and beginning families of their own.

By most standards, people in their twenties are still "young." Many are at the peak of their physical abilities, as we see in most professional sports, wherein the stars are typically in their mid- to late twenties. The adult world is new and exciting for many people in their twenties, though it is likely to prove a little frightening as well. It is a world that offers a wide variety of opportunities for provisional commitments. Adults in their twenties, as they launch careers and families, carve out an initial niche in society. While some of these commitments may last a lifetime, many may not. Major career shifts in the lives of American men and women are more the norm than the exception,[19] and many families change by virtue of divorce. Therefore, the initial commitments of the twenties are imbued with a temporary quality. Most of us realize that things may change in significant ways in the years to come. Many of us feel that we have not really settled in yet.

The individual who makes provisional commitments in his or her twenties looks forward to later years through the lens of a *dream* for the future. According to Levinson, the dream is an overall script or plan concerning what an adult hopes to experience and accomplish in the future. The dream may include visions of occupational success and enhanced prestige, the development of a fulfilling family life, the attainment of financial security or an appealing life-style, the establishment of certain kinds of relationships with friends and peers, and many other hopes and goals for the self, family, and significant others. Some research suggests that men's dreams tend to be dominated by occupational achievement, whereas women tend to manifest dreams split between occupational and interpersonal goals.[20] The dream develops over time. Major transitions in life are occasioned by important changes in the dream.

Another significant aspect of development in the twenties, according to Levinson, is the establishment of a relationship with a *mentor*. The mentor is a man or woman who is usually somewhat older and more experienced than the young adult and therefore well positioned to shepherd the young adult through some of the difficult and challenging periods of the twenties. Mentors would appear to be most valuable and most common in the professional workplace. A graduate student or junior professor heading for a career in college academia may find a mentor in his or her adviser. Through actions and advice, the adviser can teach the younger man or woman how to make his or her way in the world of higher education, how to teach effectively, do good research, obtain governmental grants, get along well with colleagues, etc.

Good mentors are hard to find, however, and I fear that many, if not most, working adults in their twenties never develop a satisfying mentoring relationship. The problem is especially acute for women in male-dominated professions, in that most young adults prefer mentors of the same sex. It would appear that mentors themselves—men and women who are typically in their thirties or forties—are used to serving as personal teachers and role models for younger adults who are of the same sex as they are. Even if we never find our own personal mentor, however, we are likely to encounter role models of various kinds in our work and family lives. A good deal of development in our twenties may involve patterning our lives according to visible adult roles that are enacted by other people we meet and know.

Levinson calls the period following the twenties the "Age 30 Transition." Young adults move in this period from a life structure centered on provisional commitments to one involving tough choices about long-term priorities and goals. We may find it necessary to reexamine decisions made in the twenties, and initiate important change. Some research suggests that the Age 30 Transition may be a more critical developmental milestone for women than for men, especially for professional women who have delayed establishing a family. In an intensive biographical study of the life stories of thirty-nine professional women, Priscilla Roberts and Peter Newton conclude that "one such remarkable finding is the apparent ubiquity of a transitional period in the years immediately around 30, and the suggestion of markedly accelerated personality change in that period."[21] Roberts and Newton found the Age 30 Transition to be

a period in which priorities established during the 20s are reversed. A major task of this transitional period for women was the reappraisal of the relative importance of career and family. Women who had stressed marriage and motherhood in their 20s tended to develop more individualistic goals for their 30s, whereas those who had focused on occupation suddenly became concerned with marriage and family at around 30.[22]

Levinson describes the early thirties as a period of "Settling Down." It is a period of relative stability wherein the adult works hard to build the nest, put down the roots, and establish him or herself within those overlapping social communities—work, family, neighborhood, church—to which he or she now feels a sense of long-term commitment. Among other challenges of the times, men and women in their thirties typically face the tasks of promoting the development of their children and other members of the next generation, achieving satisfactory occupational performance, adjusting to expanded social and civic responsibilities, developing rewarding leisure activities, and beginning to adjust to aging parents.[23] Especially for professional men, the thirties is a time to start "making it" in one's career. By the end of the decade, most professionals want to have attained considerable recognition for progress made in their roles as lawyers, doctors, professors, writers, scientists, managers, artists, businesspersons, social workers, teachers, counselors, consultants, and the like.

In his studies of professional men, Levinson found that the settling-down period of the early thirties is likely to give way to a more tumultuous second half of the decade, characterized as "Becoming One's Own Man." This period represents the culmination of early adult development. In their late thirties, many adults wield considerable influence in numerous spheres of life. By this time, many professionals in our society have begun to earn substantial salaries and have achieved certain leadership positions in work and sometimes in community life. Yet with the growing prominence comes a mounting frustration that one has not yet achieved enough, one has not yet become sufficiently autonomous. Professional women in our society presumably have the same yearnings for increased autonomy and achievement at this age. Levinson describes this period as it manifests itself among the professional men he studied:

> It represents the high point of early adulthood and the beginning of what lies beyond. A key element in this period is the man's feeling that, no matter what he has accomplished to date, he is not sufficiently his own man. He feels overly dependent upon and constrained by persons or groups who have authority over him or who, for various reasons, exert great influence upon him. The writer comes to recognize that he is unduly intimidated by his publisher

and too vulnerable to the evaluation of certain critics. The man who has successfully risen through the managerial ranks with the support and encouragement of his superiors now finds that they control too much and delegate too little, and he impatiently awaits the time when he will have the authority to make his own decisions and to get the enterprise really going. The untenured faculty member imagines that once he has tenure he will be free of all the restraints and demands he's been acquiescing to since graduate school days. (The illusions die hard!)[24]

In their thirties, many adults begin to perceive certain intransigent limitations in life and begin to realize that compromises are required. One's dream for the future is likely to become more tempered, less expansive. The boundless possibilities anticipated in the twenties may shade into more realistic appraisals of life prospects. It would appear that Levinson's professional men ran up against a number of obstacles on the road to occupational success, prestige, or emancipation in their late thirties.

The life trajectories of professional men and women are likely to diverge markedly in the thirties. While patterns of parenting appear to have become more egalitarian in recent years, women still shoulder the lion's share of child-rearing obligations, even among two-career professional couples. What David Gutmann calls "the parental emergency" mandates that in most (though by no means all) families, women and men in their thirties are likely to adopt relatively stereotypic sex roles, with women as caregivers and men as breadwinners, if children are to be raised. Therefore, a woman's professional development is likely to be less linear than that of a man's in the thirties. Women take time off to have babies and, in many cases, to raise children. Very few men take leaves from paid employment to engage in full-time, or even part-time, caregiving, even when opportunities for such leaves are available.[25] Among nonprofessional or more "traditional" American families, the sex-role divergence may begin earlier.

As we move to the end of early adulthood, we come to anticipate trouble ahead. We have made long-term commitments, tough choices, and painful compromises. We have encountered obstacles and limitations. In our late thirties, we may become more concerned with our own aging, as we see our parents move into their later years.

We are no longer "young." Roger Gould argues that most men and women in their thirties come to realize that life is not simple and not fully under their control. The realization is one of a number of developments that may set the stage for a transition into middle adulthood.

By the time we reach age forty, we are likely to have developed a much more articulated and realistic understanding of who we are and in what ways we have established ourselves as a "mature adult" in the world. Legend has it that when asked to define the meaning of psychological health and maturity, Freud responded with the simple German phrase of *Lieben und Arbeiten*—"to love and to work." Sociologically, modern life is organized within the contrasting domains of home and work. Psychologically, modern adults organize their own lives according to the twin desires for communion and agency. By the time they hit their fortieth birthday, most men and women have a pretty good sense of who they are in the realms of family and career.

The History of the Self

To create a personal myth is to fashion a history of the self. A history is an account of the past that seeks to explain how and why events transpired as they actually did. History is much more than a chronological listing of names, dates, and places. It is a story about how the past came to be and how, ultimately, it gave birth to the present. It is a truism that the historian's understanding of the present colors the story he or she will tell about the past. When the present changes, the good historian may rewrite the past—not to distort or conceal the truth, but to find one that better reflects the past in light of what is known in the present and what can be reasonably anticipated about the future.

In late adolescence and young adulthood, we begin to adopt a historical perspective on our own lives. Grandiose personal fables are a first attempt at historiography. The fanciful stories adolescents create celebrating their unique origin, development, and destiny give way in young adulthood to more serious narrative attempts to make sense of identity. These somewhat more realistic myths rearrange the past so that it can be seen to have given birth to the present.

In order to accomplish this narrative task, many of us find it necessary to pass judgment on our past and present. We seek to determine, in a very general sense, the extent to which our past and our present are "good" or "bad."

In the provocative but little-known writings of Agnes Hankiss, a Hungarian sociologist, four possibilities for "ontologies of the self" arise. Ontology is the study of being. Therefore, an ontology of the self is a person's account of how he or she came to be. Hankiss finds that young adults tend to use four different kinds of "strategies" in constructing their ontologies of self: the dynastic (a good past gives birth to a good present), the antithetical (a bad past gives birth to a good present), the compensatory (a good past gives birth to a bad present), and the self-absolutory (a bad past gives birth to a bad present).[26]

In a dynastic strategy of mythmaking, the goodness of childhood is seen to have been "passed down" to adulthood. Beginning in late adolescence, Donna Kinsey developed a personal myth according to a dynastic strategy. Today she is a thirty-three-year-old lawyer and mother of two who lives with her husband and children in an old house in a less-than-trendy urban neighborhood. Donna is soft-spoken, modest, and, in some ways, traditionally feminine, describing herself on standard psychological measures as especially "tender" and "compassionate" and scoring very high on a measure of the need for intimacy. She teaches Sunday school in a Lutheran church and has served on the church council. She is devoted to her children. In other ways, however, Donna is far from traditional. She has excelled in a profession that is still dominated by men. As a lawyer, she has worked vigorously for fairness in housing. She has defended tenants against landlords in numerous court cases and established herself as a local authority on real estate and housing issues.

For the most part, Donna's personal myth is a story of continuity. She describes a happy childhood filled with books and friends. Her father was a journalist; her mother, a writer. Both parents were "socially conscious," in her words, and interested in politics. Both instilled in her the belief that she was a member of a privileged class of people whose relative wealth and comfort bring with them a responsibility to help others. Donna traces her strong concern for social equality and justice to the early influence of her parents. For as long as she can remember, she has wanted to help others. She characterizes this motive as a "pent-up need" that energizes and directs a great deal of her behavior at home and at work. In her life story, the need is pervasive and unquenchable, and makes up the dominant theme of her myth. When her behavior is in accord with the need, she feels happy and fulfilled. In Donna's view, one can never do enough to help, if one is privileged enough to be able to help. Her religious beliefs, dating from childhood, provide her need to help with a Christian framework. Jesus is her model, as he mingles with the poor and the sick, for mature and fulfilling adult behavior. His model has for her been personified by her parents from her earliest days onward.

A second approach to mythmaking is an antithetical strategy. Here the present is seen as good, but the past is seen as bad. The contrast between the two may provide the story with its characteristic tension and movement. The proverbial rags-to-riches story is a favorite in American folklore, celebrating the belief that a man or woman can rise from humble beginnings in childhood to become a great leader, scientist, doctor, entrepreneur, or whatever. A song from my own childhood—second grade, I think—recalls this type of myth. It goes something like this:

> Young Abe Lincoln was a poor man's son,
> Never knew when his work was done,
> Made his way by honest toil,
> Grew up tall in the sun and soil.
> Young Abe Lincoln was his name
> Truth and honor were his fame.

Lincoln rose from the humble log cabin in Kentucky to become perhaps our greatest American president. We don't know what personal myth Abraham Lincoln developed for himself. But it is quite clear that Americans have since employed an antithetical strategy in constructing and celebrating their understanding of his life.

The antithetical strategy is an extraordinarily optimistic one, for it gives us faith that no matter how bad things may have been, they can always get better. This strategy may be used to great advantage in personal myth making. A person may come to treasure the deprivation and poverty of his or her youth. A bad past may become a badge of honor as one's life is mythologically rearranged to show just how far one has indeed come. The goodness of the present is magnified by its contrast with the past. In his famous autobiography, Benjamin Franklin masterfully employs the antithetical strategy.[27] In the fall of 1723, this seventeen-year-old boy, dirty and poorly dressed, walked through the streets of Philadelphia carrying "three great puffy rolls" and less than a dollar to his name. A few years later, he had become a successful printer. In his middle years, he conducted scientific experiments, founded libraries, and promoted a great number of personal and civic causes. In his advanced years, he became ambassador to France and an international celebrity. Franklin's personal myth captured the boundless optimism of early America and was a model for countless lives. His *Autobiography* and his many other writings on human behavior and government aimed to provide lessons on healthy and beneficial conduct for generations of Americans. This is precisely what Franklin intended for his writings, as he told his son in 1771:

> From the poverty and obscurity in which I was born and in which I passed my earliest years, I have raised myself to a state of affluence and some degree of celebrity in the world. As constant good fortune has accompanied me even to an advanced period of life, my posterity will perhaps be desirous of learning the means, which I employed, and which, thanks to Providence, so well succeeded with me. They may also deem them fit to be imitated, should any of them find themselves in similar circumstances.[28]

The third strategy is the opposite of the second. In the compensatory strategy, a good and positive past gives way to a bad and negative present. Here one's personal myth may suggest that the best is over, that "it's all downhill from here." In these kinds of accounts, the person affirms that life was once good but that something went wrong along the way. People speak in this regard of a "fall from grace," a "turn for the worse," or a "loss of innocence."

Growing up in Gary, Indiana, in a relatively poor working-class neighborhood, I remember many of the stories about youth and adulthood I heard as a child. I was told that "these are the best years of your life," that I should enjoy myself as a youth because life would get rougher when I grew up. My father believed this strongly. As I reconstruct it all now, I think that many of the parents of my friends were indeed dissatisfied with their lives. For the most part, they worked in the steel mills or were housewives. Growing up meant hard labor and low incomes. Many believed a good education was the way out, but few of the parents who told the stories had been able to get one in their youths. I remember not wanting to grow up, or at least not wanting to grow up like them. Their compensatory strategies for making sense of their own lives did not sit well with me. I did not feel that I was living then, as a child, in a "golden age." While I was relatively happy, I did not relish the idea that these times were as good as they would get. I was troubled, as I still am, by the tragic quality of the compensatory strategy, the sense of regret and missed opportunities. Yet such a strategy may still provide life with meaning and purpose. And it can even prove a source of inspiration in life, as when a person who believes that he or she has lost a positive past seeks in some constructive way to recapture or reconstruct certain elements of that past in the future.

Phil McGrath has fashioned a personal myth according to the compensatory strategy. Though he describes his family as very poor, Phil's childhood is filled with fun and freedom, carefree days of running around the neighborhood, playing war and playing baseball, getting into minor scrapes with other boys and, once or twice, with the law, but always coming out on top. In high school, Phil is a star athlete. He pitches a no-hitter in a key championship baseball game. He does well in football and track, too. Young women find him extremely appealing, as sexual conquests come to rival his consider-able accomplishments on the playing fields. The good times go on and on, even during his stint in the U.S. Navy, when he saw minor combat in Korea.

Returning to the United States in his early twenties, however, Phil begins to find that his stock has suddenly fallen. While he was in the service, the economy took a mild downturn, and now Phil finds it especially difficult to land a high-paying job. He has no interest in going to college, and he refuses to take on high-paying factory work, because he finds manual labor demeaning. His girlfriend gets preg-nant, and after a hasty wedding, Phil settles for a low-paying job in sales. Though he is very successful in his work, he cannot summon up the discipline to provide his family with consistent financial support. Harking back to the carefree days of youth, he spends much of his money in bars and gambling. The marriage dissolves, but not until four children have been born, and Phil is saddled with considerable child-support payments.

Many jobs and two marriages later, Phil is now fifty-five years old. He describes his life as structured around two monumental turning points: The first is his transition to marriage and parenthood after Korea, when he began to realize that life was not as fun as it used to be, that being a child is vastly superior to being shouldered with the burdens of adulthood. The second is a fateful decision he made in his early forties. Having achieved a respected status as a top-notch salesman, Phil had an opportunity to purchase a business and move to another part of the country. The purchase entailed considerable risk, according to Phil. His wife (his second) at the time strongly urged him to take the risk, but at the eleventh hour of negotiations, Phil seemed to lose faith, and he backed out of the deal. Shortly thereafter, his second wife left him. He gained a considerable amount of weight. He was diagnosed as having high blood pressure. His latest marriage seems to have been a disaster from the beginning. His friends claim that his new wife—who is nineteen years old—only wants his money. Too embarrassed by her ex-husband's latest match, his first wife no longer speaks to him. Relations with his children are also strained.

Phil's account of his life is filled with regrets about missed opportunities and time passing him by. Turning points go from good to bad; things never get better; the old days are always preferred to what follows. Young adulthood was so bad because, in part, childhood was so good. And his current situation is viewed as significantly worse than what he experienced in his first marriage, which now, in retrospect, does not appear quite as bad as it did at the time. In the compensatory strategy, yesterday is always brighter than today. And tomorrow promises the black of night.

Finally, in the self-absolutory strategy, a negative past is seen to have produced a negative present. In these kinds of accounts, the person often suggests that he or she is "paying the price" for past mistakes. Other accounts support the idea that serious disadvantages are rarely transcended over time. Poverty leads to more poverty. Childhood unhappiness breeds adult misery. The person may suggest that he or she "never had a chance," that "the cards were stacked against me" from the first day onward. Thus, life is made sensible, but the story is a tragic one.

Sara Levin is a forty-three-year-old bookkeeper and mother of three who, from a very early age onward, has been repeatedly reminded that life is not fair and that good things are likely to turn bad. She grew up in a conservative Jewish household wherein she was strongly urged to value introspection, reading, and "being quiet." Sara has always identified closely with her mother and with certain Jewish traditions carried forth by the older generation. Her identification is symbolized in her own story by the fact that she was born on her mother's birthday, which was, in the year of her birth, also a major Jewish holiday. The identification, however, is highly ambivalent. Sara sees her traditional religious upbringing as being responsible for a great deal of misery in her life. Even as a child, she felt that certain beliefs and customs that her family held dear were foolish and a waste of time. Home and family seemed suffocating to her as a child, and now, as an adult, she still feels suffocated by certain aspects of her family's legacy. She cannot escape the past—Sara finds it impossible to banish her mother, and certain patterns of behavior, from her life. Her mother has become even more domineering and obnoxious over the years, and Sara feels that she herself is becoming that way. As she gets older, Sara believes herself to be more and more "guilty of unselfish giving." In Sara's view, she has helped too many people too often. She has given too much and received too little in return.

Sara feels that she is currently experiencing the most troublesome period of her life—a "mid-life crisis" that, she believes, has been brewing for a very long time. She is quick to trace its roots to her earliest years in the family. Today, her children are doing very poorly in school, her friends repeatedly let her down despite all she has done for them, and her mother has become a burden. Though she continues to volunteer for various groups and causes, community service proves to have few rewards. Lying beneath Sara's regrets and frustrations is a profound cynicism about human life. The day after Sara was married, her twelve-year-old niece, Susan, discovered a lump in her own neck. She was dead in a few months. Since that day, Sara has refused to believe that there is a God. "I won't tell my children that God created the world in seven days, because you can't do that and kill Susan," she says. "I won't say communal prayer because God is not listening." Ever since the Vietnam War, she has refused to recite the American Pledge of Allegiance. She believes instead in what she calls "brutal honesty." Life is fated to be unfair and random; people are unfair and generally selfish. If more people were honest with themselves, they would believe what she believes, she claims. Her personal myth also suggests that if more people had been honest with her in her past, she might not find her present life so disillusioning.

The Good Myth

We work on our stories, consciously and unconsciously, throughout most of our adult years. Major identity changes may follow significant life changes, such as getting married or divorced, having one's first child, changing jobs, changing residences, losing one's parents or one's spouse, menopause, retirement. They may also correspond to symbolic watersheds in the life course, such as hitting a fortieth birthday, or even getting the first gray hairs. During these periods, we may call into question some of the assumptions of our life and our myth. We may recast the myth to embody new plots and characters and to emphasize different scenes from the past and different expectations for the future. We may set new goals. The sense of an ending may change substantially, and as the envisioned ending changes, the entire narrative may be reoriented. At other times, however, we experience relative stability in identity. During these more tranquil periods, the myth evolves slowly and subtly.

Our personal myth develops in periodic episodes that punctuate the relative equilibrium of the rest of adult life. Dramatic changes may be followed by long periods in which very little mythmaking seems to occur. Every life is different in this regard, and so every personal myth has a unique course of development.

To say that the myth "develops" is to suggest that identity is progressive, that we make progress over time in the search for unity and purpose as we move from adolescence through adulthood. We have already witnessed this progress in the transition from those fantastic personal fables of early adolescence to the more realistic and refined personal myths that young adults form. Through early and middle adulthood, the personal myth expands and matures further. To say that myths develop is also to imply that at a given point in time some myths are more "developed"—more mature, more adequate, more adaptive—than others. We must, then, ask ourselves: What is a "good" personal myth?

This is a tricky question. It can only be asked in a meaningful way when we take into consideration the particular developmental and environmental circumstances within which the myth and the myth-maker are embedded. As fantastical and immature as it may seem, a fourteen-year-old boy's personal fable concerning a glorious career in professional basketball may be an altogether appropriate aspect of identity at this time in his life. We should not be too concerned, therefore, at the primitive story he has fashioned for himself. If he has that same story at age thirty and his jump shot looks like mine, then we would have to register serious reservations about the development of his identity. A life story needs to be appropriate for a given level of development, and particular life circumstances. We do not expect the same things from a twenty-one-year-old woman and a middle-aged man. Furthermore, we should not expect the same things from a thirty-five-year-old mother of four, with no husband and an eighth-grade education, and her thirty-five-year-old professional counterpart who has degrees from two prestigious schools and whose husband is a lawyer. Opportunities and identity resources are not distributed equally over the life span and across the socioeconomic and cultural spectrum. I repeat: In life and in myth, we cannot transcend our resources.

If we think of a personal myth as developing over time, then we might do well to look for standards of maturity in life stories. Six developmental trends may be identified. Each provides a standard or criterion against which we may compare a particular personal myth at a given point in time. Over the course of adolescence through middle adulthood, our personal myths should ideally develop in the direction of increasing (1) coherence, (2) openness, (3) credibility, (4) differentiation, (5) reconciliation, and (6) generative integration. The prototype of the "good story" in human identity is one that receives high marks on these six narrative standards.

All other things being equal, the personal myth that is more coherent is better than one that is less coherent. Do the characters do things that make sense in the context of the story? Do their motivations make sense in terms of what we know about how human beings generally behave? Do events follow events in a causal manner? Do parts of the story contradict other parts? A story that lacks coherence leaves its reader wondering why things turned out in such an inexplicable, puzzling way. When the story of our life does not make sense to us, then we need to explore alternatives in identity in order to fashion a new myth.

But coherence isn't everything. Some stories seem too coherent to be true. We do not need perfect consistency in order to find unity and purpose in life. Indeed, a good life story is one that tolerates ambiguity. Such a story propels the person into the future by holding open a number of different alternatives for future action and thought. Our stories need to be flexible and resilient. They need to be able to change, grow, and develop as we ourselves change. Openness is a difficult criterion to judge in personal myth, for there is always the danger of too much openness, reflecting lack of commitment and resolve. Still, the personal myth that welcomes change and growth is superior to one that is less welcoming. Without openness, our personal myths run the risk of becoming rigid, stagnant, and brittle.

A third standard is credibility. Our life stories are about our lives. History is not simply a chronicle, but a narrative interpretation of what we believe to have happened in the past, based on what we know in the present. History may shape facts, but it is nonetheless still based on facts that are generally believed to be true. Napoleon really *was* defeated at Waterloo. No matter what interpretation we may place on it, this event really happened. So it should be with our personal myths.

We must seek credibility in our life stories. The good, mature, and adaptive personal myth cannot be based on gross distortions. Identity is not a fantasy. This is why the adolescent's personal fable will ultimately fail. We create our identities, certainly. But we do not create them out of thin air, as we might a poem or a fiction. In identity, the good story manifests more than the mere appearance of credibility. It must really *be* credible, and accountable to facts that

111

can be known or found out. While identity is a creative work of the imagination, it is still grounded in the real world in which it functions.

A good story is rich in characterization, plot, and theme. Its reader is drawn into a richly textured world in which characters develop in intriguing ways over time. Their actions define compelling plots as tension builds to climax and resolution follows. In this regard, we may say that the good story tends to be richly differentiated. Similarly, a personal myth should develop in the direction of increasing differentiation. As the adult matures and gathers new experiences, his or her personal myth should take on more and more facets and characterizations. It should become richer, deeper, and more complex. As we shall see in the chapters ahead, this is especially evident in the development and refinement of imagoes in early and middle adulthood. Our personified images of ourselves become more richly delineated and refined. As our stories become more differentiated, we bring into the narrative a greater number of factors, issues, and conflicts. We come to see that we are many things, and that some of these things may contradict each other.

As differentiation increases, we may seek reconciliation between and among conflicting forces in the story. Harmony and resolution must prevail amid the multiplicity of self. A good story raises tough issues and dynamic contradictions. And a good story provides narrative solutions that affirm the harmony and integrity of the self. Reconciliation is one of the most challenging tasks in the making of personal myth. Psychologically, we are not generally prepared to face this challenge until our middle adult years.[29]

The sixth standard for a good story of identity is what I call generative integration. The life story seeks coherence, credibility, and reconciliation to a greater extent than might some very good stories that are purely fiction. But the life story is not simply a story that one might read in *The New Yorker*. It is a mythic rendering of a particular person's life. The human life exists in a social and ethical context that does not generally apply, or apply in the same way, to other kinds of stories.[30] In mature identity, the adult is able to function as a productive and contributing member of society. He or she is able to take on adult roles in the spheres of work and family. He or she is able and willing to promote, nurture, and guide the next generation, to contribute in some small or large way to the survival, enhancement, or progressive development of the human enterprise. The good myth integrates the mythmaker into society in a generative way.

Our personal myths provide our own lives with a sense of unity and purpose. But our own lives connect to other lives, our myths, to other myths. The most mature personal myths are those that enhance the mythmaking of others. Mature identity in adulthood requires a creative involvement in a social world that is larger and more enduring than the self. It is to that world, as well as to the self, that the myth must be oriented. We must be true to ourselves, certainly. But we must also be true to our time and place. If our myths do not integrate us into a social world and a sequence of generations, then the development of identity runs the risk of degenerating into utter narcissism. Ideally, the mythmaker's art should benefit both the artist who fashions the myth and the society that it adorns.

PART II

Story Characters

Properly speaking, a man has as many social selves as there are individuals who recognize him and carry an image of him in their mind. To wound any one of his images is to wound him. But as the individuals who carry the images fall naturally into classes, we may practically say that he has as many different social selves as there are distinct groups of persons about whose opinions he cares. He generally shows a different side of himself to each of these different groups. Many a youth who is demure enough before his parents and teachers, swears and swaggers like a pirate among his "tough" young friends. We do not show ourselves to our children as to our club-companions, to our customers as to the laborers we employ, to our own masters and employers as to our intimate friends. From this there results what practically is a division of the man into several selves; and this may be a discordant splitting, as where one is afraid to let one set of his acquaintances know him as he is elsewhere; or it may be a perfectly harmonious division of labor, as where one tender to his children is stern to the soldiers or prisoners under his command.

—*William James*

Characters are the masks worn by moral philosophies.
—*Alasdair MacIntyre*

CHAPTER 5

Character and Imago

Sandy is married, has two children in elementary school, and works as a middle-level manager at a major accounting firm. She aims to spend as much time as possible with her children, and to provide them with consistent care and discipline. With her husband, she wants to be a good friend and a passionate lover. With her colleagues at work, she feels the need to assert herself confidently, to justify her behavior in terms of clear goals and rational plans, and never to let her personal feelings get in the way of sound business practice. When she visits her parents in the summer, by contrast, this same woman is playful and childlike. She defers to her father's authority in arguments, she knits and plays Scrabble with her sisters, and she never thinks about balance sheets, lovemaking, or what time her children are going to bed. Among a multitude of other things, she is a daughter, worker, wife, and mother. The roles are wildly different. But is there something in Sandy's life that ties the roles together? Is there something that integrates her different social selves into a coherent and dynamic whole?

If the answer is yes, then that something is identity. And if identity takes the form of story, then the different selves in Sandy's life, embodied in the multiple roles she assumes in daily life, may be seen as potential characters in the story. Among other things, stories are

117

about characters who act, interact, desire, think, and feel. As we move through early and middle adulthood, identity challenges us to construct a personal myth in which a sufficient number of different kinds of characters may emerge, develop, and thrive. The problem of many roles and one identity is therefore resolved through the distinction between character and story. The many are the main characters; the one is the story within which the characters are given form, function, and voice.

> Do I contradict myself?
> Very well then I contradict myself,
> (I am large, I contain multitudes.)[1]

When Walt Whitman proclaimed that he contained multitudes, he was celebrating the boundless possibilities of the adventurous American self. I can be many things, said Whitman. I may be a lover and a hater, a warrior and a peacemaker, a parent and a child. Like God, I can give life, and I can take it away. Whitman's "Song of Myself" may seem like boasting to some, but his romantic verse reminds us that being an adult in our society typically means being many things. Modern life demands that each of us act and think in a multitude of different, sometimes contradictory ways.

The Split Between Family and Work

Adults move psychosocially through their twenties and thirties by first making provisional commitments and then consolidating social roles. Commitments are made and roles are consolidated within the two very different social realms of family and work. In 1990, the average age at which American adults entered their first marriage was 26.1 years for men and 23.9 years for women.[2] While Americans are having fewer children and are starting families at later ages than in past years, most married couples have still begun to raise children by the time the woman has reached the age of thirty. By the time the woman has reached age forty, at least one child is probably well into elementary school or of high-school age, and the family system is adjusting, or will soon adjust, to accommodate the growing independence of teenage children. In the realm of work, men in their twenties and thirties are often driven by an ethic of upward mobility and accelerating advance. The masculine ideal in occupational development is to move up fast.[3] The imagery of continuous ascendancy in the realm of work proves especially problematic, however, for many women (and indeed some men) in their thirties, should they desire to have a satisfying family life. A major lesson of young adulthood, it seems, is that the public world of work and the more private world of family life offer very different challenges. If the adult is to negotiate his or her way through both worlds with any felicity, he or she must develop at least two very different ways of being.

Social historians tell us that this has not always been the case. In the small towns of traditional Colonial America, adults worked at home, for the most part, and family life was a matter of public consideration.[4] The farmers, craftsmen, educators, pastors, doctors, and other citizens of eighteenth-century America raised their families and carried on their occupations in the same place—at home. The home was a microcosm of the society at large, reflecting and affirming the puritanical and patriarchal values of American life during the century and a half before national independence. The Colonial household was a business, a school, a vocational institute, a church, and a welfare institution. Adults functioned as workers, parents, lovers, teachers, neighbors, and worshipers in a social context that blurred distinctions between an individual adult's roles and affirmed the unitary nature of one's being. Public life and private life were pretty much one and the same, so much so that private infidelities were subject to public censure. Remember Hester Prynne, the heroine of *The Scarlet Letter*. The community enforced a public shaming as punishment for sexual relations outside of marriage. What we today would probably consider a private moral issue was perceived as a public affront in a puritanical New England town three hundred years ago.

The public and private worlds of adulthood began to separate during the nineteenth century, partly as a result of the Industrial Revolution and the urbanization of America. As men (and some women) began to leave home everyday to work in factories and other distant places, the household evolved to become the exclusive domain for private family life. According to one historian, the occupational world became dominated by a masculine ethic of efficiency, automatization, and the aggressive pursuit of profit.[5] Work became what men did, away from home. By contrast, the family realm was romantically portrayed as an ideal and feminized world of intimate relationships. For men, the home became a regular refuge from work, a domain inhabited mostly by women and children during the "workday." For individual men and women, the separation of public and private—work and home—produced a great expansion in personal consciousness. The integrated Colonial community ceased to exist. Private life was no longer under public surveillance. Adults were challenged to fashion separate selves for separate domains. Today the challenge is probably greater than ever, as modern men and women find it increasingly necessary to segment their identities into many different roles in order to accommodate the many different life spheres in which they operate.

The separation of public and private in the nineteenth century became almost an obsession for many educated adults. The conflict between the inner and outer worlds of human experience culminated in Freud's turn-of-the-century argument that much of what lies within the human mind is unconscious and split off from the external world of public observation.[6] Leading up to Freud, the nineteenth-century philosophies of Schopenhauer and Nietzsche celebrated aspects of human functioning that are outside of consciousness, typically emotional and irrational urges from within. These urges were believed to be antagonistic to human reason. The nineteenth-century Romantic poets placed the person's heroic and creative powers in an unconscious, inner realm. Hypnotism was used to gain access to the unconscious mind as early as 1784, and one of Freud's teachers, Jean-Martin Charcot, employed the method with legendary effectiveness. Charcot was able to impel adults to behave publicly in bizarre ways that they could not consciously understand, by appealing to a private world of thought and feeling that was split off from everyday consciousness.

Middle-class adults in nineteenth-century Europe believed in the existence of an inner world unknowable to the conscious self.[7] Many men and women of the Victorian age were preoccupied with the involuntary revelation of this inner self to others, as can be seen in biographies of prominent nineteenth-century figures. While you might not be able to attain conscious insight into the deep secrets of your own mind, the Victorians believed, there was always the danger of inadvertently disclosing the nature of your hidden self to others, as objective observers might come to know you better than you know yourself. The social message warned of the multiplicity of self: Beware! The hidden self may explode at any moment, revealing the bestial reality behind even the most upright public persona. It is no accident that the story of Dr. Jekyll and Mr. Hyde was such a tremendous popular success at this time. A Victorian life of rectitude and responsibility required vigilance, lest the demons from within erupt violently or lustfully onto the public scene.

The three most influential intellectuals of the late nineteenth century, Freud, Marx, and Darwin, maintained respectively that human lives, human societies, and biological organisms are governed by deep and hidden forces beyond control. Whether it be the unconscious (Freud), the dialectic of history (Marx), or natural selection (Darwin), the life forces that are ultimately responsible for what happens in the world are rather secret, subtle, split off. There is a manifest level of experience that is public and generally knowable. And there is a level that remains private or hidden. What you see at one level is not the same as what you find at another.

Modern life in middle-class America derives from this nineteenth-century legacy. The public and the private realms of adulthood remain divorced, and adults recognize the existence of their several selves. The multiplicity of the self is a result of economic, technological, social, and philosophical changes that have occurred in our world during the past two hundred years. Like many aspects of modern life, multiplicity in the self is an uneven privilege. On the one hand, modern men and women would appear to have a great many more opportunities, compared to adults living two hundred years ago, for living productive, happy, and full lives. To middle-class Americans, the late-twentieth century offers a rich assortment of alternative occupational roles and life-style choices. On the other hand, wide-open choices are sometimes frightening, and adults are bound to realize, typically in their thirties if not before, that choices bring with them eventual limitations and inescapable sacrifices. Furthermore, as we seek to become many different things, we appear to be pulled in the opposite direction as well, to become one thing upon which, as William James once put it, "we can stake our salvation."[8]

Modern life invites us to be many things. Our life stories welcome the debut and development of a wide cast of characters. But ultimately we seek unity as much as diversity. We seek to be one thing, for the story, no matter how complex, must still be the single story for a single life. As a modern adult, one must find meaning at home, at work, and in all the other domains of life; one cannot and must not be everything to everybody at every place and time. But an individual *can* be some important things for important people, at particular times and in particular places. Furthermore, he or she can be these things in a way that is unique, self-consistent, coherent, meaningful, purposeful, and gratifying. Creating a personal myth that contains a rich but finite source of characterization—a suitable cast of imagoes—enables an individual to resolve the problem of simultaneously being the many and the one.

Creating the Main Characters

I call the characters that dominate our life stories imagoes.[9] Imagoes provide a narrative mechanism for accommodating the diversity of modern life. In seeking pattern and organization for identity, the person in the early adult years psychologically pulls together social roles and other divergent aspects of the self to form integrative imagoes. Central conflicts or dynamics in one's life may be represented and played out as conflicting and interacting imagoes, as main characters in any story interact to push forward the plot. The chaotic multitudes of which Whitman speaks are reduced to a manageable cast of characters.

An imago is a personified and idealized concept of the self. Each of us consciously and unconsciously fashions main characters for our life stories. These characters function in our myths as if they were persons; hence, they are "personified." And each has a somewhat exaggerated and one-dimensional form; hence, they are "idealized." Our life stories may have one dominant imago or many. The appearance of two central and conflicting imagoes in personal myth seems to be relatively common.

During early and middle adulthood, most of the psychological "energy" we expend in creating our identities goes into the development, articulation, and refinement of our imagoes. Each imago is like a stock character in our story. Each is larger and more encompassing than the specific roles we play in daily life. Indeed, each imago may serve to bring together different roles under a single narrative category. Imagoes are each unique in some way, personalized to fit a particular identity story. Various imagoes I've seen in my research include the sophisticated professor, the rough boy from the wrong side of town, the steady caregiver, the corporate executive, the worldly traveler, the athlete, the sage, the soldier, the teacher, the clown, the peacemaker, and the martyr.

Imagoes exist as carefully crafted aspects of the self, and they may appear as the heroes or villains of certain chapters of the life story. They are often embodied in external role models and other significant persons in the adult's life. As our personal myths mature, we cast and recast our central imagoes in more specific and expansive roles. We come to understand ourselves better by a comprehensive understanding of the main characters that dominate the plot of our story, and push the narrative forward. With maturity, we work to create harmony, balance, and reconciliation between the often conflicting imagoes in our myth.

In Figure 1, I have illustrated my own scheme for classifying imagoes in life stories. The taxonomy is derived primarily from research into identity configurations of men and women between the ages of about thirty and fifty years. I organize imago types according to the properties of agency and communion, which I consider to be the two central themes in stories.[10] Some imago types are highly powerful, suggesting personified idealizations of the self as an assertive, dominant, and individuated agent. Others are highly loving, personified idealizations of the self as a provider of care, compassion, and friendship within a community of other selves. Some imago types blend power and love, and others appear to emphasize neither.

Examples of some of these imago types may be found in certain world mythologies, including the well-known mythologies of ancient Greece. In their idealized exploits and adventures, the gods and goddesses of the ancient Greek pantheon personify basic human needs and propensities that are still exemplified and played out today in personal myths and human lives. Other world mythologies offer equally useful taxonomies that one might follow. Although

Greek myths are habitually used by psychological researchers, there is nothing special or universal about them. Some people whom I have interviewed present personal myths whose main characters do not fit neatly into the scheme presented in Figure 1. The scheme is no more than a rough guide. I use the Greek names simply because they will be familiar to many readers.

Four points about imagoes need to be emphasized.

Imagoes are not people. Imagoes are archetypal patterns for human thought and conduct that compose idealized personifications in personal myth. They exist as characters in life stories, not as real people in life. You are not your imagoes. Rather, your identity is a story concerning certain imagoes.

Imagoes are not "the whole story." There is more to your personal myth than the main characters. A central message of this book is that personal myths can be understood on different levels and from different perspectives. A story may be viewed, for instance, from the perspectives of theme, setting, image, tone, and plot, as well as character.

Figure 1
Imago Types: Some Common Characters in Personal Myth

Agentic and Communal
The Healer
The Teacher
The Counselor
The Humanist
The Arbiter

Agency	**Communion**
The Warrior (Ares)	The Lover (Aphrodite)
The Traveler (Hermes)	The Caregiver (Demeter)
The Sage (Zeus)	The Friend (Hera)
The Maker (Hephaestus)	The Ritualist (Hestia)

Low in Agency, Low in Communion
The Escapist
The Survivor

Imagoes may be positive or negative. My taxonomy in Figure 1 deals only with positive imagoes. These are personified idealizations of the self that contain many good and desirable attributes. However, many adults develop negative personifications as well. Sometimes these negative imagoes are opposites or mirror images of the positive ones I have listed, and in many other cases they are not.

Imagoes, like personal myths, are both common and unique. Figure 1 is merely a guide for exploring certain common imagoes. Within this framework, there exists a good deal of individuality. One person's Warrior imago may be very different from another's. Some imago types do not fit into the scheme in Figure 1. Like personal myths more generally, imagoes come in many different forms.

The Nature of the Imago

A recent advertisement for *Cosmopolitan* describes it as the perfect women's magazine for today's "juggler." From what I can tell, the juggler is a middle-class American woman in her twenties or thirties who raises her children, holds down a well-paying job, carries on a happy relationship with her husband or lover, keeps abreast with what is going on in the world, and manages to look beautiful at the same time. She juggles many different and seemingly conflicting roles at once. She keeps her roles up in the air and moving, and works furiously to assure that none ever hits the ground.

The juggler is especially skilled at what sociologist Erving Goffman called "the presentation of self in everyday life."[11] According to Goffman, the modern man or woman is like a performer enacting roles in order to manipulate the impressions of others. We provide scripted performances for each social situation, he believes. Even social situations that seem to be "natural" and "spontaneous" are typically ritualized performances designed to create a desired effect on the many different "audiences" we confront. The most successful and well-adjusted people, in Goffman's view, are those who are most adroit in selecting and enacting the appropriate performance for a given situation. For Goffman, we are the roles we juggle, and nothing more.

Psychiatrist Robert Jay Lifton employs a very different metaphor for essentially the same social phenomenon.[12] For Lifton, the juggler is like the Greek god Proteus, who was capable of assuming any guise he chose. If he needed to be a dog, he could become a dog. If a situation called for a doctor, he could become a doctor. The protean man or woman is the modern adult who tries to be everything to everybody. Such a person may appear on the surface to be well-rounded and adjusted. He or she may be actively involved in a host of interests and avocations. But the protean person suffers from a profound inner emptiness. There is no coherence in his or her life. No unifying narrative binds together his or her disparate interests and activities. The self is split, and each part is alienated from the others.

Goffman's view of social life is deeply unsatisfying because he fails to discern an integrative sense of self—an identity—behind the many different roles we play. For Goffman, nothing transcends the particular behavioral performances we enact. We are here to play our roles, and that is all. What each of us thinks and feels about the roles we play would appear to be irrelevant. By contrast, Lifton is deeply troubled by the incessant role-playing of modern adult life. The juggler may be socially effective and admired by some, but when it comes to making our lives meaningful, we each must do more than merely juggle roles. We must find a way to subsume the roles within a larger and meaningfully patterned self, Lifton argues. We must find a way to bring the roles under the partial control of an organizing identity.

The mythic challenge of our twenties and thirties is to move beyond juggling roles into creating and refining imagoes. Imagoes are larger and more internalized than social roles. The general features of a given role are defined by the society within which the role is operational. With respect to social roles, a mother is a woman who bears and raises children, providing care and counsel and endeavoring to promote her children's development in accord with her own values and society's demands. A federal judge is a man or woman who presides over a courtroom trial, hears legal arguments, renders judgments in accord with law, and so on. These roles are elaborately scripted by societal norms and expectations, and we are all very familiar with them.

If a role is to become an imago, however, the role must be broadened to function as an aspect of the self that is applicable to a wide range of life activities. A person whose life story contains a strong imago of the mother acts, thinks, and feels as does a mother in a variety of ways that go well beyond caring for biological or adopted children. He or she magnifies and personalizes the social role and situates it in a self-defining life story. Similarly, someone who develops an imago of the judge may be concerned, as a judge would be, about issues of justice and fairness in many different realms of life. The person might act and think as if he or she were a judge in situations in which even a real judge isn't one, as when with family and friends.

Imagoes may personify aspects of who you believe you are now, who you were, who you might be in the future, who you wish you were, or who you fear you might become. Any or all of these aspects of the self—the perceived self, the past self, the future self, the desired self, the undesired self—can be incorporated into the main characters of personal myths.[13] Any or all of them can become an imago that dominates a particular chapter or personifies a particular theme, or idea in the story.

In the next chapter, I will illustrate different kinds of imagoes by describing selected cases from the many life-story interviews I and my associates have done. You will probably recognize parts of yourself in these descriptions, as well as particular characters that appear to play important roles in the life stories of friends, spouses, children, parents, and other people you know. The next chapter aims to flesh out an initial classification of imago types—a standard cast of characters for contemporary identity making. To provide additional background for that description, let me conclude this chapter by laying out six basic principles of imagoes. Each principle pertains to a particular way in which any imago may express itself as a central character in a personal myth.

Imagoes express our most cherished desires and goals. What we most want in life is often expressed in our identities as an idealized personification of the self. We are able to give voice to our basic desires by constructing characters in our stories who clearly personify what we want. Consider a thirty-five-year-old nurse with a strong power motive who wants to travel to exotic lands, loves to meet new people and experience new ways of life, and strives to explore her own potential by undertaking various kinds of therapy and by regularly attending human-growth seminars. She fears getting stale or bored. Physically and psychologically, she wants to keep moving. A main character in her personal myth is the traveler, modeled after the Greek god Hermes, the messenger god who was always on the move. The woman's love of adventure and exploration, however, runs up against a competing desire to help others, to promote their health and welfare. This second and equally powerful set of desires is personified in a second main character, who might be called the healer. The woman's personal myth is a story about a traveler and a healer. The two imagoes became established as central characters in identity during her late twenties and early thirties, and their alternating passages of conflict, dominance, or harmony have determined her actions throughout her life.

Social psychologist Hazel Markus argues that our specific wants and fears are typically captured in what she calls "possible selves."[14] According to Markus, a possible self is a well-articulated image a person has of what he or she might be, wants to be, or fears becoming. In her imagination, a struggling twenty-six-year-old writer may have envisioned a possible self as a Pulitzer Prize–winning novelist, living among the New York literati, regularly contributing erudite articles to *The New York Review of Books,* getting big advances from publishers, traveling to Europe to gather material for books, and so on. She may also have envisioned a possible self as a writer who never makes it. In this contrary scenario, she is never able to publish an article, short story, or book. She receives no recognition for her talents. She takes on a series of dead-end jobs, gets further into debt, and finally slumps forever into frustration and mediocrity. Markus's possible selves appear to be potential imagoes. They are characters who may or may not make their way onto the stage, depending on how life develops and how the story comes to be told.

Like characters in stories, imagoes enter myths in specific opening scenes. In stories, characters are born, they live, and they sometimes die. They do not gradually come or cease to be. A birth is as discontinuous an experience as a death. A person springs forth on to the scene. Similarly, a character enters a narrative all at once, as does, for instance, Prince Hamlet in act 1, scene 2 of Shakespeare's play, or Moses in chapter 2, verse 2 of Exodus. So it is in personal myth. As we reconstruct the past to create a narrative that makes sense to us, we give birth to characters who personify key aspects of the self. In so doing, we often specify particular scenes in the story wherein characters "are born" or "come onto the stage." It is often at a high, low, or turning point that an imago finds a narrative mechanism for coming to be (see Appendix 2).

Imagoes personify our traits and recurrent behaviors. A trait is a linear dimension of behavior upon which persons can be said to differ.[15] For example, people differ markedly in the trait of "friendliness." Some people are consistently more friendly than are others. Even though each of us is likely to be friendly in some particular situations and unfriendly in others, we would still agree that people can be rated or ranked on this dimension, from those who appear to be "very friendly" to those who appear to be "very unfriendly." A great deal of research shows that people can be reliably assessed in terms of a number of simple trait dimensions and that these ratings are relatively stable over time. People rate themselves reliably as well—a person's self-ratings tend to correlate with ratings others give to the person. People are generally aware of their own traits.

Whereas a person's "motives" or "desires" refer to what a person wants in life, traits are more concerned with consistent styles of behavior. Each of us has spent a lifetime observing our own behavior and implicitly comparing it to the behavior of others. Therefore, most of us have a pretty good sense of how we stack up to others on such trait dimensions as "friendliness," "dominance," "impulsiveness," "conscientiousness," and so on.[16] Our self-attributed traits are likely to make their way into our personal myths. A man who sees himself as extremely "spontaneous" may create an imago that is fun-loving, impulsive, and playful, thereby translating this trait into a narrative character. Imagoes provide a narrative vehicle whereby a person can embody self-ascribed traits.

Imagoes give voice to individual and cultural values. All societies generate stock characters that personify those beliefs and standards that society as a whole (or a significant segment of society) holds in greatest esteem. The character furnishes people at a given time and in a given place with a cultural and moral ideal, legitimating a particular mode of social existence. For example, Robert Bellah suggests that "the independent citizen" served as a representative moral character type for early-nineteenth-century Americans.[17]

Reaching its culmination in the life of Abraham Lincoln, the independent citizen was the self-made, self-sufficient farmer or craftsman of small-town America who held strongly to biblical teachings and was fiercely devoted to the values of freedom and autonomy. The independent citizen captured the ideological spirit of the times; he was the moral exemplar of a young and idealistic nation.

The moral character types of which Bellah speaks are general models around which adults can pattern their own lives and articulate their own more personalized characterizations of self. Like moral character types at the societal level, imagoes often reflect personal values and beliefs. Significant aspects of an adult's ideological setting may be clearly expressed in imagoes. A fundamentalist Christian may develop an imago of the evangelist, a character devoted to spreading the Christian gospel to all who have yet to accept it. A Christian with a slightly different perspective may create an imago of "the loyal friend," seeing in Saint Paul's teachings on love and charity the ideological inspiration for his or her own life. Outside the realm of religion, imagoes may personify ethical, political, and aesthetic values. A prime function of imagoes in some personal myths is to be a mouthpiece or an exemplar for what a person holds to be right, true, and beautiful.

Imagoes are often built around significant others. Beyond the character types offered by society at large, adults fashion their imagoes on models provided by parents, teachers, siblings, friends, and many other significant people they have known. Ultimately, imagoes are forged from interpersonal relationships. A significant person in one's life may serve as a flesh-and-blood incarnation of what a particular imago represents. One's own mother may serve as a model for the imago of the caregiver. A beloved teacher who helps clear up some academic and personal confusions may prove to be the prototype for an imago of the healer.

There exists today a strong movement in clinical psychology and psychotherapy suggesting that we all "internalize" important people in our lives and structure our personalities around these internalizations. According to the "object relations" approach to personality, people for whom we feel strong emotions ultimately become represented in our unconscious minds as personified structures.[18] The infant will build up an unconscious representation of mother as a result of early experience, and this enduring representation will come to exert substantial influence on the course of interpersonal relationships many years down the road. Over time, many different objects (representations of persons) are formed within, each carving out its own territory in the unconscious. Neurosis may result from excessive conflict among different internalized objects, or from "splitting," through which certain objects seem to leave the confederation of the self and become inner mischiefmakers. Healthy development involves the integration of different objects, and the healing of splits through relationships of love and caring.

Imagoes would appear to be life-story derivatives of early object relations. In other words, certain main characters in personal myth may spring from the intrapsychic sources of internalized objects. In some cases, we write our main characters according to guidelines of which we are not consciously aware. The guidelines are embodied in those unconscious representations we have accrued as a result of a lifetime of loving, hating, and being with other people.

Psychotherapist Mary Watkins likens internalized objects to inner voices engaged in dialogue.[19] The hallmark of healthy psychological development, from Watkins's point of view, is the progressive elaboration of different characters within, and the continuous enhancement of imaginal dialogues among those characters. In therapy, Watkins encourages her clients to explore the many different personified "presences" in their minds—the lovers, warriors, sages, children, teachers, friends, and others who populate the psyche. As each presence comes to be known, its voice becomes clearer and more distinctive, and it is able to engage other internal presences in meaningful dialogue.

Watkins strongly values openness and diversity in intrapsychic structure. She deemphasizes the modern problem of the multiplicity of the adult self, for she seems to believe that being many different things is, by and large, a good thing. Her approach appears to be less concerned with unity and purpose than is the viewpoint I have been advocating. Still, Watkins's way of thinking about imaginal dialogues is useful when applied to imagoes. A personal myth may be seen as a complex set of imaginal dialogues involving different imagoes developing over narrative time.

Imagoes may signal a fundamental life conflict. Most good stories are predicated upon some sort of conflict between competing interests, goals, and characters. At the story's end, the conflict is resolved. So it is in personal myth. Conflicting imagoes are as much the norm as the exception in identity, and many life stories are organized around starkly polarized characters. For some adults in their twenties and thirties, the split between work and home selves gives rise to a parallel dichotomy in their personal myths as they try to satisfy opposing goals of agency and communion. Consider a thirty-year-old female attorney who constructs a life story in which an agentic imago of the successful and aggressive lawyer must share the stage with a nurturing caregiver. There does not seem to be room for both. Conflicts may also occur within the general thematic domains of power and love. The caregiver may conflict with the friend. The sage and the warrior may work at cross purposes. Personal myths do not always produce the most congenial imaginal dialogues.

Personal myths are frequently dominated by central conflicts through which imagoes act, interact, converse, argue, develop, do combat, and make peace. Within the context of the single story, different characters want a multitude of things. Many voices want to be heard. Between the ages of about twenty and forty, it would appear that the adult is psychologically engaged in creating a personal myth that allows various characters to establish their roles and find their voices. It is likely that the roles will eventually conflict and the voices will clash. A certain degree of narrative confusion should result, and this would appear to be good. We should not expect as adults to reconcile and fully resolve the central conflicts of identity during the third and fourth decades of our lives. During this time, characters are still seeking their unique roles within the self-defining story. And the story is still seeking its unique form to accommodate faithfully all the different characters and their different developmental paths.

CHAPTER 6

Agentic and Communal Characters

Since at least the nineteenth century, adult citizens of Western democracies have crafted their identities to accommodate the dualism of modern life. To be powerful in work and loving at home—ideally, this is what most of us want, even if we find it extraordinarily difficult to attain. But we do not all want power and love to the same extent or in the same way. Some personal myths are dominated by agentic imagoes whose forceful efforts push the plot forward. Other life stories present a more communal cast of characters who act in the primary service of love and intimacy. Some characters are agentic and communal at once. Still others seem to avoid both power and love.

Each character is a personalized representation of a particular mode of being adult. Therefore, each life story contains unique main characters. But certain common character forms may be identified across different personal myths. Under the rubric of agency are the standard characters of the warrior, the traveler, the sage, and the maker, among others. Communion's imagoes include the lover, the caregiver, the friend, and the ritualist, as well as others. Each of these imago types represents a recognizable social form in human life.

There is nothing mystical or mysteriously biological about the imago types. While I am not averse to Jungian analyses, I find unwarranted Jung's notion that an imago is derived from a deep-seated collective unconscious. Jung's concept of the archetype (sometimes termed "imago") assumes too much about the human mind, I think. It suggests that each person has access to a universal storehouse of information about human life that is biologically transmitted. To me it seems more sensible to assume that much of this information is culturally imparted to an organism who is biologically prepared to accept it. Nor should imagoes be seen as instances of "human nature" as it is encoded in our genes.[1] Imagoes arise out of the normal and expectable demands made upon adult human beings living in many different kinds of societies. Because of the nature of our minds, we are impelled as adults to make sense of our lives in terms of narrative. The agentic and communal types described in this chapter seem to apply well to the narratives of modern Western life. They would also appear to provide general templates for identity making that might have been viable in some, though by no means all, previous historical eras as well, and may well be applicable to certain other cultures today.

Agentic Characters

In literature, drama, song, and verse, there are many different kinds of characters who act, think, and feel in agentic ways. These are characters who seek to conquer, master, control, overcome, create, produce, explore, persuade, advocate, analyze, understand, win. They are described by such adjectives as aggressive, ambitious, adventurous, assertive, autonomous, clever, courageous, daring, dominant, enterprising, forceful, independent, resourceful, restless, sophisticated, stubborn, and wise, among many others.[2] Such characters may be considered "masculine," in the sense that they personify some characteristics that are stereotypically associated with the masculine sex role. But they need not be male. Whether they are personified as women or men, these are characters who tend to proceed vigorously through the world. Four common types of agentic characters are the warrior, who forcefully engages others; the traveler, who progresses swiftly over terrain; the sage, whose effort is to understand the world; and the maker, who moves body and soul in order to create.

134

The Warrior

The June 24, 1991, issue of *Newsweek* announced the arrival of a "men's movement" in the United States whose goal is to enable middle-class men to recover their heritage as warriors.[3] Influential spokesmen for the movement, such as the poet Robert Bly[4] and the popular writer Sam Keen,[5] believe that many men live weak and lonely lives, cut off from their fathers and from an archetypal masculinity celebrated in ancient myth and folklore. Accountants, executives, lawyers, and professors are unable to experience life as the spontaneous and courageous warriors their masculine nature has prepared them to be. Bly exhorts men to get in touch with their mythopoetic roots; Keen urges them to separate themselves from the world of women in order to find their own masculine voice. Organizations now sponsor weekend retreats in which men dance, sing, talk, beat drums, and reenact ancient male rituals together in the forests, deserts, or mountains.

What seems to be emerging out of the nascent men's movement is an idealized characterization of masculinity, personified by the warrior. Born to fight courageously, their warrior is also spontaneous, emotional, and able to establish bonds of friendship with other men. The image is complex, blending many personal and interpersonal qualities that are sorely lacking in the lives of many middle-class American men. At the center of the image is the active man who moves vigorously, aggressively, and unselfconsciously in a natural world that he experiences as both threatening and challenging. In order to do battle, warriors must perceive threats; in order to move forward with courage, they must experience challenges and obstacles as being manageable.

The imago of the warrior I will outline in this chapter is both more limited and more general than the one described by the contemporary men's movement. It focuses on the defining aspect of warriors, making war, and excludes the many other characteristics (such as spontaneity, brotherliness, etc.) that Bly, Keen, and others would appear to attribute to them. I believe that some people whose stories feature the warrior do attribute these characteristics to the imago, but many others do not. And unlike theirs, my general concept of the warrior imago is equally applicable to men and women, for both are certainly able to engage in courageous battle—whether physical, verbal, mental, or spiritual.

In the mythology of ancient Greece, Ares is the god of war; his name in the Roman pantheon is Mars. Ares is the personification of the impetuous and courageous warrior, of blind and brutal courage, of bloody rage and carnage. Like Ares, the imago of the warrior—a highly agentic narrative character—exists to make war of one kind or another.

The warrior is a main character in Tom Harvester's personal myth.[6] At the time of his interview, Tom was a forty-three-year-old communications worker employed by the police department. Growing up in a southeast-side Chicago neighborhood during World War II, Tom recalls a number of significant events in his very early years associated with war, death, and authority. His earliest memories concern the air-raid sirens and a childhood fear of "imminent invasion" resulting from the regular air-raid drills organized by Chicago neighborhoods. The unexpected death of his grandmother and his dog, the latter killed by a speeding automobile, were two early events associated with a feeling of rage toward those who were larger, stronger, and in authority. In 1943, Tom's family moved to a farm community outside Chicago. This resulted in considerable stress for Tom. The major conflict in his new community was between the "farm kids" and the displaced "city kids." He describes his role in the conflict as that of diplomat: "I was like Henry Kissinger doing shuttle diplomacy," negotiating fragile peace treaties between warring factions. Tom found himself assuming a similar role in the wake of family arguments.

All of Tom's childhood heroes were soldiers. He is quick to link his own life history to violent world events—the beginning of the Korean War, the construction of the Berlin Wall, the assassination of President Kennedy. Tom contrasts his glory years at the military academy where he attended high school with his subsequent "first big failure" at Notre Dame University. There he repeatedly battled a host of authority figures, unwittingly cultivating what he now calls the role of "the rebel." Soon after dropping out of college, Tom enlisted in the air force and began another glorious chapter. His life story since then alternates periods of glory, when he moves forcefully and successfully in the world as the noble warrior (in the guise of good citizen, dedicated husband, or courageous politician), with times of depravity and shame, when he falls into heavy drinking and generally irresponsible behavior. His warrior seems to have lost the battles during life chapters associated with the failures at Notre Dame, recurrent bouts of problem drinking, divorce, and periods of unemployment.

Tom's personal myth is a story of warfare—there is always some battle to be fought. The warrior is victorious when he is able to channel disciplined aggressive energy into the arts of preparing for war, negotiating treaties between warring factions, and making war so as to keep the peace. In Tom's unique myth, the imago of the warrior is the self-controlled vanguard of domestic tranquillity whose work and life promote peace and stability through strength. But when he fails to live up to an implicit warrior code—a regimen of conformity, impulse control, and Spartan austerity—the story lapses into dereliction and defeat.

For Tom, the warrior serves to embody his agentic goals of attaining power over others and control over himself. Hints of the warrior's emergence appear in childhood scenes of war preparation and violence. Tom perceives himself as a dominant and aggressive individual, and values courage and discipline as central tenets of his personal warrior code. His role models include strong and disciplined men such as John Kennedy, Henry Kissinger, and his early war heroes. In keeping with the imago of the warrior, Tom tends to be somewhat combative and wary when engaging in new relationships with others. Friends and acquaintances are "allies." Many others, especially people in authority, are adversaries Tom must fight. Relationships provide opportunities for heroic action. They challenge Tom to remain "strong" and "true," to fight the good fight and win the battle in the end. The warrior signals the central conflict in his personal myth—between self-discipline and losing control.

The Traveler

Margaret Mead (1901–1978) traveled to the South Seas as a twenty-three-year-old to study primitive cultures. She returned years later, having authored her first book, *Coming of Age in Samoa*. Her descriptions of adolescent sexuality and apparently guilt-free love shocked many readers and made her famous, associating her name forever with sex and freedom. During the next fifty years, Mead established herself as one of the preeminent social scientists of the twentieth century, and probably the greatest popularizer of anthropology in the English language. Hers was a rich and complex life story within which a number of prominent characters seemed to emerge. Chief among them was the traveler.[7]

In her autobiography, Margaret Mead reports that as a first child she was "wanted and loved."[8] Though her father's university job made it necessary that his wife and children repeatedly move—"like a family of refugees"—Margaret recalled an essentially happy childhood. She delighted in being something of a favorite in the eyes of relatives, friends, and acquaintances. "There's no one like Margaret," her parents often said. As a child, she was encouraged to develop this perceived special nature, to explore her self and her environment to a greater extent than is probably true for most American children, especially little girls growing up in the early years of this century. In each new neighborhood Margaret found that there were new people to meet and new territories to explore. Recurrent themes for her childhood years are learning through exploration and constant movement, and in many instances the themes are merged:

Looking back, my memories of learning precise skills, memorizing long stretches of poetry, and manipulating paper are interwoven with memories of running—running in the wind, running through meadows, and running along country roads—picking flowers, hunting for nuts, and weaving together old stories and new events into myths about a tree and a rock.[9]

As a freshman, Margaret enrolled in DePauw College in Indiana. Here she was stifled in her movement and her exploration—it was the first environment she found to be intolerant of her special nature. In her mind, DePauw was provincial, oppressive, and too traditional for a free spirit like herself. She thought the social life—dominated by fraternities and sororities—was dull and rejecting. Her peers and her classes seemed boring. So she left after a year and enrolled in Barnard College, in New York City, where she soon found acceptance, excitement, and close friendships with a group of college women.

At Barnard, Mead arrived at a vision of who she was and who she might become, and she was able to tie this back, in a very satisfying manner, to her perception of who she had been in the past. By the time she graduated from Barnard, she knew that she wanted to devote her life to the study of human cultures so as to learn something of the various "homes" in which people around the world lived. Mead's newly fashioned identity as an anthropologist who continually moved from one home to another was formulated according to a perceived special relationship between "travel" and "home":

> For many people moving is one kind of thing and travel is
> something very different. Travel means going away from home and
> staying away from home; it is an antidote to the humdrum activities
> of everyday life, a prelude to a holiday one is entitled to enjoy after
> months of dullness. Moving means breaking up a home, sadly or
> joyfully breaking with the past; a happy venture or a hardship,
> something to be endured with good or ill grace. For me moving and
> staying at home, traveling and arriving, are all of a piece. The world
> is full of homes in which I have lived for a day, a month, or much
> longer. How much I care about a home is not measured by the
> length of time I lived there. One night in a room with a leaping fire
> may mean more to me than many months in a room without a
> fireplace, a room in which my life has been paced less excitingly.[10]

Throughout her life, Mead was a woman on the move. Her anthropological studies took her all over the globe—from the South Pacific to collect field data, to London to report her findings, to New York City where she served as a museum curator. One biographer writes that Mead "rushed across oceans, continents, time zones and networks and disciplines, knocking down barriers and redefining boundaries."[11] Gregory Bateson described his marriage to Mead as "almost a principle of pure energy. . . . I couldn't keep up, and she couldn't stop. She was like a tugboat. She could sit down and write three thousand words by eleven o'clock in the morning, and spend the rest of the day working at the museum."[12] One of Mead's mottos in college was "Be lazy, go crazy."

For an academic engaged in scholarly research and writing, Margaret Mead was remarkably unreflective. She was more of a restless observer than a sedentary philosopher. She had little patience for leisurely speculation about anything, even about herself. Mead adamantly refused to undergo psychoanalysis to examine her own life in depth. Such an adventure in self-reflection would have been too time-consuming and intangible for a traveler whose mind tended toward the practical and concrete. After completing a field study in July of 1932, Mead found she had too much free time on her hands and complained, "I had too much time to think—too many empty spaces." Writes a biographer, "Unstructured time, all the rest of her life, was a prospect that would fill Mead with dread."[13]

Like the ancient Greek god Hermes, Mead was a messenger, always exploring, always communicating what she learned to an audience lagging behind her. By fashioning a personal myth around the protagonist of the traveling anthropologist, Mead was able to put into practice her mother's values of social activism and her father's emphasis on becoming an intellectual. Like her grandmother, too, she could delight in children and the domestic rituals of everyday life, observing these practices and often taking part in them, in the different cultures she studied. And like the child who ran through the meadows, adult Margaret could stay on the move. Just before leaving for her first anthropological expedition to Samoa, Mead celebrated the inauguration of her new adult imago in a poem she wrote about herself entitled "Of So Great Glee":

She used to skip when she was small
Till all her frocks were tattered,
But mother gently gathered up
The dishes that she shattered.

Her skipping rope got caught in trees
And shook their blossoms down,
But her step was so lighthearted
That the dryads could not frown.

And when at last she tore a star
Out of the studded sky,
God only smiled at one whose glee
Could fling a rope so high.[14]

The Sage

I remember a class in graduate school in which one of my good friends—a fellow student—was leading a discussion on maturity in adulthood. He asked everybody in the class to describe their ultimate goals in life. I do not remember what my response was, but I remember my friend's very clearly. He said that his goal was "to become enlightened" and that this had been his goal for as long as he could remember. He found it difficult to believe that everybody in the class did not have the same goal. My friend was referring to the attainment of a deep knowledge of the self and the world. His own brand of enlightenment was colored by Hindu philosophy and his explorations in meditation. But certain other adults hold similar life goals, and strive long and hard to find truth, understanding, knowledge, wisdom, sagacity, acumen, expertise, or know-how. Above virtually everything else in life, some adults want to learn—this desire drives the sage.

All cultures put a premium on the attainment of knowledge, but each culture defines knowledge in its own way. Although Americans are especially taken with scientific and technological knowledge, we also tend to value forms of understanding found in religion, literature, and human relationships. Americans tend to value practical knowledge over knowledge that lacks "real-world" application; still, both are believed to be good. We also value wisdom—the knowledge gained from lived experience—but it is probably true that many traditional societies, less technologically oriented than ours, value it more. Virtually all societies offer models of adulthood that extol the pursuit of knowledge or wisdom. Especially wise men and women are generally believed to be somewhat older than many, if not most, citizens, for learning comes with experience, and experience takes time.

The sage is an extraordinarily agentic imago. Through knowledge come power and mastery, and knowing the world (or the self) can be likened to conquering one's own external (or internal) environment. The link between knowledge and power is clearly displayed in ancient Greek mythology: Mighty Zeus is the wisest of the gods. But Zeus also personifies a host of other agentic qualities. He is a judge, a ruler, a seducer, a patriarch, and a celebrity. The Homeric Hymns praise Zeus as "the best god and the greatest. . . . You're the most famous of all."[15] Other figures in Greek mythology personify wisdom as well, as in the case of the blind prophet Tiresias, who knows the deeply buried truth of Oedipus' lineage. The goddess Athena portrays a highly pragmatic wisdom that proves especially useful in peacemaking and adjudicating interpersonal conflict.

The college campus is one place where the imago of the sage may find a hospitable home. Christina Wilkens is a fifty-year-old college professor whose personal myth bears the stamp of the sage. One of the first African-American women to attain prominence in her academic discipline, Christina was recognized to have special intellectual and artistic talents at a very early age and was encouraged to develop them fully. Raised by her great-grandmother—her own mother worked full-time, and her father was away from home for long periods of time on military service—Christina was a "somewhat lonely but relatively happy" child whose "main job was to go to school every day" and learn. She says:

> Despite some inauspicious beginnings, I was the apple of my family's eye. I was the person whom they taught. My great-great-grandmother taught me to tell time. And I can remember them showing me off to company for the long words I could spell. My father reported that on times when he was home from the military taking me someplace on the bus he would have conversations with me as if I were an adult. He said at one point on the bus the woman who was one row behind us stood up and looked down to see if he was insane or not because he was having this very adultlike conversation with somebody whose head could not even be seen. I was pretty little.

Christina was the first in her family to go to college. On her first day, visiting the college library, "I saw all these tall guys, these tall white guys with spectacles, looking extraordinarily scholarly and orderly and I said, gee, this is for me!" In graduate school during the civil rights movement of the 1960s, Christina fell in love with a young black man who was active in campus politics. What attracted her most to him was his power as a speaker and a thinker. For Christina, he personified a worldly and sophisticated wisdom to which she herself aspired.

I heard him give a speech about something or another, and he was a powerful orator, and I thought, this guy really has the right vision. We should be trying to establish our own African-American institutions. We should be trying to, you know. And his energy, his looks, his ideas, his aggression just bowled me over, and I thought Lord, you know, this is what I ought to do. I ought, you know, but how can I get there? Well there were so many ways that I felt inferior and inadequate, but certainly I was as smart as anybody. However, I didn't have the social savvy that he had, or that I feel I have now. And I was not nearly as politically astute as some of the girls who were close comrades around him. In other words, I couldn't engage him in a conversation about politics and get him to pay any attention to me because I really didn't know anything about that, and that's why I was so fascinated about what he was saying, about the situation of black people and the community and the larger world picture and this and that. And I read, and I read. And I studied to know more.

Christina's relationship with the young man never developed further, but she went on to receive her Ph.D. and to establish an impressive career in academia. Despite her close ties to her family and to friends, Christina's identity is a strongly agentic tale in which the sage grows in knowledge, influence, and independence. Partly as a result of her substantial investment in scholarship, Christina did not marry until her late forties, shortly after her father died. Curiously, she married a man from another culture who is twenty years her junior and who has virtually no formal education. He is a quiet craftsman—a maker rather than a sage. While her main job is still "to go to school every day," she has now taken on the additional task of helping her husband adjust to a radically different culture, helping him find work, learn the customs, become acclimated to an American college town. Her imago of the sage appears to have expanded in the process, as she now sees herself in the role of the older and wiser woman providing sage advice and counsel for her younger man. And she continues to learn from him, too, to widen her understanding of self and world through this bold new relationship.

The kind of knowledge that Christina values is a blend of the scientific, the artistic, and the mystical. The science has been developed through her formal education and in her professional work. Her artistic and mystical traits were nurtured in her family and have become associated with her cultural heritage as an African-American woman. The interesting mixture can be seen in her description of her religious beliefs. She suggests that she is somewhat skeptical about conventional religion because it does not fit well with her commitment to scientific inquiry. Yet, she reports a growing interest in Catholicism, and she believes that she is able to communicate, in subtle but powerful ways, with her dead ancestors through certain spiritual experiences.

For Christina, the sage finds knowledge as much through personal experience and emotional expression as through study and scholarship. She places a premium on the pursuit of knowledge. Her pursuit is an organic blend of the tough and the tender. She has defined herself through a highly agentic narrative of the self in which a main character strives to know and to learn, and in the process, to become more powerful, expansive, and self-affirming.

The Maker

In the mythology of ancient Greece, Hephaestus is the divine artificer. A skilled craftsman who works with fire and metal, Hephaestus makes wonderful, magical things. He is lame, but he proves that a person with a physical disability may still contribute to society in powerful ways by moving his hands to manufacture objects. In less obvious ways, Zeus and Hermes are also involved in the making of things. Zeus is the creator god who is ultimately responsible for providing many of the essentials for life. Hermes is an inventor—he invented the lyre on his first day out of the womb—and a capitalist who masters the economic world of goods and services in order to make a profit.[16]

Most adults are involved in making things. Preparing a dinner, building a garage, producing a business plan, designing a course of study, sewing a dress, painting a portrait—the list of things we make and our ways of making them is almost endless. In that making is such a pervasive human activity, it seems to have the power to become appropriated into human identity through readily recognizable characters. For some of us, the maker is a central aspect of our personal myths. As creators, producers, inventors, entrepreneurs, artists, and the like, some adults write their own identities around the character of the maker.

The maker presents an imago type that can be less interpersonal than most of the others. Making is often done alone. The things we make are typically inanimate objects to be used, in one way or another, by animate beings like ourselves. Of course, we can also make "love" or make "decisions," but the imago of the maker usually focuses on the making of tangible products, or on their repair, refinement, or distribution. Therefore, the selling and buying of merchandise fits in here, even though neither sellers nor buyers make the merchandise themselves. If the warrior seeks his place on the battlefield and the sage takes up residence in the university, the maker may eventually find himself in the marketplace. It is in the rhetoric of the business world where the maker finds many of the most compelling images, terms, standards, and frameworks. The maker seeks to be productive, to be efficient, to maximize profit and minimize cost, to invest time and resources in a profitable manner, to make something that works and sells. Making connects thematically to the agentic motive of achievement, more so than to power. The person with a strong need for achievement is not necessarily concerned about having a large impact on the world. Instead, he or she wants to do things well, to be successful, efficient, and productive.

Going as far back as he can remember, Curt Rossi has wanted to make beautiful things with his hands. He grew up as the younger of two brothers in a very religious family in southwestern Ohio. Curt's brother was a star athlete and high-school valedictorian. Though he was also a good student, Curt could not match his brother's accomplishments in math and science. And he expressed no interest whatsoever in sports. (Today, Curt claims that he knows less about sports than any other middle-aged man in America.) Curt's interests turned in the direction of making things, and he learned very early on that he could distinguish himself in the family through painting and sculpture, as well as through his talents in music, literature, and poetry. Both of Curt's parents were models for him in this regard. His father was a teacher, but on weekends he spent most of his time in the garage doing woodwork of various sorts. While Curt's brother organized the neighborhood baseball games, Curt helped his father with his projects in the shop. He also spent countless hours with his mother in the kitchen. By the time he went to college, Curt was an excellent cook.

The maker can be an especially nonsocial imago. Curt is by no means a loner, but he has cultivated a life-style that assures a consistent distance between himself and most other people and allows him considerable periods of solitude. Now forty-four years old, he has never been married, though he has dated many women. Many people are drawn to Curt for his charm and enthusiasm as a conversationalist, but even his closest friends report that they cannot break through a certain personal barrier he erects. In his life-story interview, Curt concedes that he does not let people get too close:

> It's not that I am afraid to open up. I just think that those kinds of conversations get real sappy, real fast. I try to avoid the mush of it all—all the maudlin moments about how bad we've all got it. People's lives are real messy, for the most part—mine too, I suppose. But why do we have to talk about it in great earnest? For me, it's better to keep a kind of clear, clean distance.

There is a quality of clarity and cleanliness to the work that Curt does and the things he makes. As an editor for a textbook publishing company, Curt works hard to transform sloppy manuscripts into well-organized and coherent texts. Some of this work involves "pruning things" and "tightening things up," he says. He also works closely with authors in early stages of a project, wherein he can help them shape their initial vague ideas into a well-formed pedagogical product. He finds great satisfaction in his work as an editor, but the peak experiences in Curt's life come when he is making things in his free time. In the furniture he builds, in the tapestries he weaves, in the Christmas cards he designs, in the gourmet meals he prepares, Curt's creations are always elegant and distinctive. His style favors clean and simple lines, laconic expressions, a muted sensuality living within an orderly universe. It is a style expressing a faith in the clarifying power of simple truths, a style that follows naturally from Curt's steadfast religious beliefs and lifelong involvement in mainline Protestant churches. For Curt, the greatest inspiration for his making is his religious faith. This is the source of the beauty he creates. "There are many great stories in the world," he says, "but the Christian story is the most beautiful. A lot of what I do connects in one way or another to my being in the church since I was a kid, knowing the stories there, and the music, and appreciating the beauty."

A prime function of the imago is to bring together many different aspects of the self under a single character umbrella. In Curt's personal myth, the maker integrates a distinctive assortment of artistic, religious, and life-style elements in Curt's life. It is the maker imago who

1. Acts in ways that are creative, imaginative, somewhat bohemian, but always refined

2. Builds furniture, involves himself in a wide variety of arts and crafts

3. Enjoys classical music, regularly visits art galleries, sings in a church choir

4. Prepares sumptuous meals, enjoys experimenting with new recipes

5. Teaches arts and crafts in schools and churches

6. Loves to travel in order to sample indigenous art and cuisine

7. Decorates his apartment in the most tasteful of fashions

8. Feels inspired by grand liturgy and majestic hymns

9. Works alone

The most glaring shortcoming of the maker, in Curt's life story, is that it does not afford him the opportunity to make much *money*. This is the greatest source of frustration and tension in his life story. As Curt tells it, recent years have witnessed the emergence of a new and troublesome character in his identity, what he describes as "the successful, worldly, money maker." "I look around and I see that most of my friends have a lot more than I do. They've got houses, high-paying jobs. I like what I do, but I can't buy anything." Curt resents the fact that he rents an apartment rather than owns a home; that his car may not make it through another winter; that his brother pulls in a huge paycheck and enjoys great success, as well, in the stock market. How can you dedicate your life to beauty and be a wealthy man at the same time? Curt points to a few people who have done it. One of them is an older friend who has been fabulously successful in writing children's literature conveying religious themes. Curt admires the friend greatly. He hints that he might like to try his own hand at writing children's literature, creating beauty in simple stories. But would they sell? Curt looks forward, with a mixture of doubt and hope, to the next ten years of his life, wherein he will (1) work to integrate the maker with other competing tendencies in his life story and/or (2) seek to enlarge the maker in such a way that it can bring him some of the satisfactions that have eluded him in the shop, at the office, and in the kitchen.

Communal Characters

There are numberless characters who act, think, and feel in communal ways. Oriented toward love and intimacy, these are characters who seek to unite with others in passionate embrace, who love and care for others, who nurture, cooperate, encourage, communicate, and share with others. They work to provide settings for love and intimacy, and to cultivate the best in human intercourse. They are described by adjectives such as affectionate, charming, altruistic, enticing, gentle, kind, loyal, sensitive, sociable, sympathetic, and warm, among many others.[17] As they personify stereotypically feminine sex roles, such characters can be considered "feminine," but they need not be female. Whether they are personified as men or women, these characters seek to be with others in mutually gratifying ways. Four common types of communal characters are the lover, the caregiver, the friend, and the ritualist.

The Lover

The most beautiful and enchanting of the ancient Greek goddesses is Aphrodite, whom the Romans renamed Venus. She is the goddess of passionate love in both its noblest and most degraded forms. She is the inspiration for the amours of deities and mortals alike. She is married to Hephaestus and has lain with Hermes and Ares, but the dearest object of her affection is probably the mortal Anchises, father of Aeneas. Lucretius wrote that the heavens were overwhelmed with the beauty of Aphrodite, and the sea cast its smile upon her. She is the mistress of playful and seductive repartee, and the sweet deceits and delights of love.

"I live for love," says Michelle Bradley, a thirty-two-year-old mother of two and manager of a small and very successful business. "I have accomplished a lot in my work; I was smart in school; but the only thing I've cared about since my father died is loving and being loved. And I've paid dearly for this." The dear payments are a string of failed relationships, including two divorces. Michelle dated one boy steadily through high school, but on the night of the senior prom he told Michelle that he had gotten her best friend pregnant. They broke up; he left town; the girlfriend obtained an abortion. Shortly thereafter Michelle married a young man whom she had known since childhood. They had two children. But her husband became extremely erratic and abusive and was eventually diagnosed as a schizophrenic. Drug therapy and repeated hospitalizations did not seem to lessen his problems; their divorce was finalized on the younger son's second birthday. "Right after that I fell helplessly in love with a guy I worked with," and they were married within a year. Before the younger son's fourth birthday the second marriage was also in a shambles.

Michelle has had at least two serious relationships with men since the second divorce, both of which ended precipitously. At the time of our interview, she is engaged to be married to "the man of my dreams," as she describes him. Insisting that she has learned important lessons about men in the last fifteen years, Michelle believes that this new relationship will succeed where all the others have failed. When Michelle was a freshman in high school, her father dropped dead of a heart attack at the age of forty-seven. As she looks back on it now, Michelle sees that the unexpected loss of her father launched her on a roller-coaster course to find his replacement. With the benefit of two years in psychotherapy, Michelle now believes that she is no longer desperately seeking a man in the image of her father. She feels that she is much better positioned these days to make a discerning evaluation of a prospective lover. She tells me that she has learned how to transfer her rational and analytic skills from her work life into the realm of personal relationships, an accomplishment she credits to the help of her therapist. She says that she knows what she is doing this time.

Michelle's personal myth is sharply split between a dynastic plot of success in school and work (a good past begets a good present) and a self-absolutory plot of failure in relationships with men (a bad distant past begets a bad recent past). Michele hopes to rehabilitate the lover—her dominant but failed imago—in a new marriage founded on a better understanding of who she is and what she wants. Whether or not she will be able to do this is a tough call to make. Michelle appears to have a good understanding of the ways in which she was victimized in past relationships, and how certain of her own behavior patterns set her up to be victimized. She appears to have matured considerably since her high-school days. But like Aphrodite, the lover imago can be capricious and tempestuous. It is difficult to predict what it will do, or what will happen to it. At age thirty-two, Michelle is again "helplessly in love."

Sara Nowinski is a forty-three-year-old high-school counselor who was formerly a Catholic nun. Her personal myth celebrates the life of a passionate and loving woman of God. The main character in the story is an interesting variation on the imago of the lover. For Sara, a woman whose psychological profile shows a very strong intimacy motivation, being a woman of God involves cultivating a passionate orientation to life. The imagery in her story is both religious and erotic. A key nuclear episode was her college baptism into the Catholic Church—it took place on Valentine's Day.[18]

The lover imago has its roots in Sara's childhood relationship with her grandmother. Never very close to her parents (both of whom were fundamentalist Protestants), Sara considered her grandmother to be her first heroine. She was "the perfect human being," Sara says, "loving, independent, feisty, committed to God and to others." After joining the religious order, Sara worked to integrate faith in God and love for people. She developed the reputation among her Catholic sisters as "the earthy one"—the nun steeped in the world and people rather than abstractions and Church dogma.

Throughout her life story, Sara describes many very close relationships in unabashedly sensuous terms and states that these serve as the greatest source of satisfaction in her life. Virtually all of the major changes in her life involve some major influence from those she loves, from her early rendezvous with Catholicism to her decision to leave the Church in her thirties and become a school counselor. She also found herself involved in romantic relationships in her earlier years, falling in love with at least two men. In one episode, laced with irony and missed opportunity, she fell in love with a priest just as he was deciding to leave the religious life. She had decided to enter the religious life largely because of the example he had set for her. She declined his marriage proposal and became a nun.

Sara's dream for the distant future is to set up a religious community in Wyoming where people can live in peace with each other and with God. She speaks of ministering to others both in her work as a school counselor and in her play. Summing up, she states, "I see my life as becoming more and more integrated—to be able to be a space for ministry in my work and with friends, and to enable people to grow and be who they are." Her "life theme" is, in her own words: "A lot of living, dying, and loving."

The Caregiver

The children call her "the T-shirt lady." Betty Swanson decided that the students in her twelve-year-old son's school needed appropriate clothing for gym class. She designed an elegant school logo, made arrangements to have the T-shirts and gym shorts made, and established a distribution and payment plan. Now, school sweatshirts and jackets can also be purchased. When her son enrolled a few years ago, the school cafeteria provided no menus. Children found out what they were going to eat when they arrived in the lunchroom each day. Betty felt that parents should know what was going to be served for lunch well in advance, so that they could make informed decisions concerning when their children were to bring bag lunches to school and when they were to purchase a hot lunch. Fighting intense opposition from the cafeteria employees and the school administration, Betty established a program, and now at the beginning of each month she sends a menu to each parent. In 1989, the parent-teacher organization voted Betty "mother of the year."

Betty's accomplishments are impressive but perhaps not all that dramatic until one learns more concerning her present circumstances. At age forty-eight, Betty has already suffered a massive stroke and two major heart attacks. In addition, she incurred injuries and brain damage after falling out of a window and landing on her head. Once a well-paid accountant, she can no longer add or subtract. She is able to walk only with assistance from others; she speaks very slowly and gently, for she tires easily when talking with people; for each active day in her life—wherein, say, she attends church or collects T-shirt orders or volunteers to staff a neighborhood food pantry—she must rest in bed for two days afterward. She spends an enormous amount of energy trying to appear relatively "normal" when she is out in public, masking her disabilities to the greatest extent possible. "You have to be healthy and strong to be sick," Betty says, "because it takes so much just to live when you've been abused, when your body has been stricken like mine."

Betty's personal myth is the story of a mother who never knew her own. Her parents divorced shortly after she was born. Her father—who apparently was not at all involved in caregiving—remarried soon thereafter, and Betty was raised by her stepmother and her father's parents. She does not remember her biological mother. But she learned as an adult that the woman who once bore her had been employed as an accountant too, and had been convicted of embezzlement. Her mother died in her early forties. Betty tracked down some facts about her mother's life and eventually found her grave in a nearby cemetery.

I never saw her; I never saw what she looked like; I never knew who she was. When you have a *bad* mother—and it turns out that my mother was an accountant, and she had embezzled money, and none of this was ever told to me—in her younger years she was bad; she went to prison, and for a woman to go to prison in the forties, you had to have been pretty bad—when you have a *bad* mother, it is never talked about, and I still don't know much about her, except that I really think that she was this incredible person who must've been very bright and creative and really needed. But I think that her choice of my father as a husband and a mate was totally wrong, because my father was a *stick*, my father was a typical Swede, who has great difficulty showing any emotion. I don't have any conscious memory of ever having any discussion with my father about anything important in my life. He never talked. He would discipline us with his eyes. He would do things with his face. But my mother, well, I think that I must be the way she was, in some way. I talk and share things, and nobody else in my family does. I think I got that from her. I did find out that my mom had a couple of really great escapades before she was sent to prison, and it allows me, you know—well, what she did *was* awful, and she did it at the expense of her children—but it allows me to connect with her. She is a part of me that I lost, but I think I found it again when I found her grave.

Betty was a good student in school. She went to college in the early 1960s, and she studied mathematics. In her twenties, she was gainfully employed as the only female accountant in a very large company. She dated a businessman for two years, and at age twenty-seven she married him. He was thirty-five. Their early years of marriage were very happy:

> I thought it was a perfect existence. I mean I had been afforded a wonderful education. I had come from a good home. My parents were very supportive. There had been no financial burdens. My parents hadn't been alcoholics, you know, or anything like that, which makes people crazy in their early life. I didn't experience anything like that. I was very healthy. I was very athletic. I married a man with whom I had so many interests. So we were able—I was able—to continue to enjoy a very special life. Worked very hard, but it was by choice. But also had time to enjoy life, traveled a little. There was a lot of joy, a lot of pleasure.

Like many professional women today, Betty began to feel a strong need to have children in her early thirties. For reasons that were unclear in the interview, Betty's husband was adamantly opposed to having children. When at age thirty-five she became pregnant, he threatened to divorce her if she did not obtain an abortion. She refused to terminate the pregnancy, and he left. Betty's son was born. She quit work to be a full-time mother. She lived very conservatively, stretching the child-support payments and other monies from her family to make ends meet. During this time, former business associates offered Betty a number of different opportunities for part-time work. She repeatedly turned them down, but after three years at home with her son, she began to think that such a part-time arrangement might be feasible. She received a good offer to work for an attorney. She would be able to do the work at home. She would be paid handsomely. She would also be able to continue as the good mother her own mother had never been. So she began to make preparations. The house needed to be cleaned from floor to ceiling, and she needed to organize an office upstairs.

> I have my own list of priorities, and one is I would never clean a closet if I could play with a three-year-old. Those things were always—not that I disregarded them—but I was really clear on what was important to me. Going to the park every day was very important. And if you do those important things, then you don't have time to clean closets and wash walls and windows. So I thought maybe I should take this next week and really get these things done, because then I won't have to think about them for another, maybe, ten years. So I decided to wash the windows, and I landed on my head and it was really, really awful. Awful in so many respects I can't begin to tell you, because it changed my life in every respect—physically, mentally. I sustained severe head injuries, which ended up to be permanent brain dysfunction in some areas, left me paralyzed. It was so awful. I mean the only good thing was that I survived, that I was still alive, which meant there was hope, and I started an incredible fight to—not just survive. I went into the rehab institute and they told me I would never walk again, never, and I couldn't imagine living like that, and I wasn't able to understand that I couldn't do it, and I left there walking, and it wasn't easy.

Betty made a strong but slow recovery. Just as she was beginning to show substantial progress, she was struck down again, with a massive cardiac arrest and stroke.

> They couldn't fix this. I was in my early forties. . . . I was told that I was not a candidate for bypass because my arteries and heart were seriously diseased. . . . They said good luck, you know, and in the next breath they said go out and get your life in order, and I said what does that mean . . . Well, you go out and buy a cemetery plot is what that means.

Years later, Betty hangs on. As far as I know, she has yet to buy a cemetery plot. With considerable help from some devoted friends and her church pastor, Betty continues to raise her son and to contribute to his school and their community. She can no longer teach Sunday school, but she has organized field trips for the church youth group. As I write this, she is recovering from a third cardiac incident, eight years after her first heart attack and ten years since her fall. Betty reports that she has already experienced death, in a sense. She says she has no fear of it anymore, but she feels driven to remain alive by a "will to survive," so that "I will be there for my son."

In the mythology of ancient Greece, Demeter is a mother goddess who knows what death means. The goddess of fertile and cultivated soil—the earth's caregiver, in this agricultural sense—Demeter is stricken with grief when she learns that her only daughter, Persephone, has been abducted by Hades and transported to the underworld to be his queen. Disconsolate and vengeful, Demeter curses the ground and its fruits. A terrible famine ensues until Zeus arranges a return of the daughter to the mother. Their reunion is pure ecstasy, but later both learn that Persephone must return for one season of each year to the underworld, because she has eaten a forbidden fruit. During that season (winter), the earth remains barren, but when the beloved daughter returns every spring, Demeter makes the fields blossom and the flowers bloom.

Demeter is the devoted caregiver, ready to sacrifice herself and her domain to save her offspring. She is the all-giving martyr who must first experience deprivation (separation, grief, winter) in order to become enhanced (reunion, joy, spring). As a model of the caregiver, Demeter reminds us that caring for others may require great sacrifices and that one must have supreme patience if one is to see the efforts of one's own care bear fruit. In Betty's personal myth, she must sacrifice her marriage and her health in order to become the good caregiver. She would never have fallen out of the window if she hadn't needed to go back to work to support her son. There is bitter irony here, for by cleaning in preparation for the new job, Betty implicitly violated her own code of behavior—never clean house when you can play with a child. Of course, she had no choice. She does not blame herself for cleaning the window. But the irony is not lost on her.

The caregiver is one of the richest imagoes in adult life stories because it can connect thematically to so many different aspects of adult life. Betty identifies "caring for others" as the most important value in her life. Her image of God is that of the benevolent parent. She does not hold God responsible for the bad things that happen in life. God is "what a good parent should be." God "doesn't make tiny babies die; God doesn't do things like that; those are things that just happen." In her volunteer work at school, church, and a local food pantry, Betty always plays the role of the caregiver. She is a vocal advocate for neighborhood parents over and against a local school system that she considers to be corrupt and bloated. "I have never met a parent that I didn't really feel cared about their child. What I have found is that the school makes it difficult for that parent to be committed to that school."

A few years ago, Betty was recruiting other mothers to help her organize the school menus. She called a black woman who had three children in the school. The woman was uneducated and very poor, and she lived with her children in a run-down housing project. She said she was unable to work on the menus, but Betty kept her name and number and gave her a phone call now and again because "she seemed to be a very caring lady."

> She always left me with this feeling that she wanted to do something. So one day I called her again for something and all of a sudden she started sobbing on the phone. And she said, "You know, I really don't feel that I have a place in the school." She does not read or write. I decided I was gonna find something that she could do, and lo and behold, I did. She is now the official—and this is now several years—she is in charge of *all*, how can I say it, cupcakes, cookies, cakes. She coordinates. This is a lady who is, when I say poor, and I don't mean just in dollars and cents, I mean very poor—she has very little resource to draw on. She is now the coordinator, and I don't even think she can say that word, of all the teacher breakfasts. She does the menus. She cooks a lot of the foods. She does all the cupcakes for the kids for their birthdays. She comes into that school proud. And that's probably one of the greatest stories for me.

For Betty, the greatest heroines and heroes are caregivers like herself. For this woman, who now coordinates the cupcakes, and for the children in the school, Betty is more than the T-shirt lady. For the friends and family members who see her through her worse times, who take her to church and assist her in walking, she is more than the grateful object of their generosity and love. Betty herself is the ultimate caregiver in a world that benefits both from her care and from the effort of caring for her.

The Friend

The psychiatrist Harry Stack Sullivan believed that there was nothing more wonderful in the world than a close friendship.[19] The
intimacy experienced by two "chums" represents the pinnacle of
human experience. Yet we are very fortunate, Sullivan lamented, if
we experience such intimacy more than once or twice in our lives,
especially as adults. Sullivan believed that a person is most likely to
experience the beauty of an intimate friendship in the years just
before puberty, as a preadolescent whose sexuality has yet to be
awakened. For many reasons, life gets more complicated afterward,
Sullivan maintained, and true friendship in adolescence and adulthood is very difficult to find. We adults are left groping for connections with other people, ever longing and ever frustrated by the
limitations of human communion.

Yet there are differences among us. Some people seem to be much
more optimistic about friendship, reporting many close and satisfying relations with friends throughout their adult years. Although
they too may experience loneliness and alienation from time to time,
these people also celebrate the possibilities of close friendship in
human life. They may even understand their own personal myths as
primarily tales of friendship. The prototype of the friend in the
mythology of ancient Greece is Hera. Wife and helpmate to Zeus
and queen of Olympus, Hera repeatedly proves to be loyal, coopera-
tive, and friendly. Her steadfastness and loyalty to Zeus distinguish
her from all other deities in the Greek pantheon.

Married for twenty years, Susan Daniels is a part-time speech
therapist and mother of two teenagers. In her life-story interview,
she divides her narrative into ten chapters—beginning with "Infancy" and ending in the present with what she entitles "Mid-life
Crisis." Each chapter centers on her description of an important
person in her life at that time, either a family member or a friend.
Chapter 1 emphasizes how her father doted on her as a baby. She still
thinks it remarkable that in her first year of life he regularly rolled
out of bed to provide her with the 2:00 A.M. and 6:00 A.M. feedings.
Chapter 2 centers on her description of her mother, cast in the form
of a rigid taskmaster who kept order in the home. What Susan sees
as most remarkable about this chapter is that in spite of her mother's

coldness, little Susan was still able to make many good friends as a preschooler. Chapter 3 encompasses her very happy years in elementary school, filled with fun and friendship. Chapter 4 begins with an incident in fourth grade. On the first day of class, she met a new girl, and they became best friends. Like many of the friends she has made over the years, her fourth-grade chum has remained a lifelong friend.

Susan states, "If you have one best friend, you can survive everything else." The proposition may be put to the test in her current career crisis. As the children go off to college, Susan hopes to shed her primary role as mother, quit her part-time job, and begin afresh. She hopes to start a business of her own and do more traveling with her husband, whom she counts as one of her best friends. Because of the uncertainty surrounding her future, however, Susan feels that these are very trying times. Without her children at home, how will she spend the next thirty years of her life? Some of Susan's friends, whose children are about the same age as hers, are also facing this challenge. Susan talks with her friends about these problems, and she looks to their lives for answers to the problems in her own. All in all, loyal and long-term friendship is the major theme of Susan's personal myth. Even though children leave, jobs change, and people grow older, Susan's friendships endure as the one constant amid the many variables of life.

The Ritualist

The last imago we will sample in this chapter is embodied by the Greek goddess Hestia, the deity of the hearth. For the ancients, she was felt to be present in the living flame at the center of the home, temple, and city. Her fire was sacred, providing illumination, warmth, and heat for cooking food. Hestia provided the sanctuary where people bonded together into the family. She represented the keeper of the house, the guardian of domestic tranquillity. More generally, Hestia is the ritualist who preserves the domestic traditions that bring people together in family and community.

Terri Barnes grew up in a small Wisconsin town where she learned the value of taking life one slow step at a time and savoring its simple delights along the way. Early memories of fishing, sailing, swimming, backpacking, and playing in the fields with other children are the highlights of the opening scenes of her personal myth. Today, Terri works as a medical technician at a large university hospital in the Chicago area. She fights the traffic to drive in to her job every day from a distant suburb, where she lives in her new house with her two-year-old son and her husband Michael. Her husband is also from Wisconsin; the two met as students at the University of Wisconsin in Madison. Both in their late twenties, Terri and Michael are busy finding their adult place in the worlds of family and work. They report that, overall, they are happy with their successes on the job, very satisfied with their marriage, and thrilled to be new parents.

Terri has strong work ambitions. She hopes to return to school in the near future in order to obtain a second degree, which would enable her to assume a position of greater responsibility in the medical setting and make more money. When she was a child, Terri's mother and uncle served as strong professional role models. Terri describes her mother as "having it all." Beautiful, well-educated, and well-liked, Terri's mother is a successful businesswoman. Terri believes she is also a first-rate mom and wife. Her uncle is an artist and entrepreneur, whose paintings have appeared in galleries. She describes him as an extraordinarily talented and adventurous man who has done "exotic things."

Terri admires her mother and her uncle, but she does not see herself as following in their paths. For Terri, there is something off-putting about their achievements. When asked to describe a hero or heroine in her life, Terri recalls instead a woman she saw on a television show when she was a child. Although the memory is fuzzy, she thinks that the woman appeared on the *Tonight* show to display how she works with animals in the San Diego Zoo. "I always remember her as somebody who was doing something important," she remarks. In her dedication to animals and her concern about the natural world, the woman was living what Terri has always seen as the kind of simple life she yearns for herself.

Terri's personal myth is a story about leaving paradise and longing to return. The simplicity and fun of childhood are difficult to recapture in the Chicago suburbs, Terri maintains. Her dream for the future is to return to Wisconsin so that she can enjoy a slower-paced, less materialistic, and more natural life-style. Yet she would want to live close enough to an urban center so that she could continue her work in medicine. In Terri's story, that which is simple and pure is what comes from nature. Hiking in the woods is natural and good. Building your own furniture, planting a garden, singing songs around a campfire—these are all wholesome things that good people do together. By contrast, going to a museum, visiting an amusement park, shopping at a mall, all involve too many people cramped into artificial places doing things that are, in some sense, not natural. It also means waiting in lines, and lines are one of the many alienating symbols of modern urban life that Terri has nothing good to say about.

As romantic as Terri's view can be, she is not so naive as to think that she can fully recapture the simple life of her youth. What she needs to do instead, she says, is carry on the best traditions of that simple life, and to pass them on to her children. Every chance they get, she and her husband pack up the car and head for a state park or to the small towns and campsites of the Midwest. Terri grows her own vegetables; she makes some of her own clothing; she quilts. She stays in close contact with siblings and friends in Wisconsin. She has already begun telling her son stories about her childhood.

In her strong desire to conserve the innocent past and carry on the best rituals and traditions of small-town America, Terri is like Hestia, the ritualist. To recreate the simple life for herself and her family and to pass on the skills and attitudes that make the simple life possible are the primary life goals that she has established as a young woman in the modern world. Rejecting the ambition and materialism she perceives in her mother and her uncle, she opts for what she considers to be a humbler but ultimately more satisfying way of being. She acknowledges that making life simple can itself be very complicated, and that she must do more than simply repeat what was done in "the good old days." The creative ritualist needs to adapt worthy old traditions to new situations to bring forth the best from the past through means that are viable in the present. Terri wants a simple, loving home wherein people are tied closely to each other as part of a natural order. The main character in her self-defining life story is the ritualist, the character who makes of her home the best possible setting for human communion.

To be an adult means to understand one's own life in mythic

terms, as an evolving narrative of the self in which different characters, or self-personifications, interact with each other in purposeful ways over time. The characters are idealized imagoes that personify the general agentic and communal tendencies in human lives. They are internalized incarnations of power and love—narrative representatives of how each of us chooses or desires to live as an adult in our own time and place.

The Mythic Challenge of Adulthood

How does one transform the grittiness of the world into the fable of life? Far from being an aesthetic afterthought, the creation of form is at the very heart of both life and art. The shaping impulse is coextensive with life itself; not so much jars, but our very identity must be made. And there is considerable drama in such efforts.

—Arthur Weinstein

The way to become human is to learn to recognize the lineaments of God in all of the wonderful modulations of the face of man.

—Joseph Campbell

CHAPTER 7

Identity, Malaise, and Faith

If God is dead, then we are "condemned to be free," wrote the existentialist philosopher Jean-Paul Sartre. Each of us is "thrown" into the world with the daunting task of responding creatively to our own freedom. We do not know who we are, nor why we are here. We are free to define ourselves. Our freedom is a condemnation because of the anxiety we go through in constructing our personal myths.

The anxiety stems from the possibility that our life may mean nothing. Sartre and other existentialists refer to this feeling as "angst." In order to find meaning, we must wrestle with angst. We must consciously and seriously consider the possibility that nothing is meaningful, that all of life is random and without purpose. We must reject society's pat answers to questions of meaning, lest we find ourselves living hypocritically and in "bad faith." Meaning must come from within ourselves and through our own actions. With each thought, word, and deed, we define the self. We must never forget the possibility of nothingness and meaninglessness lurking behind every action and thought. If we forget the possibility that our lives are meaningless, then they will indeed become meaningless. But if we make it our "fundamental project" in life to create, redeem, and sanctify ourselves and our world, then we will find meaning, and we will become like God.

A person does not have to believe, with Sartre, that God is dead in order to find his words convincing. The point applies to most all modern Western men and women who are unwilling to accept conventional meanings by blind faith. Christians and Jews tend to be more skeptical today than were our ancestors of two hundred years ago. Christian and Jewish existentialists believe that each man or woman is responsible for creating meaning in the world even if God is alive and well and thriving. Whether we are Christians, Jews, Muslims, agnostics, or "other," we are each alone responsible to engage in the heroic battle for meaning, waged on a precipice above the void.

To make meaning in life is to create dynamic narratives that render sensible and coherent the seeming chaos of human existence. To fail in this effort of mythmaking is to experience the malaise and stagnation that come with an insufficient narration of human life. Meaning and malaise may be viewed from many different standpoints in the personal myth, such as the quality of imagery, the nature of themes, the characteristics of imagoes, and the viability of the ideological setting that situates the myth in an ethical and religious context. As I suggested in Chapter 4, the most mature and psychologically valuable personal myths display coherence, openness, credibility, differentiation, reconciliation, and generative integration. But many of us, during many times in our lives, find it difficult to meet these exacting standards of identity development. In many cases, our personal myths seem to stagnate in the face of the forces of convention, limitations of personal and environmental resources, and the inability we experience at times to comprehend consciously the particular features of the myth we are creating. Let us, then, consider some of our failures.

Malaise and Stagnation

At thirty-five years of age, Sam Sobel stays in touch with a great number of his buddies from high school and college. An avid sports fan, Sam regularly attends professional baseball, basketball, and football games with his male friends. He and his wife join a number of married couples for regular picnics, trips, and outings of all sorts. Sam is a good friend, and he prides himself on this. Compared to most American men, he spends an inordinate amount of time on the telephone making social calls, both at work and at home. He knows a great deal about each of his friends. He memorizes their children's birthdates. As with Susan Daniels of Chapter 6 the imago of the friend lies at the center of Sam's personal myth. The difference between them is that for Sam the friend seems to be his only well-articulated imago, and consequently his identity as a whole seems underdeveloped.

The imago of the friend is a relatively common one in the life stories of both men and women in their twenties. As young adults make provisional commitments in the realms of work and love, friendship links them back in time to experiences that are more familiar and comfortable. A freshly minted lawyer in his twenties may not know yet how to play the role of a lawyer. A newly married man may find the current role of husband and the anticipated role of father to be strange and somewhat scary. But both of these men know how to be friends, and have known how to be since at least late childhood. It is not unusual, therefore, to carve out a major role in one's emerging personal myth for the character of the friend.

Friendships remain important, but the character may fade some-what in prominence as people move into their thirties and begin to consolidate their identities in the realms of work and family. For adults who develop strong friendship networks in their teens and twenties, it appears that successful psychosocial development in their thirties involves revising the personal myth in such a way as to give the imago of the friend a smaller part to play. These adults may end up articulating new imagoes that are more closely tied to their work or family roles.

Friendship continues to provide Sam with a major source of life satisfaction, yet he reports that in recent years he has felt increasingly ill at ease with who he is and how he fits into the adult world. He has been successful in his work as a salesman, but for him the job is merely a way to put food on the table. If he won the state lottery, he reports, he would quit the job and never work again. While his marriage is relatively happy, and he is proud to be the father of two sons, Sam is unable to articulate an identity around the characters of lover or caregiver, or the like. Husband and father are social roles for him, but they are not imagoes. He has not appropriated them in meaningful ways into his identity. By contrast, Susan Daniels's central imago of the friend remains an enriching one, because she has also managed to incorporate the roles of wife and mother into her myth.

Sam's life story reminds us that the contours of modern American life for men and women in their twenties and thirties are significantly shaped by work and by family. Most of us make our identities in these two spheres. When we have trouble finding main characters for our personal myths in what we do on the job or how we are with our families, then it is likely that we will experience a certain dissatisfaction or malaise as we move in our mythmaking toward mid-life. The friend has been a sufficient imago for Sam for many years, but he is faced now with developing other integral imagoes to better round out his own character and his personal myth.

The way we use imagery in our personal myth can also influence our feelings of unease. Joan Kaminski, a twenty-six-year-old mother and graduate student in a prestigious university department, believes that the most compelling images she has collected in her life have come from the novels she has read. Joan began reading voraciously at the age of six. She enjoyed reading for the vivid characters she encountered, and for the power of escape it offered. Joan's father suffered from a series of nervous breakdowns during her childhood years. As a way of coping with the tension and avoiding the shame, Joan developed an ability "to get outside" of herself, to distance herself from inner worries and concerns by adopting the perspective of the observer. She says, "I had to be outside of myself in public," suggesting that she frequently approached life as a playactor, enacting scripts and observing herself in the process. In private, reading became her dominant means of accomplishing the same thing, as she observed and identified with the characters in novels and imported them into her private fantasy. What may have begun as a coping strategy came to characterize a style of life in adolescence, she remarks. Her preoccupation with being outside of herself, with "the otherness of life," as she puts it, kept her from experiencing real life in a direct and vivid way. "I lived in what I read," Joan comments. Some of the most significant people in her life story are fictional characters in literature, such as Tolstoy's heroine Anna Karenina, whom she adored and emulated as a college student.

But while she alludes to an assortment of vivid images drawn from her extensive reading in the past, none of these seem to hold Joan's attention for long. She tries images out and discards them without ever incorporating any into her personal myth. There is a sense in which Joan has yet to find the "right" imagery for her life. Because she has felt herself to be the outside observer for so long, she seems unable to bring what she has observed from afar into the personal domain of her own life and life story. "I don't feel passion about too many things," she remarks. What she is saying, in part, is that she has yet to find or create images for her life that do what she wants them to do. She does not even know yet what she wants them to do. Still, she is hopeful that she will be able to harness her rich and well-nourished imagination in the service of creating a coherent and vitalizing personal myth. Joan believes that she has recently begun to shed her role as the observer. The experience of giving birth to her son and the day-to-day care she provides for him seem to bring her back into herself. "This is the first time in my life I feel that I'm not outside myself," she says. In the past, "I've been a lot like my father"—watching rather than living, remaining "not completely there." But now "I love being there."

Another whose new baby seems to be urging on the mythmaking process is a twenty-four-year-old woman I interviewed a few years ago. Kate Tucker struck me as a nice but surprisingly childlike woman. She employed expressions and ideas that you often hear young children use. Her mother and father were good parents "because they gave me the most toys and the most clothes." Kate provided an account of an embarrassing moment in grade school: "I had an accident—I mean I went number one." From her entire past life, only two other incidents stand out in sharp detail—having to clean out her desk in second grade for Parent-Teacher Night, and tripping in the school hallway and having to go to the principal's office.

A major theme in Kate's life story is "being watched." In all three of the key incidents from childhood, she was humiliated as people looked on. In elementary school, she was "the class clown" who was watched because of her ability to make others laugh. Her life heroes are Harry Houdini—who performed amazing feats as others watched but could not see—and Meryl Streep. Kate has always

169

wanted to be an actress herself. Kate believes in a God "who is always watching us" to protect us and make sure that we do good. Her greatest moment in high school was passing her driver's test as her father watched. Her biggest problem these days is that people do not treat her as an adult. For this reason, she maintains, she was fired from her last two jobs. She believes that others are unduly influenced by her childlike appearance.

Kate feels she has never been adequately mirrored. People have not watched her at the right moments or in the right light. They have only seen the bumbling child who pees in her pants, not the glamorous actress and mature adult she wishes they would see. About having a baby, Kate says, "I think it's real neat, but I still feel like I'm a kid." She says, "I look at this child and realize that this little kid thinks the world of me. It's pretty scary, but I like it." Perhaps Kate will look to the baby for the mirroring she needs as she mirrors the baby in return.

Kate's personal myth is an oddly primitive one for a twenty-four-year-old woman. There is very little in her story about her current and future roles as mother and wife. She never once mentioned her husband in the interview. The central imago in her life story appears to be the child. For Kate, the world seems to be made up of two kinds of people—children, who are watched, and adults, who do the watching. Adults are "smarter" than children, and, of course, bigger. Beyond that, they are pretty much the same. She found it "totally amazing" in the previous year to discover that her parents were not as wise as she had always believed them to be. She could not come to grips with the fact that she might know more than they about certain areas of life. We do not have firsthand knowledge of the quality of Kate's early family experiences. We are in no position to make conclusions about her past. But it may be worth speculating that her lack of self-confidence and esteem and her obsession with being watched stem in part from inadequate mirroring experiences in her earliest attachment relationships. In any case, her tentative self seems to have retarded her own personal mythmaking. Kate has not as yet entered a psychosocial moratorium. She has yet to break with her past, and therefore hers seems to be a rather undifferentiated and childlike identity.

If a person tells a story but dawdles over the descriptive details, he might well be asked to "cut to the chase." An obvious borrowing from Hollywood, "cut to the chase" is the simplest advice a movie editor can give for improving a film whose plot lags behind its natural course of development. Action gets a stuck narrative moving. Obviously, the action taken may be more or less appropriate; there are many false moves Kate could possibly make at this moment in her life. But something needs to happen, and Kate's increasing distress at being watched, and her positive experiences with her new baby, are both prodding her to take some action.

Some individuals develop narrative characters that support the shirking of any uncomfortable action. One character that does not appear to derive motivation from either agency or communion I call the escapist. Unable or unwilling to take on the responsibilities of work and home, the escapist lives for diversion and amusement. In a personal myth, the escapist often plays a harmless and subsidiary role, as a fun-loving part of the self who comes out on weekends and vacations or during periods of playful regression. Its origins are often found in a fondly remembered childhood, filled with fun and play. But there are more problematic expressions as well. The desire to escape from the responsibilities of adulthood may become a central motive in daily life, manifested in endless television viewing, dangerous substance abuse, and so on.

Julie McPherson is a thirty-nine-year-old market analyst, married with no children, who tells a life story that seems bereft of concerns for power or love.[1] At the beginning of our interview, Julie shows very little emotion and appears mildly depressed. Her account of her life is very brief, and is mostly a collection of vague generalizations. Toward the end of the interview, she is asked to describe the "underlying theme" of her life story. She says:

Well, we talk a lot about stability and stuff like that, or relinquishing responsibility. That's my utopia. I want to be taken care of. I will tell you a story that will tell you where I want to be when I grow up. About two years ago, I was in the hospital for two weeks. I was sick, but I wasn't in pain. I was in a room by myself; I was in isolation. I couldn't have any visitors. I wasn't on medication; there was no discomfort. I was there for two weeks, and I chose my meals off a menu. I got up every morning at six o'clock and took a shower, put on a little makeup, put on a clean nightgown, sat down, had my breakfast, read the paper, read a book till noon, watched Julia Child at noon, turned off the TV, read a book or whatever till five or so, and then my husband came to visit me or I had dinner served. That couple I talked about earlier in the interview would come to visit. Then everybody'd leave. At ten o'clock, I'd turn off my lights and go to sleep. After two weeks, I didn't want to go home. I didn't want to go home and be faced with laundry and housecleaning and dogs that had to be taken out and a husband that had to be waited on. And that to me was like I was taken care of. I didn't have to cook a meal. . I told them what I wanted. I only had to take care of myself personally, and other than that, I went to bed at ten o'clock; I went to sleep; I didn't have to take a pill or anything; I woke up promptly at six, without an alarm. And I know I was really upset when I had to go home. That's the theme.

Julie appears to be a disgruntled and alienated woman whose life dream is to escape from her daily responsibilities. Julie wants to be taken care of. On the brink of mid-life, she wants to remain passive as others minister to her needs and whims. Stuck with a frustrating job and a dismal marriage, Julia personifies her life hopes in the character who lives to escape. But beyond the cameo appearance in the hospital, it would appear that the escapist is rarely on center stage. Rather, the escapist beckons from the wings, seductive and sedating.

Sleepwalking through her daily routine, Julie has managed to suspend her life. She takes no action to change her present circumstances, as her fantasies are occupied by the escapist. But she is unable to commit to any real escape, either, because she has defined escape as doing nothing instead of doing something new and different. Thus, she has written herself a central imago that keeps her stuck in exactly the place she doesn't want to be.

There are other ways in which an individual can get stuck. We are all familiar, consciously or not, with the fact that character determines episode. A character's actions are motivated by personal desires—we each attempt to bring about the things we want. The things we want, and the things we do to get what we want, are the things that describe our characteristics. Most memorable stories concern the way characters are frustrated from achieving their desires by their own characteristics. Aristotle's theory of tragedy hinges upon this conception—he believed humans respond most deeply to hearing of an exceptional man being laid low by the very trait that makes him exceptional.

We are satisfied by such tales because they remind us of the way in which self-defined characteristics can get us into trouble. In some cases, a single negative identity from a person's past can completely dominate the self-defining myth, well into the adult years. I once interviewed a twenty-seven-year-old man, a new father, who was employed as an assistant director of a university athletic center. Bob Shaver is an extremely personable and cheerful man who enjoys his family and his work and speaks fondly of the many close friendships in his life. The psychological test data we collected corroborated my personal impressions of Bob's personality. He is friendly, easygoing, sincere, honest, and altruistic. He appears to have a strong need for close and warm relationships—a high level of intimacy motivation. He has a strong commitment to making life better for other people. His own personal myth for making sense of life celebrates good cheer, good works, and companionship.

But the spring for all of it appears to be the primary villain in the story—Bob's alcoholic father. Bob defines himself in opposition to his father. He has worked hard to make himself into the opposite kind of person—caring where his father was cruel, responsible where his father was dissolute. Not surprisingly, narrative tension usually occurs in his personal myth when something or someone reminds Bob of his father. Two of his former bosses and the Church embody characteristics that, to Bob, are strikingly similar to those shown by his father. All four of these authority figures represent a grand negative identity. Bob accordingly has trouble dealing with authority.

Bob has been able to go a long way toward achieving what he wants in his life by defining himself in opposition to his father. He is young enough that his difficulty with authority hasn't led the plot of his personal myth either to crisis—a direct confrontation with an authority in a position to frustrate Bob's efforts—or to stasis—where the natural development of Bob's story is held up by his unwillingness to deal with an authority in a position to help him. But sooner or later, Bob's myth will reach a point of crisis or stasis. He will then be challenged to revise his myth to accommodate an ideal of legitimate authority, whatever that might mean for him.

Not surprisingly, many of the same problems that plague badly told stories can be discerned in narratives of human identity. In the context of the personal myth, underdeveloped characters, inopportune images, childish themes, or stalled plots are not mere aesthetic concerns—they result in real human malaise. In the preceding examples, identity malaise results most generally from difficulties in making wholehearted commitments to vital life projects. Wholehearted commitment in life and in myth requires a fundamental *faith* in some aspect of the human enterprise. Condemned to be free, adults must transcend their angst to find something in life to believe in. The stories we live by are enhanced by our faith and our fidelity to something larger and nobler than the self—be that something God, the human spirit, progress through technology, or some other transcendent end.

Ministry of a Madam

When I first saw Shirley Rock at a neighborhood meeting, she looked like a battle-scarred veteran of the city streets. She appeared to be a chain-smoking, tough-talking woman of late middle age with very few economic resources but an intimidating personal demeanor. Shirley was one of a small group of community volunteers who had consented to be interviewed for a research project I was conducting. The research examined the life stories of adults who have committed their lives to promoting, teaching, guiding, or assisting the next generation.[2] I was not looking forward to interviewing her and was therefore rather relieved when one of the graduate students working on the project—Ed de St. Aubin—agreed to conduct the interview. To our surprise, Ed came back with a mesmerizing story.

Shirley Rock tells a dramatic life story indicative of a woman who, as much as anybody I have ever known, truly understands who she is. Looks are indeed deceiving, in many ways. Shirley turns out to be a church pastor! But that's deceiving, too, for she reports that she was once a prostitute, has operated a number of extremely profitable brothels, has been deeply involved in organized crime, and has done time in a state prison and federal penitentiary. Some of this time was served in solitary confinement—"in the hole." She also says that she is a recovered alcoholic and drug addict. But throughout the sudden turns and dramatic transformations in Shirley's life story, her identity seems to have been sustained by a coherent set of personal beliefs and values. These have changed very little since her adolescence. Hers is a story of tremendous changes in life circumstance played out on a stage of ideological continuity and stability. It appears that Shirley has always known what is true and good. Her personal myth derives its power from her wholehearted ideological certitude. "I don't think that if I had life to live over, I would change a day of it," she says. Even in her role as a madam in the brothel, there was continuity: "I've been in ministry, I guess, all my life."

She was born to an Orthodox Jewish father and a Roman Catholic mother whose own mother was a member of the Pentecostal clergy at a time when virtually no women held such positions. Shirley grew up in a determinedly ecumenical household. Her parents each suffered considerable criticism for their decision to marry outside of their respective faiths. In consequence, they raised their children to be tolerant of all religions and accepting of all ethnic groups. "We were raised to believe that all people were equal, and so therefore, as I was growing up, my house looked like a little junior League of Nations, all colors, all languages, all nationalities . . . all mixed up." Shirley is caucasian. Her first boyfriend was black, "but this didn't cause any problems" for her parents. Everything seemed to be fine until Shirley told her parents that she wanted to marry a black man. Their reaction was "like the Hiroshima bomb."

> I didn't understand it. I was twenty-two years old, and I really did not understand how they could change overnight. I truly believed that my mother and dad should have understood an interracial marriage—probably better than anyone else—because of things that had happened to them for an interreligious marriage. But they didn't, and I had to make a big decision at that point. But they took care of it for me and sent him away, not knowing I was already pregnant. And Pearl—my daughter (that's her in the kitchen)—is the product of that union.

Shirley's parents drove her boyfriend away by telling him that they had sent Shirley to Europe and that she would not return for a very long time. Shirley was horrified by her parents' hypocrisy. They had betrayed the values of tolerance and acceptance that they had once so strongly emphasized. Although nonconformist with respect to their own life choices, they were embarrassed by the degree of their daughter's own nonconformity, and deeply ashamed of her pregnancy. Shirley left home and finally caught up with her boyfriend. The two were married in St. Louis. On the night they were married, Shirley's husband was arrested for violating an old law prohibiting interracial marriage. Her parents' betrayal together with her husband's arrest undermined forever her trust in earthly authority. She felt scorned and persecuted by middle-class society as her money and her prospects ran out.

> That was the period in my life that I really experienced being homeless and being on the street, being hungry, and finding out that people will buy you a drink before they'll buy you something to eat, that there's not a lot of milk and peaches and kindness and love and honey in this world, that if people did something for you they had an ulterior motive and wanted something in return.

She moved from job to job, working as a waitress, cook, bartender, restaurant manager.

> But it seemed like every time I'd get a job and I'd get stable, somebody'd call and say, you know, she's married to a nigger, and there would go the job. They'd call me in. "How come you didn't tell us you were married to a nigger?" I'd say, "You didn't ask me. You asked if I was married; I told you yes. You didn't ask me what color is your husband, so I didn't bother to tell you." So they'd fire me for undesirable character, all kinds of reasons.

Desperate for money, she became a prostitute. Shirley quickly found the work disagreeable, however, and moved on:

> [Prostitution] didn't last very long, because I didn't like it. It was against just everything I am, you know, so I became a madam. After a year, I had built enough of a book with names and telephone numbers to open a business. By then I had established syndicate contacts, and so I owned syndicate houses and worked as many as fifteen, twenty girls. We did operate with some ethics. My girls were clean. They went to doctors regularly. In fact, doctors came. Men were sure they were safe, because there was no thievery in the house. And I learned many, many things the years that I was a

madam, in conversation about people, men and women, about marriage, good and bad, business, how people think, what motivates people, what makes people respond, and I am probably a natural study of people and things.

As she became more successful, Shirley became more deeply involved in organized crime. Throughout the 1960s, she worked in the syndicate's "confidence game," duping unsuspecting people and organizations into giving large sums of money to the syndicate. In 1972, Shirley was arrested, tried, and convicted of crimes associated with this activity, and she was imprisoned. The day she heard the prison gates slam behind her represents the lowest point in her life story. Now in her early forties, Shirley decided it was time to turn her life around. She became involved with an organization called New Hope, "which is ex-offenders helping offenders get their heads screwed on straight." She joined a Christian group and when she left prison in 1974, began to do volunteer work for the church. She swore off alcohol, drugs, and her "money habit." Since 1974, she has "not committed an illegal act against ordinance or against law."

Personal myths often contain fascinating foreshadowings. When Shirley was ten years old, her grandmother told her that God was going to "call" her when she got to be fifty years of age. "I always thought she meant God was going to call me home, and I was going to die." But what she must have meant, Shirley now believes, is that God was going to call her to the ministry. After leaving prison, Shirley worked in a number of paid and unpaid jobs providing various kinds of social services to disadvantaged people. From scratch, she organized and administered a food pantry for a church congregation; she provided counseling and education for resident aliens; she ran an after-school program and a summer camp for children. And she managed to raise three children and launch them into adulthood with only modest assistance from her husband. Finally, on October 8, 1984, she received the call, just one year later than her grandmother prophesied:

The day before I had gone to the altar and said to my pastor, my friend, my mentor, "I don't know what's wrong with me but you have to pray with me, something's wrong." He sent me to read the Books of Samuel, which is when Elijah was called by God, and I read 'em and I came back and I said no, no, this is not what's going'

177

on. I'm, you know, I'm fifty-one years old. I'm sure he's not callin' me to go back to school and do all of that—no, you gotta be mistaken. So I went home, and that night, for the first time in weeks, I slept very soundly. The next day I came to church, and the Head Start and all the programs were gone, and I was the only one in the church, and I was putting together a directory and trying to undergird each ministry of the church, biblically, and it seemed like no matter where I went in the Scriptures that day, it pertained to God's call, and so, as I came to confirmation, I couldn't find anything biblically to undergird confirmation, and so I opened a book on church practice. And, as I held the book, it just sort of fell open by itself and it went to prerequisites for the ordained clergy. And I said, okay, you know, if this is what you want, you've got it, and all of a sudden it was as if I could float. Every care, everything went off of my shoulders and out of my body, and my head was clear and the room was bright white. I mean it was just luminous, and I sat awestruck. I have never felt like that before, and I have never felt like that since, and from what I understand, I will never feel that way again. But I knew exactly what had happened, and I knew that I had been touched and that I was in the presence of God.

Today, Shirley works as a half-time pastor for an inner-city congregation. In addition, she works "full time" for an interdenominational coalition that coordinates all of the city's "warming centers." Most of her work is what the church deems social ministry, involving her in a wide range of activities ultimately aimed at serving the poor. The ministry puts into action central beliefs and values about God and the world that Shirley has held dear since her adolescent years. As her grandmother prophesied, Shirley's acceptance of the call represents something of a return home. Her ministry enables her to live out the values of tolerance and acceptance that her parents preached but, in Shirley's opinion, failed to put fully into practice. Shirley's personal ideology has deepened and become more fully articulated through her life experience. It has been enhanced and reinforced by relationships she has had with ex-convicts like Marge, who in her capacity as coordinator for New Hope arranged for Shirley to see her children on weekends during the time she was incarcerated. Fellow clergy have also been important to her. She particularly values Albert, a black pastor and a mentor, a "man of wisdom and a good listener," a man who also "carries an awe of God." Yet, throughout her adult life the fundamental character of Shirley's values does not appear to have changed. Her faith has served as a stable setting for her identity.

Human Faith and Religious Ideology

In his book *Stages of Faith,* James Fowler argues that faith is a universal human phenomenon.[3] For Fowler, though all human beings are not religious, all live by faith. It is part of human nature, says Fowler, to ascribe some kind of order or pattern to the universe and to live according to the ascription. Faith involves a relation to and an understanding of an ultimate environment—what Fowler calls "faith as relating" and "faith as knowing." It is this second aspect of faith as knowing that becomes part of the ideological setting for every adult's personal myth. How do people understand the ultimate reality within which they live?

In my own research, my associates and I have examined the development of faith as knowing in college students and older adults.[4] The college studies were conducted at Saint Olaf College (a small, Lutheran-affiliated school in Northfield, Minnesota) and Loyola University of Chicago (a middle-sized, urban university associated with the Catholic Church). Older adults were sampled from a Lutheran church, a Jewish synagogue, and an organization for atheists, all in the Chicago area. Taken together, the different studies provide a sketch of four qualitatively different structures of religious belief and value—what I will call Positions A, B, C, and D. The four positions apply to people of varying religious persuasions and are equally applicable to those who profess no religious affiliation. Virtually all people formulate some kind of understanding of an ultimate reality, even if that understanding includes no reference to God or any forces beyond natural laws.

In Position A, a person's understanding of faith is confined to a few specific rules about good behavior, or vague beliefs about God, nature, or the like. For example, a Catholic woman may report that she believes in God in general and prays to the saints but does not attend church anymore because she believes that the Catholic stand on birth control is wrong. A man raised in a Baptist church may assert that he does not smoke or drink liquor because the Church prohibits it, but his personal theology is no more delineated than his general conviction that "Jesus is my savior." A young man who professes no religious persuasion may say that people should love each other and try not to do harm, but his belief in love is not integrated into any coherent system that addresses issues of ultimate concern.

The cardinal features of Position A are its concrete and unsystematic qualities. For the most part, religion is reduced to concrete behaviors such as being baptized at birth, fasting on holy days, eschewing premarital sex, or saying prayers before meals. To the extent that beliefs and values are enunciated, they are expressed in very vague and general terms, and they are not organized within a larger system. While the person's beliefs may be strong and genuine, they tend not to relate to each other in clearly articulated ways. Ideology seems somewhat scattered and diffuse, as we hear in this college student's description of her own religious beliefs:

> I believe in God and faithfully attend Roman Catholic mass. My religious beliefs center around my personal commitment to God and the humanity He created. My beliefs are expressed in what I do and what I think. I don't believe that one can separate beliefs into time slots. I pray whenever it occurs to me to do so, in times of happiness, sadness, and need. Mass attendance is my only ritualistic concession, possibly out of habit, but I do feel a certain closeness to God and rejuvenation. My beliefs are simple. Not quite as simple as "do good and avoid evil," but I do seek out the good in myself, in others, and in the world God created.

At a more complex level, Position B describes faith structures that are built around a systematic creed or conventional theory. In Position B, the person gathers up scattered beliefs and values into a coherent conceptual container—a system—that is provided by some external authority, such as the Church or the scientific establishment. The person may commit him or herself to an external doctrine that spells out clearly what is right and true and worth believing. For the most part, the doctrine goes unquestioned.

Fowler calls Position B the "synthetic-conventional" stage of faith, and he believes that it is a very common structure among adolescents and young adults. My own research supports his claim.[5] To illustrate Position B, here is an account of a young man who once strayed from the straight and narrow path but then returned to conventional beliefs about God:

> I search for what is real. At Saint Olaf College, my previous
> assumptions concerning the Bible, the nature of God, and my
> personal beliefs and experiences were questioned and—as I
> perceived it—threatened. The Bible was said to be nonauthoritative,
> only a book. God was more a concept and an idea that was real, and
> not a friend. My personal experience of conversion and of sensing
> God was considered to be a subjective emotional experience. I
> prayed and prayed and read a variety of books presenting a variety
> of ways of looking at God. My search was led by a sense inside me
> that said Jesus is real, God is alive, and the Bible is his Word.
> Looking at people's lives was the main reason for reaccepting my
> first views. I looked at people and watched their lives to see who was
> different in a good sense—who really cared and loved others. Then I
> looked at what they believed and listened to them. They also
> confirmed my inner yearnings. The academic look at God lacked life
> and life-giving potential. It was interesting and logical, but it didn't
> have what I was looking for in my life.

A person may organize his or her beliefs and values in a synthetic-conventional way even when he or she has not been indoctrinated within a particular religious tradition. For example, some adults dismiss all religious systems as invalid, antiquated, or antiscientific and substitute for them systems of belief that are thoroughly secular. A hard-nosed scientific approach to understanding an ultimate reality provides a synthetic-conventional structure for some people. Such a position is synthetic-conventional to the extent that the beliefs and values represent a well-organized system provided by an external authority (e.g., the political, intellectual, or scientific establishment). It is a system that, for the most part, is not questioned in any serious way.

In Position C, a person moves beyond conventions and begins to fashion a personalized and unique faith structure. The person begins to question the creeds and dogmas of Position B and to search for a more encompassing and personally relevant ideology that can account for the contradictions and complexities encountered in life. The move from Position B to Position C may involve a good deal of soul-searching, for it is very difficult indeed to reject conventions that one has grown up with, and to strike out on one's own in the search for a higher truth. A student at Saint Olaf College describes her move from Position B to Position C as beginning with a rejection of the simple answers of childhood in the face of the deeply troubling questions she encountered as a young adult:

> I think most of the serious questioning evolved out of ethical problems—friends aborting fetuses, shady practices at my place of work, etc. Right and wrong were no longer clear—if they ever had been. These single issues were maybe resolved one by one, but greater ones arose. I guess one's appreciation (in the pure sense) of evil increases proportionate to age and experience. I stood at the ovens of Dachau and asked how my Sunday-school-class God could have let it happen. The questioning has not yet been resolved, nor has it been abandoned. I rejoice in the opportunity to rail like Job against my God.

Fowler describes Position C as the stage of "individuative-reflective" faith. The individual reflects upon the validity of conventional beliefs and ultimately rejects some of them while accepting others. The individual reorganizes his or her ideology in such a way as to address issues and problems that defy simplistic pat solutions. In Position C, the person may initially rebel against all the accepted beliefs of childhood and sample many new systems and understandings that come from traditions that were previously alien to him or her. For example, a fundamentalist Christian may reject his Sunday-school teachings and explore another religious system or transcendental meditation. A girl raised in an Orthodox Jewish household may come to doubt the usefulness of some of the traditions she has known and move to a more humanistic perspective on issues of ultimate concern. Below, a Catholic college student describes in detail her move toward Position C. Her gradual questioning of her faith was followed by a careful selection of those aspects of Catholicism that in her mind are worth holding on to:

> I was brought up in a family that was strictly Catholic. We have always gone to church every Sunday and on most of the holy days also. During these masses, there was always a lot of ritual and symbolism used. I began to question religious beliefs at about the same time I began to have a feeling of emptiness every time the more ritualistic parts of the mass were performed. (This was in

182

seventh grade.) At first I felt I was missing something—wasn't trying hard enough to feel what everyone else was. I was sure they were experiencing something mystical. Eventually, this led to an argument I had with my mother over whether the host was changed into the body of Christ [in the Christian sacrament of communion]. My mother felt that the host was actually the body of Christ. I said it didn't matter if it was really changed and thought of it more as a reenactment of the event. After this I began to question the validity of the Bible (eleventh grade). This has developed to my present view that there are some very good things in the Bible, but a lot of it is unhealthy and responsible for the present degraded state of Western man. I do still have a reverence for Jesus—I've always been awed by the figure—but I don't think that it's for the same reason that most Christians do. I don't care if he died on a cross in regards to the "saving" context. People have died in concentration camps, too. The Jesus of the prodigal son or the woman caught in adultery is the one I respect.

Position C blends a commitment to a self-constructed ideology with a tolerance for the tenets of other people's faiths. The person at Position C may acknowledge that different ideological points of view may be right for those people who hold them. Typically, the person at Position C tries to reconcile inconsistencies within his or her own faith, or between his or her own and the faiths of others, through the use of reason or logic. The person at Position C tends to believe in the power of human reason to successfully address most problematic issues. For the person at Position C, the world would be a much better place if everybody were a bit more reasonable, a bit more judicious, a bit more tolerant of competing points of view.

From the standpoint of Position D, however, reason is not enough. A very small number of people, beginning probably in mid-life, reorganize their beliefs and values in order to accommodate paradox and inconsistency in life. They begin to see the limits of human reason and the inadequacies of their own reasonable systems of beliefs. Ultimate issues concerning truth and goodness come to be viewed from a more complex and ironic perspective. In addition, the person may attempt to recapture some of the elements of faith that were lost in the moves from Positions A to B to C. They gain an appreciation for the primitive stories of faith they cherished as a child but then rejected as they became more sophisticated in adolescence and adulthood. Position D is sometimes described in terms of recapturing some of the simple and beautiful truths that have been lost over time. The person may exhibit a second naïveté, but it is an ironic position that is fully cognizant of the complex world within which it exists.

Fowler calls Position D "conjunctive faith" because the person is able to conjoin ideas and images that are usually kept separate. Ideas such as innocence and experience, an almighty God and an all-merciful God, the goodness of Hitler, the evil of Gandhi, can be considered and comprehended from Position D. The position allows for complex ideological structures that make room for paradox and irony. Shirley Rock provides compelling glimpses of this kind of faith in her acceptance of her own crimes and her commitment to attacking the crimes of society, and in her understanding of herself as a madam with a ministry. Shirley is not blind to the contradictions of human life. Fully aware of the inconsistencies, Shirley plunges headfirst into her ministry. What sustains her is a conjunctive ideo-logical setting for her identity that joins together a unique and sometimes baffling array of personal beliefs and values.

Shirley's ideology begins with the firm belief that the world is filled with injustice, and that everybody is implicated. There are no pure and virtuous people, although some people are better than others. While she believes that she was pushed into a life of crime by the persecution she experienced because of marrying a black man, she does not excuse her crimes as a simple product of victimization. While she tried to run a "clean house" and gave her call girls loving advice when they came to her with their problems, she recognizes that she participated in their victimization as well. She—and not just the syndicate—is to blame. She sees that in refusing to be a prostitute herself while profiting from the prostitution of others she was just as hypocritical as her parents and the middle-class society that shunned her for marrying outside her race. Shirley does not excuse her criminal activity. Like her greatest hero, the New Testament's Saint Paul, she has sinned boldly, and recognizes that there is no way to cover that up. Furthermore, she knew she was sinning *as* she was sinning. Her decision to swear off crime, drugs, and alcohol during her time in prison was not stimulated by a sudden revelation that she was a "bad person." She already knew she was bad. Her decision was more pragmatic, even strategic. Simply put, the costs of her criminal activity were outweighing the benefits. Despite the lavish life-style she enjoyed with the syndicate, two prison terms convinced her that crime wasn't paying very well.

All people are bad. All are implicated. But two factors redeem humankind, in Shirley's view. First of all, some people are sensitive to, or aware of, the injustice and victimization in the world, even as they participate in it. She believes she has always been one of those people. In responding to a question about her current life stresses or problems, Shirley says, "What makes me stressed is not my own personal problems; it's the problem of the world, and it's injustice. This has bothered me since the time I was a little girl." The second and more important factor for Shirley is that God forgives and accepts all people, and God empowers them to do good works, even as they remain implicated in evil. Shirley sees herself as a vehicle for the ministry of a higher power. Like Saint Paul, she believes that she has opened herself up to that power by accepting "the call" and continuing to fight what Paul called "the good fight." In the good fight, Shirley battles injustice and oppression. She works on behalf of the underdog sinners, never forgetting that she is and always will be one of them. Because God forgives all, Shirley does not have to invent an elaborate justification for the criminal behavior of the past. In her mind, she was and is a criminal, just as she was and is an alcoholic and a drug addict. Despite the dramatic changes in her life, Shirley has constructed an identity that celebrates continuity. Even though she is now a pastor rather than a madam, she is still the same old self-aware sinner, conscious of her weaknesses and committed to helping others deal with their own weaknesses as well. God enables her to be who she is and always has been because God accepts all, she says.

Shirley's personal ideology as an adult specifies beliefs and values that connect her to the family of her youth, reinforcing once again the continuity of her personal myth. Shirley's current ministry enables her to recapture the ecumenical spirit of her earliest years at home, in her "little junior League of Nations":

I think the thing I like about or appreciate about the branch of Christianity that I'm a part of is that it does not condition people to

a doctrine. That it has room for people to work out their own
theology, their relationship with God. That was a long time coming
over the years. Part of my theology and who I am comes from my
Jewish heritage, my Pentecostal heritage, my Roman Catholic
training and schooling, and the Baptist church that I went to, and the
Sikh temple that I worshiped in, and in searching. And because I saw
so much diversity in my own family, it gave me the ability to reach
out and be able to worship with other people, and in ways different
from my own and still feel the presence of God.

But who is this God? Shirley says:

I believe there's one God that created all that is, all that was and all
that ever will be. I believe that God is my heavenly father. I also
believe that God is my nurturing mother. I believe that God is my
sister, my brother, my aunt, my uncle, my friend, my lover, that God
is all I meet. I believe that—in the triune God, so I have to believe
in Jesus Christ as the son of God. And the Holy Spirit as the
comforter and the third part of the trio . . . My religious beliefs are
to love my God with all my heart, soul, mind, and strength, and to
love my neighbor as myself. . . . Well I think the Bible says it very
clearly when it says all those who hallowed the Lord will not be the
ones to enter the kingdom. I think what's judged is your heart, and
the bottom line will be your consideration and your participation
with the poor and the oppressed.

We do not need to believe that Shirley's God is our God, and we
do not need to adopt her religious beliefs, to understand that this is
what is right and true for Shirley. This is the bedrock of her ideology.
It provides a foundation for her identity. Of course, we can find fault
with this foundation. We can question its validity. We can ask, for
instance, how it can be that people are fundamentally bad while God
is everywhere, existing, as Shirley puts it, "in all I meet." We can
wonder about the inconsistencies of a God who judges people with
respect to their contributions to the poor and the oppressed but who
reigns over a system that appears to be inherently oppressive. We
may want to see her belief in the existence of any kind of God as
basically naive or overly romantic. But there is no getting around the
fact that this is what Shirley believes to be true and to be good and
that these beliefs undergird her identity.

A Yuppie's Search for Meaning

If it is more difficult to understand identity today than it was in earlier times, it is because, in part, the matter of ideology has become extraordinarily complex and confusing. Modern secular societies are not built on the kind of monolithic Christian worldview that was prevalent in Europe throughout the Middle Ages and into the seventeenth and eighteenth centuries. As one scholar writes, "As long as men and women believed in a soul created and sustained (continuously known and seen) by God, there could be no question about the unity of the self."[6]

While many men and women in modern societies continue to adhere to traditional Christian viewpoints, there is certainly no widespread consensus about God and the nature of God's plan for the universe today. The synthesizing power of Christianity has eroded considerably in the last two hundred years. The triumphs of science and technology, the rise of the Industrial Revolution, widespread urbanization, the proliferation of capitalism, the alienation of worker and work, the discovery of the unconscious, two world wars, the atom bomb, the advent of mass media, increasing global awareness, and a host of other developments have come to shape our modern and postmodern consciousness. Today we are faced with a rich assortment of alternative and competing ideological frameworks, and a pervasive attitude of skepticism about the power of any traditional or institutional belief system to address all of our ideological concerns.

Ted Belize grew up in a suburban community outside St. Louis, Missouri, the oldest of four children in a middle-class household. His father was a businessman, and his mother stayed home and raised the children. Ted was very close to one brother who was only a year and a half younger, and they spent a great deal of time playing together. His early memories center on outdoor activities, the family, and the Church:

> I spent a lot of time outdoors. The area we were growing up in was being developed, so there was still a lot of forests and trees, wilder areas around, and there was a lot of things to do in the woods that

you couldn't do in the city. And I remember spending a lot of time around houses that were being constructed, climbing in them, taking wood and bringing it home to build forts, taking it into the forest to build forts, a lot of things like that. I have real good memories of going to my mother's parents' home in southern Illinois. They had a farm, and I remember seeing the pigs and the soybeans and getting the soybeans in your nose, and those memories are still very strong. And I think I developed a very close attachment to the land, the earth, and I still find that a lot today. I've got a strong feeling there. Also, another big part of that, I think, was our parents were very active in their church, and therefore we were, too. We spent a lot of time there.

Ted's parents were active in a congregation affiliated with the Lutheran Church—Missouri Synod. Historically, the Missouri Synod is a relatively conservative church body within Lutheranism, with ethnic roots in Germany. Like many Missouri Synod congregations in the 1950s and 1960s, Ted's church emphasized a strict and literal interpretation of the Bible. To them, the Christian God is the one true God, and Jesus Christ is his son and humankind's savior. This Lutheran Church body tends not to be ecumenical, and is relatively intolerant of dissenting points of view. In the 1970s, the Missouri Synod experienced a great deal of doctrinal tumult, and a more liberal wing of the synod split off from the main body. Ted accepted the doctrines of the Church as a child and adolescent and reports little tension and few disagreements with the Church through his high-school years. For the most part, religion remained in the background in his life. He rarely thought about issues of ultimate concern, even into his early adult years. His daily thoughts tended to center on outdoor activities and sports, on schoolwork, and as he moved through his teenage years and into his twenties, on "an overriding obsession with work and success."

Since his high-school years, Ted has distrusted his overriding obsession. The obsession with personal success makes his life "un-balanced," he contends. The struggle to find balance is a recurrent theme in Ted's personal myth. For Ted, the struggle is couched in terms of the conflict between individual and group. In describing his athletic activities in high school and college, Ted repeatedly points out that with the exception of college lacrosse he excelled in individual sports, not team sports. He details clear memories of long and solitary hours training for track meets. The most vivid episode in his entire life story is a mile-long race he ran in high school:

> I wanted to win. I knew I could win. So I went out and I set up and I was leading. I set a very fast pace. And what happened in the fourth lap—there are four laps in a mile—on the fourth lap, coming down to the fourth turn, my legs had oxygen depletion, my lungs weren't able to get it, and my legs just stopped. I couldn't pick 'em up. I fell over, 'cause I was still moving forward of course. I fell down, and I was in the lead at the time. Well, my own schoolmate came around me. I remember I was laying on the ground; I remember my coach screaming, get up, get up, and I remember my teammate came around me and won the race, but one of the other runners from one of the other schools also passed me, but I was able to basically drag myself down the last quarter eighth of the track. I don't know why it's so, I consider that a peak experience, except that I remember it, I recall it over and over. I dream it, I dream about it all the time.

The memory expresses Ted's deep ambivalence about the pursuit of individual achievement. He wanted to win that race as much as he has ever wanted anything. After countless hours of training and three and a half perfect laps around the track, he was ideally positioned to win. Yet at the last moment, his body gave out. His individual pursuit was for naught. Interestingly, his own teammate won the race. Symbolically, the collective team triumphed, even though the individual lost out. This critical memory stands in sharp contrast to Ted's account of his experience participating on the college lacrosse team. Though he was not a star in lacrosse, his experiences playing this sport with his teammates and traveling to other colleges to play other teams are among the most positive memories of his life.

Part of Ted's ideology is the belief that untempered individualism leads to an unbalanced life. Ted believes that balance is good for all lives, not just his own. After graduating from college, Ted worked for three years for a major accounting firm. He was extremely successful, putting in tremendously long hours and making a great deal of money. Much of his time was spent traveling. The fast-paced and ever-changing work that he did for the firm was fun but exhausting. It was an exhilarating but "difficult and hardworking life-style, what I call an unbalanced life, where you're totally devoted to work and at the expense of everything else." He spent the next three years working for a private consulting company, occupying a prestigious office on the fiftieth floor of a downtown skyscraper. Around the same time that Shirley Rock accepted her call to the ministry, Ted and a coworker started their own manufacturing consulting company. Again, Ted has been very successful, as the company has grown significantly over the last eight years. During this time, Ted married a woman who is also employed in the business world. They bought a comfortable home, and they are raising two young sons.

The years between 1983 and 1988 were a lot like the first three and a half laps of that high-school race, as Ted ran fast and free and in the lead. But in 1988, his spirit began to give out. He felt the same restlessness that had moved him to leave his two previous jobs. In addition, his wife's parents suddenly became quite sick. For a period of several months, she went home to care for them every Thursday and returned on Monday mornings, leaving behind the two children (one of whom was an infant) with Ted. Up until this time, Ted had not been primarily involved with child care, so he found the new role as full-time parent for half of the week to be extremely taxing. Ted reports this to be an extremely difficult time in his marriage and hints that he and his wife considered a divorce. His wife's parents eventually died. The marriage survived and may have ultimately been strengthened.

During this time, the old issue of balance came to the fore once again. Ted was forced to spend less time at work and more time with his family. Despite the increased level of family tension, Ted found new satisfactions in caring for his sons and in helping his wife cope with the death of her parents. He became more involved in a local Lutheran church and even taught some Sunday-school classes. As his life became more balanced, he became increasingly dissatisfied with his professional work. Today he would like to quit. But he does not know what he would do next.

The whole concept of balance runs counter to another of Ted's deeply held beliefs, that people need to make commitments in life. Ted feels committed to his family, but outside the domestic realm he has made no commitments whatsoever. And this, for Ted, is not right. Ever since high school, Ted reports, he has searched for something to which he can make a wholehearted commitment.

"Before high school, it was like I was just going along; I really didn't have a mission or a purpose in life—maybe I still don't." The problem is partly ideological, for it is impossible to believe wholeheartedly in both balance and commitment at the same time. A thoroughgoing commitment to anything or anybody involves some kind of imbalance. Ted's high-school race may symbolize for him what happens when one is committed wholeheartedly to a particular life endeavor. His commitment to winning the race was total, and it took his life out of balance. And he did not win the race.

Ted has reached a point where he is ambivalent about both of the two central tenets of his personal ideology, that life should be balanced, and that people should make commitments. Ted is still searching for a way to reconcile the conflict between these two central beliefs. His search for an ideological resolution contrasts sharply with the ideological journey we see in Shirley Rock's life. For Shirley, nothing is more alien to her ideology than the notion of balance. Her behavior on the streets, in prison, in church, and in her own family is repeatedly characterized by extremes. Whereas Ted searches for the golden mean, seeking a reasonable way to be a good family man, a good citizen, and a productive worker, Shirley swings wildly from 100 percent rebel to 100 percent criminal to 100 percent pastor and so on. Like Saint Paul, she throws herself completely into everything she does, and she believes strongly in everything she believes. Ted and Shirley differ in other ways, too. Shirley's embrace of mainstream Protestant religion and social ministry symbolizes a coming home to what she has always held dear. For Ted, the search for what is right and good involves leaving behind the parochial viewpoints of his parents and their church, and finding something better, broader, and more balanced. Where Shirley has consolidated a coherent ideological setting for her personal myth, Ted is still searching.

For one thing, Ted is searching for a new and more fulfilling line of work. He has considered many alternatives, including some that might involve getting back in touch with farming and the land. Yet it is now much more difficult to leave the security and the ample earnings of his current job than it was before, when he was unmarried and had no children and no mortgage. Despite his ambivalence about individual achievement and material success, it is quite clear that Ted enjoys his status as a thriving professional with a good income and a nice home.

Ted also appears to have become increasingly concerned in recent years with philosophical and religious questions. Though he and his family attend a Lutheran church, their relationship to the church is very different from the one enjoyed by Ted's parents in Missouri. In some ways, Ted's current church is strikingly different from the church he grew up in. The current church considers itself to be an extremely "progressive" congregation, with an inclusive theology and a strong social ministry. Ted's own theology appears to have departed dramatically from his conservative Lutheran origins. In recent years, he has become increasingly interested in a spiritual movement founded in the early part of the twentieth century by the German philosopher Rudolf Steiner. While the tenets of this movement are not clearly presented in Ted's interview, it would appear that the movement supports many traditional Christian and Jewish beliefs but adds pieces from humanistic psychology and certain Eastern religions. An important feature of the movement is the belief in reincarnation. Ted finds himself drawn strongly to these views. He finds very appealing the new movement's "spiritual dimensions." And he argues that reincarnation is really not very different from the Christian idea of resurrection:

> Steiner believed that there's a science of the spirit, that you could actually perceive and communicate with these spiritual beings, that they're all around us. The indications that he pulled from his research he translated into ways to live your life and ways to nurture the earth and ways to teach children. So that has had a lot of influence on me. . . . All Christians believe in the resurrection—that there's a resurrection, you know, that the spirit lives on. But the question is where does the spirit go? And doesn't it maybe come back, even if it doesn't remember? And how soon does it come back and why does it come back? These are the kind of questions that Rudolf Steiner was interested in. Of course, he wasn't the first. It goes back to the ancient Egyptian and Greek mysteries.

Ted argues that Steiner's eclectic brand of spirituality provides valuable lessons in human growth and development. In that Ted sees the main motif in his own life to be "constant evolution, constant growth," he believes that the spiritual framework provided by Steiner is more in keeping with his own life story than traditional Christianity might be. "I think most religions bring the spiritual down to the human being, but this approach teaches us to take ourselves up to the spiritual level, to become more spiritual ourselves," he says. "I think I see myself going that way."

It is a way that seems to affirm the quest for balance that centers Ted's personal ideology. Ted's new spirituality would appear to be a balanced blend of the traditional Christian frameworks of his youth and the more esoteric approaches he has been drawn to as an adult. For Ted, the new spirituality does not contradict his Christian heritage. It remains to be seen, however, if the new spirituality of which Ted speaks will help him with the wholehearted commitments in life he longs to make. Ted believes that it will. He implicitly ties his recent commitments of time and money to a local community organization to his broadened humanistic perspective. Nonetheless, he admits that he is still searching for the right faith upon which to build his adult identity. Optimistically, but with some caution, he keeps moving on, looking for a better balance of truths to which he can commit his life and his energy.

CHAPTER 8

Putting It Together in Mid-life

The mid-life crisis is an example of a good concept that has been trivialized by popular culture. Since the 1930s, social scientists such as Else Frenkel,[1] Carl Jung,[2] and Elliott Jaques[3] have provided thoughtful accounts of how certain men and women in their middle-adult years experience important shifts in their life perspectives as they evolve toward greater psychological maturity. In the 1970s, Daniel Levinson made the mid-life crisis a central feature of his new theory of adult development, based on interviews of forty men.[4] Popular writers such as Gail Sheehy, author of *Passages,* next urged adults to go out and experience their own mid-life crises, lest they become stagnant and boring.[5] The press jumped on this sexy idea, and used it to explain everything from marital infidelity to intergenerational conflict. By the mid 1980s, Americans were joking about enjoying their mid-life crises, or enduring them, or hoping that their spouses would soon get through them so that life could return to normal.

The popular view of the mid-life crisis is that adults either go crazy or become extremely irresponsible shortly after they hit their fortieth birthdays. Buttoned-down bankers leave their wives for exotic women. Mid-life mothers sink into melancholia as they anticipate their children leaving home, and leaving them with nothing but "the empty nest." Upstanding men and women all of a sudden become afraid—of death, of getting older, of never accomplishing anything in their lives, of accomplishing too much professionally to the detriment of families and friendships, of having extramarital affairs, of never having extramarital affairs, of repeating the mistakes of their parents. Although the mid-life crisis may lead to personal growth, it is the popular view that the growth generally comes at the expense of others. There seems to be something narcissistic about the mid-life crisis, almost as if it were an American middle-class luxury.

As the concept of the mid-life crisis has become popularized, certain behavioral scientists have come to view the idea with greater and greater suspicion. Some suggest that there is nothing especially traumatic about mid-life and that many people move through this period in their lives with ease. A substantial body of research suggests that most American men and women do not become overly depressed and anxious in their mid-life years as a result of their children's leaving home for college or work. The "empty nest syndrome" appears to be relatively rare.[6]

Research psychologists Robert McCrae and Paul Costa, Jr., reasoned that if adults tend to experience a crisis in their early forties, then their scores on questionnaires indicating "emotional upset" should peak at that time in their lives. They administered short personality questionnaires to nearly ten thousand men and women between the ages of thirty-four and fifty-four and found no evidence of a pervasive mid-life crisis. McCrae and Costa argue that people may experience crises at any point in development, not just in mid-life. They believe some people are dispositionally geared to experience lots of crises, whereas others rarely, if ever, go through them. The two psychologists have gathered additional data to suggest that those few individuals who do report crises in their mid-life years tend to score high on the enduring trait of "neuroticism," which means that they have probably experienced crisis at many points in their lives, and will continue to in the future.[7]

Because the mid-life crisis has been popularized by the culture and correspondingly minimized by scientific researchers, we have lost sight of important developments in personality that do often occur in the mid-life years. These changes do not necessarily produce the kind of dramatic "emotional upset" that would show up on a short personality questionnaire. They are changes that are more subtle and probably more private than what we typically imply when we use the term *mid-life crisis*. But they are profound changes nonetheless, and they may signal substantial development in the personal myth. Adults move forward in their forties and fifties to confront conflict and ambivalence in their identities, and reconcile mythical opposites in light of an envisioned ending for their own life stories.

Mid-life

In contemporary American society, mid-life is considered to last from roughly age forty to age sixty. Certain biological changes, such as menopause, play a role in demarcating this period of life. But for the most part, mid-life is socially defined, based on the assumptions that most Americans have about the human life cycle. Mid-life is situated according to what the eminent social scientist Bernice Neugarten has called "the social clock."[8] A set of expectations about age-appropriate transitions, the social clock is the standard against which individuals evaluate the extent to which their lives are "on time." Graduating from college in the early twenties, raising a family in the twenties and thirties, seeing the children leave home in the forties, witnessing parents' deaths in the fifties and sixties, retiring at age sixty-five or seventy—these are a few of the transitions in the life cycle that in contemporary middle-class society are considered "on time." Many Americans expect to live well into their late seventies and eighties. The mid-life chunk of time is seen as comprising that period following early adulthood and preceding the retirement years.

For many, the "on-time" experience of mid-life in the forties involves a curious blend of resurgence and decline. On the one hand, the person in his or her forties may be at the height of power and influence in work, family, or community life. Especially for men on professional career tracks, the forties may be a time of peak earning potential and enhanced visibility and prestige. Historical studies of artists, scientists, and other creative adults show that these individuals typically reach the peak in their creative output between the ages of about thirty-five and forty-five.[9] On the other hand, the person in his or her forties has begun to experience certain undeniable signs of aging. Even among the most athletic adults, body strength and speed are noticeably diminished. For most men, the hair begins to thin. Women go through menopause, typically in their late forties. Children grow up and begin to compete more vigorously for power and influence in the family. The parents of mid-life adults now become elderly as they move into their seventies and beyond.

To believe that one is now at the "midpoint" in life is to believe that at best there is only as much time left in the future as there is time past. This is why adults sometimes "celebrate" their fortieth birthdays with an "over-the-hill party." The realization that one is now at about the halfway point in life may lead to an increased concern with mortality, as death becomes more "personalized."[10] The sense of middle age may also affect relations among generations. Mid-life adults may feel more responsibility to provide care and support for both the generation ahead (their retired parents) and the generation behind (their children).

Daniel Levinson has argued that the adult in his or her forties looks both backward and forward in time, and begins a concerted reassessment of life. Adults undergoing the most intense mid-life reevaluations live through what Levinson considers a state of crisis:

> Every aspect of their lives comes into question, and they are horrified by much that is revealed. They are full of recriminations against themselves and others. They cannot go on as before, but need time to choose a new path or modify an old one. . . . A profound reappraisal of this kind cannot be a cool, intellectual process. It must involve emotional turmoil, despair, the sense of not knowing where to turn or of being stagnant and unable to move at all. . . . Every genuine reappraisal must be agonizing, because it challenges the illusions and vested interests on which the existing life structure is based.[11]

Levinson overdramatizes the experience to emphasize its characteristics as a "crisis." And he overgeneralizes to imply that virtually all of us go through a period of mid-life reassessment. Yet the points he makes are valid when seen in a more tempered and qualified context. For many (though not all) adults, the forties can be a time of reassessment and revision of the life story. The revisions are probably not so dramatic as to be experienced as a crisis by most people, but they nonetheless involve significant changes in self-understanding that have profound implications for mythmaking.

In a fascinating paper entitled "Death and the Mid-life Crisis," Elliott Jaques suggested that mid-life may mark significant changes in the adult's efforts to be creative. Jaques examined biographical information and artistic productions for 310 painters, composers, poets, writers, and sculptors "of undoubted greatness or of genius."[12] Included in his list were Mozart, Michelangelo, Bach, Gauguin, Raphael, and Shakespeare. Jaques found that before mid-life the artists are more likely to produce masterpieces in a rapid and passionate fashion, as "hot-from-the-fire" productions. Their work tends to be highly optimistic and idealistic, laden with themes of pure desire and romance.

After the age of about forty, however, artists of genius appear to work more deliberately, creating refined and considered masterpieces. With the increasing concern over mortality at mid-life, youthful idealism gives way to a more contemplative pessimism and a "recognition and acceptance that inherent goodness is accompanied by hate and destructive forces within."[13] As a result of the artist's own confrontation with the prospects of evil and death, creative products demonstrate a more philosophical and sober cast. Shakespeare produced most of his lyrical comedies before he was thirty-five, whereas the great series of tragedies and Roman plays— *Julius Caesar, Hamlet, Othello, King Lear,* and *Macbeth*—were begun later, in his late thirties and early forties. A similar change is evident in the writings of Charles Dickens, whose novels become much more tragic and realistic with the publication of *David Copperfield* at age thirty-seven.

Roger Gould suggests that the great illusion to be exposed in one's forties is the false belief that "there is no evil in the world."[14] Based on her life-history interviews of Europeans living in the 1920s and 1930s, Else Frenkel concluded that adults tend to become much more philosophical and concerned about the ultimate meanings of life and death after they turn forty.[15] The forties may mark a move from the youthful and passionate perspective we have cultivated from adolescence onward to a more tempered, refined, and philosophical orientation. The passion that has driven us to engage our worlds of work and love with fervor and ambition becomes subject to a more exquisite form of sublimation. We may become more choosy in how we plan to expend our psychic energy. This does not mean that artists, writers, doctors, businesspersons, and homemakers become less passionate as they move through mid-life. But the personal myth often adopts a narrative tone that incorporates more tragic and ironic elements. The shift is subtle. Optimistic adults are not transformed into brooding pessimists when they turn forty. But the on-time experience of being at the halfway point in life, of living through important losses and compromises and anticipating many more to come, gradually changes identity's color. From the bold primaries and light pastels of the first half of adulthood, we move to darker mixtures that suggest ambiguity, ambivalence, complexity, and a new uncertainty about the world.

The sublimation of passion goes hand in hand with a subtle shift in thinking patterns, which some psychologists have theorized is especially characteristic of mid-life. Recall that with the development of formal operational thinking the adolescent is able to reason in an abstract manner. The ideological settings we establish for our life stories in late adolescence and young adulthood often contain abstract assumptions and propositions about what we believe to be good and true. Some cognitive psychologists contend that as we move into mid-life some of us go beyond formal operations to engage in "postformal" modes of thinking.[16] Postformal thought rejects the absolute truths of formal operations and focuses instead on situationally specific truths, on solutions and logical inferences that are linked to, and defined by, particular contexts.

In postformal thinking we realize that no objective statements of eternal truths may be made in many domains of life, such as the domains of interpersonal relationships and the self. We instead must struggle to formulate useful statements and viewpoints that are true for the time being and in a particular place. Our thinking about certain issues becomes more contextualized and more radically subjective. We come to accept "local truths" rather than universal ones; we grow suspicious of general laws about domains of life that now seem to have multiple and even contradictory meanings. Because certain kinds of knowledge are now seen as thoroughly contextualized, we see how each context must be examined if we are to understand the truth. We recognize each context is a uniquely organized system. We must struggle to understand how each part of the system affects, directly or indirectly, every other part.

The sublimation of passion and the contextualization of thought are two manifestations of a general movement in the human life cycle away from the absolute. Neither the passion of youth nor the power of reason is quite enough for mid-life, for they cannot handle the paradox, irony, and contradiction facing the man or woman who is now moving through the middle and anticipating the end. Life requires more nuance now. It requires that a person look at two contradictory propositions about life and pronounce them both to be true; abstract logic does not allow this. To take the most celebrated example, logic says that light cannot be both a particle and a wave, and yet physicists have had to defy logic and yield to paradox in order to model the properties of the universe. Physicists have here rejected demonstrative logic in favor of dialectical thinking, through which truth is found in opposites.[17] In a dialectic, both thesis and antithesis may be true in some fundamental synthetic sense, even though they are in diametric opposition to each other, as "A" is to "not A."

Following the sublimation of passion and the contextualization of thought comes the confrontation of opposites. According to Jaques, the mid-life artist comes to realize and accept that "inherent goodness is accompanied by hate and destructive forces within"—as stark an opposition as one can find. James Fowler describes "conjunctive faith," which is not generally experienced until mid-life, as the acceptance of inherent contradictions or paradoxes in life, even though they cannot be fully understood or logically reconciled.[18] Carl Jung argued that in mid-life, men begin to explore their unconscious feminine selves—their "anima"—while women begin to explore the hidden inner male—their "animus."[19] By confronting the opposite of one's own conscious ego, the mid-life adult moves toward greater wholeness of the self, which Jung termed "individuation." David Gutmann submits that because adults in their forties and early fifties have launched their children into early adulthood, they are now freed up to explore their contrasexual selves. Having weathered what Gutmann calls "the parental emergency," men may now explore the world of femininity. They are free now to engage in more communal and expressive behaviors than they were able to experience in early adulthood. Similarly, mid-life women may now move toward more masculine and agentic behaviors.[20] Levinson, too, speaks of the integration of masculine and feminine energies as one of the central challenges of the mid-life period.[21]

The opposition of masculinity and femininity mirrors the distinctions between work and home, agency and communion, that are central to my theory of personal myths. In his or her twenties and thirties, an adult explores and develops the various characters that personify the different needs for power and love and the often conflicting demands of work and home. The problem of "the many and the one" is resolved by dividing up different aspects of the self into the personified characters of a single personal myth. The resolution, however, is only temporary. In mid-life, we come to identify fundamental conflicts in the myth. As the story develops, tension builds. In our forties, we identify the tension and begin to address it. We may seek to resolve the tension by reconciling opposites. Or we may learn to live with the tension and even turn it into a kind of advantage in our lives, perhaps because it provides us with added perspective or deepened wisdom. Or we may despair over our inability to handle the tension effectively. In any case, we become familiar with the tension, and realize we have created it by virtue of the opposites built into our identities and our lives.

Finally, the forties bring with them the growing realization that good lives, like good stories, require good endings. Even though the adult is only halfway through the life cycle, the belief that there is now less time ahead than behind may push a man or woman to think more seriously and more often about the sense of an ending. Adults seek to create legacies of the self that will initiate new beginnings.

The sublimation of passion, the contextualization of thought, the confrontation of opposites, and the apprehension of a sense of an ending are four cardinal features of mid-life that emerge for many of us in our forties. These developments challenge us to recreate our identities in ways that enhance our sense of unity and purpose in life. The extent to which we successfully address these four identity challenges in our forties influences the facility with which we move through our fifties and early sixties.

Levinson argues that the mid-life transition experienced in our forties is followed in the fifties and early sixties by a more peaceful period of "restabilization." Other theorists speak of a mellowing process in the fifties, as men and women become increasingly comfortable with who they are. In a provocative cross-cultural analysis, David Gutmann contends that young warriors evolve into senior peace chiefs as men sublimate their aggression in their fifties and beyond to assume positions of mature leadership. Women move in somewhat the opposite direction, though still in a maturing way, as they leave the communion of domestic life to assume more agentic roles in the family and in society at large. In addition, Gutmann says, both men and women come to enjoy a playful and diffuse sensuality in their fifties and beyond, a childlike appreciation for what feels, smells, and tastes good in everyday life.[22] As adults who have now "made it" in life, they are able to relax a bit and enjoy some of the fruits of their strivings.

In a study of male mid-life as expressed in modern fiction, Sharan Merriam observes that a number of American novels portray the forties and fifties in highly negative terms for men.[23] Salient themes in the literature include obsession with the loss of youth, search for meaning, and career malaise. Nonetheless, Merriam observes that male protagonists frequently evolve in the direction of "ego rejuvenation" as they move through mid-life. One means by which they become rejuvenated is to establish a mentoring relationship with younger characters:

> Middle-aged men are in a unique position to be mentors. By mid-life most have achieved, through experience, the status and power younger men aspire to. Rarely, if ever, is a young person a mentor, and herein lies the dilemma for middle-aged men: one cannot be both young and have accumulated the years of experience necessary to offer guidance to others. Assuming the role of mentor to a younger man allows for the middle-aged man to operate from a coveted position of authority, while at the same time vicariously reliving young adulthood.[24]

Teaching and mentoring are valuable experiences for both men and women. They enable us to exercise the authority that comes with age in a way that puts us intimately in touch with youth, and even innocence. In addition, teaching and mentoring in adulthood may be manifestations of generativity, and generativity is central to creating a satisfying sense of ending. Teaching and mentoring—like only a handful of other adult endeavors—are ideal vehicles for integrating our competing needs for agency and communion. And with the movement through our middle years in adulthood, we become increasingly concerned about conflict and reconciliation among different narrative characters embodying different mythic aims. Our myths evolve to confront fundamental oppositions and to accommodate the paradoxes of our lives.

Integrative Imagoes: Power and Love

There are complex imagoes available to men and women in early and middle adulthood. These character types personify both agency and communion at the same time. Power and love may be integrated in the imagoes of the teacher, the healer, the counselor, the arbiter, and the humanist. Because they personify opposites, these imagoes are more indicative of developmental issues confronted in mid-life than are purely agentic imagoes, like the warrior, or purely communal imagoes, like the lover.

Since his elementary-school days Richard Krantz, a thirty-eight-year-old attorney, has valued the life of the mind. For years, the sage has been the central imago in his life. For him, the enlightened sage is the man who can think clearly and solve problems in a logical and coolheaded manner. Richard works hard to arrive at precise and reasonable answers to complex questions. To convey his political orientation to me, Richard arrives at a formula: "I am twenty percent Libertarian, forty percent progressive Democrat, and forty percent Socialist." On the topic of religious beliefs, he provides a framework that is cerebral, intellectualized, and impersonal:

> I think that if there is a God, that God probably was created by man, and is not a supreme being, apart from its existence by man. If men cease to be—or humans cease to be part of this world—then God would probably die along with them. God is the internal belief we all have in our selves, or many of us have in our selves, that represents the force for good. God is the good motivating force in our lives—if there is such a thing, and I'm not even sure there is such a thing, but if there is such a force in our lives, that's what I would call God.

Richard was the only child in a family that prized education. "I spent a lot of my childhood alone, and my companions were books more than they were other kids." Books have catalyzed the growth of a keen and precise intellect, a mind that values clarity and organization over everything else. In all things, Richard seeks to be organized and clear. A high point in his life story is his wedding, which he and his wife-to-be organized all by themselves:

My wife and I entirely planned our own wedding. From A to Z we did it all completely. We moved into a new apartment and invited sixty people over for six weeks later and we had the wedding in our apartment. We arranged for somebody to marry us; we arranged for the catering; we arranged for the chairs; we arranged for everything. We chose the ceremony; we did everything. It went without a hitch. It took ten minutes and it was over with. We had a party afterwards, and I loved it because I wasn't really nervous. I knew I wanted to marry this person. I thought everything had been really well planned out, and here was the high moment of our lives at that point in time, and we were in control, our show, nobody was telling us what to do. . . . It was this wonderful experience of getting married and being married with no glitches. . . .

In Richard's life story, the clear and well-organized mind is the most powerful tool available to a human being. It is what makes the sage a powerful force in society. But things don't always get resolved without a glitch, even for the sage. Among the many different goals Richard has for his life, one of the strongest is "to make the world a better place for somebody or some people." This goal is a prime motivator in his work as a class-action attorney. He represents clients who feel they have been cheated or abused by industry or government. It is also a prime motivator for his volunteer work in a local food pantry. "You have to make an effort, big or small, to leave the world a better place than you found it." The problems he faces because of these efforts, however, are not always resolved by rational thought, and this causes Richard considerable grief. Richard's need to make a positive social contribution and his need to perfect a rational mind do not go well together. The first need pushes him to become more involved in community work, but the second pushes him toward cynicism—intellectually he believes that the work will not do much good. The rational sage is repeatedly frustrated by intractable and irrational human problems. As he approaches mid-life, Richard sees the conflict in distressingly stark terms:

> I admire Clarence Darrow [a civil rights attorney who defended John Scopes in the famous 1925 trial concerning the teaching of evolution in schools]. He was incredibly cynical about things. He was asked how somebody who was as big a cynic as he was could do what he did. He would still take on these cases involving supposedly hopeless people fighting against the system to keep from being in prison. Why did he do this when he was so cynical about human nature and he believed people were not necessarily born good and were not necessarily motivated by good? And he said, "It's because my intellect hasn't caught up with my emotions yet." I've found that I'm a lot like Darrow in that regard, because I'm incredibly cynical—I'm not at all positive that the world is going to be a better place when I die than it was when I was born into it. . . . I'm not sure that we won't find ourselves at the brink of annihilation through our own stupidity, and I'm very concerned about that, and very cynical. . . . I'm not that far from being so cynical that I'm going to say the hell with it all.

It is hardly surprising that a rational man who wants precise solutions to complex human problems would find it difficult to sustain a commitment to helping others when the situation seems so objectively hopeless. It's not like planning a wedding, Richard admits. If the sage comes to dominate the story, then Richard may just say the hell with it all and retreat to the world of books he knew as a kid. But this seems very unlikely, for there are too many forces pushing Richard to develop a new character in his life story that may successfully integrate his agentic mind and his communal heart. Richard invokes Martin Luther King, Jr., as a great hero, a man whose life proves that "standing up for what you believe in can make a difference." An even more significant force may be his own mother. He describes her as the most important person in his life. "She taught me about my heritage, and she taught me my values," he says. "My mother was the social activist in the family, as well as the organized person in the family, and I think I've inherited some of that from her, and I think that's probably something I'm passing down to my son, as well, so it's continuing the lineage."

Richard's mother personifies what we might call the organized activist. This would appear to represent a potentially integrative imago for Richard himself as he refines his life story to address the difficult demands of mid-life. But if Richard is to create this kind of character for his life story, he will need to surpass Clarence Darrow in at least one sense—by pushing his intellect to catch up with his emotions. Perhaps he will need to move away from the absolute truths cherished by the sage and develop a more refined and realistic form of problem solving. In Richard's plans for his mid-life years, we catch a glimpse of a movement in this direction:

> In the rest of my life I want to be able to fulfill the goals of being a good family member, husband and father, and trying to make a positive impact on society. I think I'm trying to do that through my volunteer work at the food pantry and through some of the work I do on the job. . . . My plans for the future enable me to be creative because they call upon me to exercise abilities and skills I have that I really may not have been using as much as I could. I think I show a lot of creativity in my family life and in terms of being a member of society involved in social and political work. The kinds of creativity that I'm going to need to apply are intellectual and social—motivating people to help feed the hungry or help deal with other social skills, social issues that call for skills. There are lots of ideas out there waiting to be found that haven't even been thought of, whether it's tactics in community organizing or methods of child rearing. And I've got some modesty, but I'll tell you what I think: I'm reasonably smart, and I've got a lot of ability to put that smarts to work. And sometimes I look at problems and I say, gee, you know, why don't they do this? If they did this, they could solve the Chicago school crisis, or they could throw this bum out of office, or something like that. That's what I could do.

The organized activist of which Richard speaks is a variation of the humanist. In ancient Greek mythology, Prometheus personifies certain characteristics of the humanist. As punishment for teaching mortals how to use fire, Prometheus was bound to a cliff for thirty years. Each day a winged monster pecked away at his liver, but every night the liver grew back. Prometheus may be seen as a great but suffering benefactor and advocate for humanity. The father of the arts and sciences, Prometheus inspires the cultivation of human-kind's noblest achievements. Also a defiant rebel, Prometheus champions the underdog and the enemy of oppressive authority. He tends to be idealistic, helpful, generous, inventive, persevering, outspoken, and somewhat rebellious.[25] His actions and characteristics are reflected in Richard's work as a class-action attorney, and in the attributes of Richard's heroes, his mother and Martin Luther King, Jr. Both were activists aiming to preserve the best of humankind's heritage while working tirelessly for positive social change.

Imagoes that blend agency and communion tend to shade into one another, so clear distinctions among different types cannot be readily made. The humanist works for social change while preserving good traditions from the past; the teacher passes on knowledge and skills to those who are younger or less experienced; the counselor provides personal guidance, advice, or therapy to help resolve emotional and interpersonal problems in human lives; the healer cures disease and seeks to assure health and organic well-being; the arbiter makes crucial decisions about right and wrong. Ideally, healers, teachers, counselors, arbiters, and humanists exercise substantial personal power for the betterment of other people. Highly agentic and highly communal, these characters are blends of oppositions, dialectically crafted like Richard's organized activist.

The teacher is the central imago in the personal myth formulated by Gail Washburn, an elementary-school teacher in her mid fifties. Recently, Gail won a major award for excellence in teaching. Visitors to her classroom marvel at the ingenious ways through which she engages her children in a wide variety of learning tasks and subjects. Gail says:

> A teacher must convince her students that nothing is impossible in life. I have learned that all things are possible; students must also learn to believe that. I think that if a teacher can do that you've already given headlights to the dark road ahead. . . . I love teaching. There's always a new challenge. There's always a new way to do something. I tend not to repeat; I might take certain aspects and use them again, but I try to do it in a different way each time. I have classes that have personalities just like individual students do, and you know, what you do for one you're not going to do for the other. Or maybe one's going to respond and the other is not, and that's when I learn something different that I haven't used as an approach before. I do things in an interdisciplinary fashion, so that enters into my unique style too. I've broadened my scope in teaching over the years, and I'm still learning.

Gail suggests that a key to good teaching is finding what works for each unique group and individual. Again, we are confronted with that kind of contextualized approach to knowledge rarely encountered before the mid-life years. There may be few universal truths about being a good teacher, but there are many local truths. In Gail's personal myth, a good teacher is a good learner, too. Gail takes pride in her belief that as an exceedingly self-reliant child she taught herself many of her most valuable lessons. She continues to teach herself new techniques for reaching her students. She looks forward to learning new methods of influencing people in positive ways after her retirement from teaching, during which time she hopes to do some volunteer work and perhaps even serve in the Peace Corps. It is clear that for Gail being a teacher means more than what one does in the classroom. For her, the teacher is a personified and idealized image of self that functions as a main character throughout most of her life story, in both work and family life. In commenting on some of her creative hobbies, Gail says:

> Well I think there's no value in doing a lot of these creative things unless you can share them, and in sharing, you're giving. I like to do origami [Japanese paper-folding] art and when I'm showing children I try not to use a lot of words. I show them and simply say that it has to be exact. I tell them, "You've got to do this well." "Why do I keep saying this?" I ask them. "Does anyone know?" Maybe I get a few answers, but then I'll always conclude with, "You see, I'm teaching you it this way because you are going to teach somebody else. And if I don't teach you well, then you won't have the lesson to pass on." And, that's what it's all about.

There is a second imago in Gail's life story whose origins go back even farther than her childhood lessons in self-reliance. It is one I call the survivor. Concerned with neither agency nor communion, the survivor is a primitive character personifying Gail's struggles with childhood health threats, and later with her efforts to teach white children before the civil rights movement. The survivor is a character from the early chapters in Gail's story. But it is still an integral part of her personal myth, an undeniable part of who she still is today. The survivor is born in Gail's earliest memory:

> I was three years old. I picked up part of a sewing machine that was plugged into the wall outlet. I picked it up thinking it was a whistle

and put it into my mouth. My mother was visiting with my aunt, and they were baking pies in the kitchen. Well, my sister walked around with a little hum most of the time, and they heard this hum, but it wasn't my sister's hum. It didn't dawn on them for a while that this was a monotone kind of thing. They found me on the floor, so how long I'd been there I don't know. And doctors were amazed that I survived it.

The current burned a hole in her tongue the size of a quarter and severely disfigured her mouth. "I know that I had a bottom lip that reached to the end of my chin, and I know that I still have a big bump on my tongue that bothers me from time to time when there is severe cold weather." She was in the hospital for more than three months. A few years later, she underwent serious surgery to remove sections from her bronchial tubes. "I had to be observed very closely until I was an adult because the bruise on the lung could cause tuberculosis." In a third childhood mishap, she was run over by a car, resulting in a fractured skull.

The three traumatic events from childhood are Gail's mythic proof that she is a survivor. She is able to persevere in the face of life-threatening obstacles. Each confrontation left its scar. The imagery of scarring and disfigurement appears again in Gail's account of her life. Gail was the only black student enrolled in a small midwestern college in the early 1950s. She arrived for freshman orientation by rail. As she stepped off the train on the first day, she found herself facing the American Legion, which had organized an angry mob of white protesters.

> You get off the train, and there they are. The kind of feeling wasn't one that brought tears to my eyes. It was being tense and scared. But the tears came later. It was like, well, I would describe it by saying that in a fearful situation adrenaline takes over. You may not tremble. It's the trembling that comes after the fact, when you realize what kind of situation it was, how vulnerable you were. And so, the stab causes a wound. But the wound is, well, it festers a bit before it truly heals, if it ever heals. I mean the scar is there; it cannot be eradicated. That is a terrible thing.

In Gail's personal myth, the survivor is defined through injury and discrimination. It is a main character whose legacy is scarring and pain. As a victim of accident and cruelty, the survivor cannot find space in life for power and love. It is enough simply to make it from one day to the next. Gail's is a story about teaching and surviving, about surviving in order to teach. The two imagoes seem to work well together; they are main characters in an impressive story of personal triumph and mature generativity.

In general, the survivor appears to be a type of imago whose ultimate narrative purpose is to make it possible for other characters to perform. In some life stories, however, the survivor may be the only main character. In situations of repeated abuse, unmitigated poverty, chronic illness, severe mental illness, and other overwhelming impediments to the expression of human power and love, the survivor may sometimes be the only viable candidate for the personification of the self. In these instances, tremendous human potential is either squandered or squelched, in some cases because of a cruel or harsh environment, in others because of factors that reside within the individual person.

One Woman's Story: The Evolution of Karen Horney

Karen Horney (1885–1952) was a pioneer in the psychoanalytic movement who became internationally famous for her eloquent and revolutionary writings about neurosis and the human mind.[26] An early disciple of Freud, Horney broke away from the psychoanalytic establishment in her mid-life years and articulated a new theory of human behavior that emphasized social relationships and interpersonal conflicts in human lives. She was a therapist and training analyst, and she taught classes for clinicians on theory and technique. A mother of three daughters, Horney was especially sensitive to how the life experiences of women differ radically from those of men. She was an engaging writer who made difficult psychological concepts come alive for the professionals and nonprofessionals alike who read her books. Because her ideas did not fit well into the patriarchal orthodoxy of American psychoanalysis in the early 1940s, Horney was expelled from the New York Psychoanalytic Society. She soon established a rival group of her own. In the two years before her death, she became interested in Zen Buddhism and hoped to incorporate ideas from Eastern philosophies into her evolving theory of the human personality.

She was born Karen Danielson, the second child and only daughter of a ship captain and his wife, who lived just outside Hamburg, Germany. From an early age, Karen was prized as an intelligent and energetic girl who surpassed her older brother in schoolwork. Growing up in Hamburg, Karen witnessed a good deal of social ferment in the 1890s, including a strong movement in support of women's rights. She may have found support for some of the highly unconventional goals she formulated for herself as an adolescent in this nascent women's movement. She sketched out elaborate plans for studying at the *Gymnasium* and ultimately becoming a doctor.

Karen was a passionate and fiercely independent teenager. Rejecting the strict Christianity of her parents, she favored "the riotous sensuous exuberance" of the Greeks in their Dionysian festivals.[27] "Passion," she declared, "is always convincing."[28] Karen's views about sexuality and women's place in the world were much closer to those of our current age than to the Victorian era in which she grew up. Women should be able to achieve all of the professional goals that men achieve, she believed. Women should engage their worlds in an openly sensual manner, unashamed of their sexuality. Karen's idealistic and romantic engagement of her world is evident in this passionate section written for her diary at age seventeen. As you read it, pay close attention to the recurrent and powerful imagery of movement and light:

Everything in me is storming and surging and pressing for light that will resolve the confusion. I seem to myself like a skipper who leaps from his safe ship into the sea, who clings to a timber and lets himself be driven by the sea's tumult, now here, now there. He doesn't know where he is going.

Homeless am I
With no sheltering abode I rove about.
Safe and quiet
I lived in the old masonry
stronghold that thousand of years
had built for me.
It was gloomy and close—
I longed for freedom.
A little light only, a little life.
Quietly, driven by an inner urge,

I began to dig.
Bloody my nails, weary my hands.
Mockery from others and bitter scorn
the end reward for the endless toiling.
The stone came loose—
one more powerful grip and
it fell at my feet.
A ray of light pressed through the opening
greeting me kindly,
inviting and warming,
waked a shiver of delight in my breast.
But hardly had I drawn into myself
this first shimmer
when the rotting masonry broke to pieces
and buried me in its fall.
Long I lay
thinking nothing
feeling nothing.
Then my strength stirred, so freshly drunk-in
and I lifted the fragments with muscular arm.
All aglow with strength,
bloom of the storm,
delight flowing through me
I looked out far and wide.
I saw the world,
I breathed life.
The brightness of light
almost blinded me—
yet soon I was used to its brilliance.
I looked about.
The view was almost too wide,
my sight could roam to unlimited distances.
Oppressive almost
the New, the Beautiful invaded me.
At that an all-powerful longing seized me,
almost bursting my breast,
and it drove me forth to wander
in order to see, to enjoy
and to know the All.
And I wandered—
restlessly driven
I rove about,
released from the dungeon
I joyfully sing in jubilant tones

the old song of life,
to freedom, to light.
Only an anxious question often hems me in:
toward what goal am I striving?
A gentle longing, a mild lament:
When at last will you come to rest?
And I think I understand the answer
in the murmuring of the woods:
"Rest is only behind the prison walls,
life, however, does not know it."
Watchful searching
with no cowardly complaints,
restlessly striving
with no weary despair:
that is life—
dare to endure it.[29]

The personal myth that Karen began formulating in late adolescence draws liberally upon the imagery of movement and light. Karen's adolescent diaries, and the letters she wrote in her early twenties to her future husband, Oskar Hornvieh, are filled with this kind of imagery. In love for all of two days with Ernst Schorschi—a young man with "sunny sparkle" in his eyes—she finds herself "chasing after happiness in every form."[30] Months later, as she comes to reflect on Ernst's rejection of her, she writes that her "blood flowed sluggishly after the great loss, but it is already beginning to pulse more rapidly."[31] The Swedish writer Ellen Key—an early heroine for young Karen—"lit the sacred flame of enthusiasm for me." She was "the lustrous star toward which my soul directed its way," the one name that above all "shines brightly" above me.[32] With a new lover later in medical school, "we naturally romped around like two dogs."[33] In contrast, her husband-to-be seems to move more slowly and clumsily, as if movement does not come naturally to him; he is more inclined "to splash through life in heavy rubber boots."[34]

A biographer reports that in later life Karen Horney claimed that she traveled to South America as a nine-year-old girl on one of her father's steamships.[35] The biographer doubts the validity of the story. Still, even in the fantasy Horney employs the imagery of movement, travel, and adventure. The same biographer reports that Karen's best-loved resource for her frequent flights of childhood fantasy were the stories of Karl Friedrich May. Karen's hero in these was the fictional American Indian named Winnetou. Winnetou is "a noble savage, capable of swimming faster, creeping through woods more softly, and covering his tracks more deftly than any other mortal."[36]

For Horney, rapid movement signifies youth, vigor, passion, taking the challenge of life on with no doubts and no fears. When things go badly, one feels sluggish, and movement seems as unnatural as if one were wearing Oskar's heavy boots. Pregnant with her first daughter in 1911, Karen repeatedly complains of feeling languid and unable to move. "I do so desperately want to be active," she writes in a letter to her analyst.[37] One must always keep moving if one is to find happiness and fulfillment. And if one must indeed rest on occasion, then it is best to rest in the sunlight. After two days of hiking through the deep snow, Karen and friends take a break:

> At noon we lay in the sun and ate our provisions. Yesterday our resting place was a little pine wood, snow all around on a slope—in it a little round clearing in full sun, moss-covered with a few great stones; and my only wish was to lie there for my whole life, staying in the sun.[38]

For Horney, light seems to symbolize truth, understanding, and clarity. This is a familiar linkage for all of us, as we often speak of something being "illuminating" or "enlightening." But more than most of us, Horney invested images of light and movement with particularly strong emotions. She employed such images often to convey her ideas and feelings. The themes, plot, and characters of her story reflect this basic fact of her personal imagery.

The thematic lines of Karen Horney's evolving personal myth begin to show themselves clearly in her early adult years. After completing her studies at the *Gymnasium,* she enrolled as a medical student at the University of Freiburg. She was one of only a handful of women in medical studies at the time. In 1909, she married Oskar, and they moved to Berlin. There he began a successful business, and she continued her studies in psychiatry. Freud was beginning to enjoy a wide audience in Europe and America, and Karen became enamored of his psychoanalytic theory. She found Freud's ideas about neuroses, the unconscious, and childhood sexuality to be the most exciting concepts she had ever encountered. They became

integral parts of her therapeutic orientation and of her overall ideological setting. For a time, she was in therapy with the famous
psychoanalyst Karl Abraham. In 1915, she completed her psychiatric
training. She began to psychoanalyze patients, and to write papers
concerning their courses of treatment.

At the same time, Karen and Oskar were struggling to raise a
family. In 1911, her first daughter, Brigitte, was born. Two more
daughters, Marianne and Renate, followed shortly thereafter, during
the frightening years of World War I. After the war, Oskar's business
began to fail, and the marriage did as well. Apparently, both Karen
and Oskar had numerous sexual affairs during this period; the marriage finally ended in 1926. At about this time, Horney began also to
separate herself from the mainstream of the psychoanalytic movement. Between 1922 and 1935, she wrote a series of fourteen papers
on the psychology of women, culminating in a total rejection of
Freud's ideas on femininity and the female Oedipus complex. In
1932, she moved to the United States, and by 1940 she had established herself as a powerful and independent voice in the world of
psychoanalysis.

As a young woman, Karen already shows herself to be strongly
motivated by both agentic and communal needs. She wants power
and love, and she wants them fast. In Karen's personal myth, there
are two very different kinds of movements she can make, and each
is tied to a corresponding motivational theme. The first is the agentic
and self-expansive move toward independent control. If she was to
become the accomplished doctor promised by her brilliant student
years, she might be able to express the controlling power of her
rational mind. In order to do so, however, she would need to free
herself from feminine sensuality. At age 20, she writes:

> To be free of sensuality means great power in a woman. Only in this
> way will she be independent of a man. Otherwise she will always
> long for him, and in the exaggerated yearning of her senses she will
> be able to drown out all feeling of her own value. She becomes the
> bitch, who begs even if she is beaten—a strumpet.[39]

As a young woman, Karen feared that her impulses would get out
of control—that love would destroy her freedom. To enhance control, she watched herself carefully. She cultivated what she called "an

unremitting, ever more refined self-observation that never leaves me, even in any sort of intoxication."[40] Yet she also longed desperately to escape from this controlling state, to free herself to the "brutal naturalism" of impulse. According to her myth, a woman is inexorably drawn to sensuality. She cannot help but surrender, Horney believes, time and time again.

Surrender is the second kind of movement in Horney's self-defining myth. It is indicative of a communal need to merge with others in self-effacing and passionate bonds. Writes her biographer, Horney "wanted to experience abandon, to be tossed about in the stormy seas of passion, under the sure lead of a man who would be skillful enough to awaken her."[41] Surrender is Horney's characteristic mode of eroticism and intimacy. It is the way Horney chose to connect with others on what she called "a more elemental level." In her psychoanalysis, Abraham called this Horney's "inclination to passivity," and he identified it as the governing force in her love life. She surrendered again and again in a remarkable series of sexual and emotional involvements. Surrender also seems to be the dominant mode of her love affair with psychoanalysis, which she accepted totally uncritically at first. For Horney, surrender meant moving quickly, lest the "ever-refined" function of "self-observation" catch up, and reason recover the reins. Horney believed that she could not live without her impulsive surrenders. As with her agentic desire for control, she had to be quick with them.

Lurking beyond agentic control and communal surrender is a third thematic possibility in the life story of Karen Horney. It is resignation. During the most difficult periods in her life—when she felt trapped at home with the birth of her first daughter, when she felt abandoned and cut off with her emigration to the United States, when she was rejected by the New York Psychoanalytic Society— Horney sank into deep depression, became listless, and succumbed to what she called in her theoretical writings "basic anxiety." These were periods in which control and surrender no longer provided thematic coherence for her life. Thankfully, these periods were relatively infrequent and short-lived. For most of her life, Horney remained on the move.

In 1945, Horney outlined in her book *Our Inner Conflicts* three solutions to neurotic struggles. She called them "moving against," "moving toward," and "moving away from" others. The three would appear to correspond to her mythic themes of control, surrender, and resignation, respectively. The three motivational themes in her own identity appear to have been transformed into more general categories for explaining the behavior and experience of others. Her theory is an outgrowth of her myth.

Karen was extremely proud of all three of her daughters. Brigitte grew up to be a glamorous movie actress in Germany during the years of the Third Reich. Marianne became a psychiatrist. Renate raised a family. In her later years, Horney told a friend that she had wanted as a child to be either an actress, a doctor, or a mother—"you see I'm already living on through my children."[42] But Karen Horney managed to live out each of these roles personally, too, through the imagoes she formulated. During her twenties and thirties, Karen Horney struggled to realize her needs for control and surrender in the realms of work and family. By the time she reached mid-life, she had formulated three imagoes—the actress, the doctor (or healer), and the mother (or caregiver).

The actress was the least well developed, and her roots were in Karen's childhood dreams to be a star on the stage. The actress was a personification of Karen's restless and flamboyant nature, a child-like incarnation of spontaneous movement and fast escape from reality and reason. An actress can surrender to the momentary role. No long-term commitments are necessary. She acts with great passion, for passion is always convincing. But next month, she can play a different role, with a new leading man. In her last writings, Horney spoke of a neurotic tendency to split off parts of experience from the real self.[43] The actress seems to have been split off from Horney's self. Manifest mostly in a lifelong impulsivity in romantic relationships, the actress played a minor role in the drama Karen Horney made of her life.

By the time Karen Horney was in her thirties, the imagoes of the doctor and the mother were well integrated into her personal myth. In adolescence, she had planned to be a doctor, and as a young adult she accomplished those plans. A professional psychiatrist, she treated many of her clients in her own home, as her well-paid nannies helped her care for the children. Horney effectively healed broken lives and psychic wounds. She juggled the roles of doctor and mother about as well as a woman could do in the 1920s. Her role as mother extended beyond the home. Karen Horney "was like a mother to me," remarked a young companion who accompanied her to Japan.[44] "She was one hundred percent maternal type," remarked Dr. Leon Saul, who enjoyed some kind of affectionate relationship with Horney during her first few years in the United States.[45] Before she broke with Freud, Horney was a mother figure in psychoanalysis in the 1920s and 1930s. One of the few women of prominence in the movement, she nurtured and promoted the development of many young analysts in Chicago and New York.

The most profound and intriguing way in which her personal myth influenced her work concerns the imago of the mother. By becoming one herself, Horney helped to move the mother to the center of psychoanalytic thinking. In thematic terms, by surrendering to the social demand to become a mother, she was ultimately able to determine changes in her profession. For Horney, the communal imago of the caregiver proved to be extraordinarily agentic as well! According to Freud, childbirth was a woman's symbolic substitute and partial compensation for the lack of a penis. Horney's first creative breaks from the psychoanalytic establishment involved her thorough critique of Freud's view of motherhood. Her biographer writes:

> There is a wonderful irony here. Like most women pioneering in a male world, Karen Horney had devoted a great deal of energy trying to be one of the boys. And she had felt trapped, in the beginning, by the undeniably feminine position in which pregnancy placed her. And yet, as a result of the experience of birth, she felt compelled, for the first time in her professional life, to take an independent position. It was because the experience differed so strikingly from analytic theories that she was forced to propose an alternative theory. Birth was too remarkable to be only a substitute or a sublimation. In the end, because she was a truth seeker, she couldn't deny her femininity. And it was her femininity that led her to her first original, and important, conclusion.[46]

Horney's conclusions appeared in her essay "The Flight from Motherhood." Written at the age of forty-one, the essay marked Horney's move into mid-life and heralded her emergence as a creative psychoanalytic theorist. At this time, she moved beyond the conventional universals of Freudian orthodoxy to a more nuanced theory of human behavior, illustrating a movement toward the contextualized kind of thinking often associated with mid-life.

The essay also symbolized an evolution in Horney's personal myth. In her mid-life years, the opposing imagoes of the doctor and the mother merged to form a larger and more generative character that I would call the visionary teacher. This most integrative and influential imago is an adult incarnation of a prescient statement that Karen made in one her earliest diary entries. "School is the only true thing, after all," she wrote on January 3, 1901, at the age of fifteen.[47] Writes her biographer, "Horney's most important contribution to the history of psychoanalysis grew out of her teaching role."[48] Her down-to-earth and empathic style of presentation made her students feel that she was speaking and listening especially to them. People came away from lectures given by leading male analysts feeling that they had encountered a brilliant mind or a dazzling argument. But as Horney's biographer puts it, "They came away from Horney's lectures feeling they had encountered themselves."[49]

In mid-life, Karen Horney appears to have refined her identity to capture in myth the ever-widening influence she had on the world around her. As the opposing imagoes of the doctor and the mother came together in mid-life to form the teacher, Horney shifted her energies away from direct caregiving and healing to the formulation of new ideas that she could pass down to her students and the readers of her many influential books. Through teaching, she created a legacy of scholarship and practice that survives vigorously today. Movement and light remained her strongest images, as she moved deftly and creatively in her mid-life years to enlighten others with the insights she had gained. Control, surrender, and resignation remained the central themes in her personal myth. As she moved through mid-life, she reworked these images and themes after the emergence of new characters, who were amalgamations of the old. Some conflicts were resolved, but others remained problematic. While the story evolved smoothly to accommodate the visionary teacher, the actress remained split off from the plot.

In mid-life we endeavor to put the many pieces of our life story together into a more integrative and generative whole. As we reach what we perceive to be the halfway point in our lives, our thinking may become more subtle and nuanced, and we may begin to confront fundamental oppositions in the identities we have been creating since our adolescent years. These developments are apparent in the life of Karen Horney. The emergence of the visionary teacher in her personal myth marks a significant step toward wholeness, integration, and generativity. The teacher seeks to leave a legacy of the self for the next generation—Horney's new mid-life character signals her growing apprehension of a sense of ending, and of the new beginnings an ending may generate for her children, students, and readers.

CHAPTER 9

Generating
New Beginnings

Living organisms are time-bounded entities. Their lives have beginnings, middles, and ends. But DNA, the most narcissistic of molecules, the molecule that carries life's intricate code, is able to create itself over and over again. Because living organisms replicate themselves, their endings are not as discrete as we might initially conclude. New forms are generated from the old; progeny carry into the future the cultural and genetic legacies of the previous generation. Endings are qualified, mitigated, blurred, by the beginnings that are left behind.

Self-replication drives the evolution of the natural world. The *raison d'être* of what the biologist Richard Dawkins calls "the selfish gene" is to carry on, to propagate to the greatest extent possible, from generation to generation.[1] Genes carry on through individual organisms. Therefore, those organisms who are most genetically fit, from the standpoint of natural selection, are those whose genes directly or indirectly cause the prolific reproduction of themselves. In the harsh and random world of natural selection, the fittest species are simply those best able to reach maturity and replicate.

As human beings, our own desires to replicate are given their most obvious expression in the bearing of children. Flesh of our flesh, carriers of our genes, our biological children are the offspring whose beginnings we set in motion and whose lives will carry on, we dearly hope, long past our own end on earth. They are flesh-and-blood proof that we can leave something behind, that our own deaths are, in some sense, not final. The "something" we leave behind is created in our own image. In the Book of Genesis, God creates man and woman in his own image; they are the mortal beings who are most like him. Adam and Eve are separated from the rest of creation by their unique position. They have a special status in the story, like our own children have in ours.

Why do we have children? Just as theologians through the centuries have offered many theories to explain why God created the world, so might we identify many plausible explanations as to why men and women create children. But one biological and psychological underpinning of parenthood appears to be the need to carry on, to produce something that will outlive the self. The same need challenges us to fashion personal myths that defy the most basic convention of stories—that an ending is really the end. We seek endings that furnish new beginnings through which the self may live on. In our endings, we seek to defy the end, like the genes that replicate themselves from one generation to the next. As hopelessly narcissistic as it may seem, we are all looking, in one way or another, for immortality.

On Immortality

The hero of one of Jonathan Swift's poems, "Cassinus and Peter," describes an absurd paradox of human life.[2] Swift's hero is tormented by the realization that his beautiful and idealized lover, Caelia, must, like all other animals on earth, occasionally relieve herself. It's enough to drive him to the brink of madness:

> Nor wonder that I lost my wits;
> Oh! Caelia, Caelia, Caelia shits!

Swift's hero is troubled by more than a neurotic peccadillo, argues Ernest Becker, the Pulitzer Prize–winning author of *The Denial of Death,* published shortly before his death.[3] Becker asserts that Swift's hero has articulated the essential paradox of human existence. The fact that his lover, Caelia, must obey an urge common to all creatures demonstrates that a human being is at once a transcendent god and a defecating animal. In their imaginations, humans can go anywhere in the natural world, and even soar above it. "This immense expansion, this dexterity, this ethereality, this self-consciousness gives to man literally the status of a small god in nature, as the Renaissance thinkers knew." Yet at the same time,

> as the Eastern sages also knew, man is a worm, and food for worms. This is the paradox: he is out of nature and hopelessly in it; he is dual, up in the stars and yet housed in a heart-pumping, breath-gasping body that once belonged to a fish and still carries the gill marks to prove it. His body is a material fleshy casing that is alien to him in many ways—the strangest and most repugnant way being that it aches and bleeds and will decay and die. Man is literally split in two: he has an awareness of his own splendid uniqueness in that he sticks out of nature with a towering majesty, and yet he goes back into the ground a few feet in order blindly and dumbly to disappear forever. It is a terrifying dilemma to be in and to have to live with.[4]

In the unconscious, writes Becker, the human mind is associated with the immortality of the spirit, with soaring above nature, and with escaping clean away from the earth. The body is what connects us to the mortality of the flesh. The mind is reason, and the body, emotion. The mind is abstract, and the body, concrete. The mind is represented by the Sky God; the Earth Mother represents the body.[5] These associations are evident in myths and dreams.

The human being is the only animal who anticipates and dreads its own mortality. The fear of death is the fundamental motive in human life, Becker argues. Although we are transcendent beings who can soar above our bodily casing, we all know that we are not long for this world, that worms will eventually enjoy our flesh. Our fundamental response to this paradox is to engage in "activity designed largely to avoid the fatality of death, to overcome it by denying in some way that it is the final destiny for man."[6]

Our denial is accomplished through what Becker calls heroism. Heroism is "first and foremost a reflex of the terror of death."[7] In order to deny the inevitable death of the body, the human mind invents ways to be heroic and thereby attain a kind of immortality. From this perspective, human societies have always existed as symbolic systems designed to cultivate and condone human heroism. Individual adults "serve" society in order to earn a "feeling of primary value, of cosmic specialness, of ultimate usefulness to creation, of unshakable meaning."[8] To be a hero is to do something that matters in the larger scheme of things—to do something that lasts and lives on after the body is gone:

> They [human beings] earn this feeling by carving out a place in nature, by building an edifice that reflects human value: a temple, a cathedral, a totem pole, a sky-scraper, a family that spans three generations. The hope and the belief is that the things that man creates in society are of lasting worth and meaning, that they outlive or outshine death and decay, that man and his products count.[9]

The psychiatrist Robert Jay Lifton adds further detail to Becker's ideas by identifying five different strategies that human beings typically employ in their quest for immortality.[10] The first is biological—producing children and continuing a family line. The second is a cultural strategy: We achieve a certain cultural immortality through works of art, science, technology, and through the humbler influences that we all have on those around us, as we pass on knowledge or skills. The third strategy is religious. Beliefs about an afterlife figure here, as do religious traditions that move men and women to a sense of union or communion with an immortal deity. The fourth strategy occurs among cultures and individuals who venerate the natural order for its perceived limitlessness in space and time. The fifth is located in personal mystic or ecstatic revelations, through which an individual experiences a sense of eternity or ultimate value. Episodes of this fifth strategy may overlap with any of the other four categories, as when a woman or man feels intense joy, even a kind of divine bliss, at the birth of a child, or the production of a cultural legacy, or during a religious or natural epiphany.

By all five strategies, human beings take part in an enterprise that is perceived to be exalted and enduring. In the biological and cultural strategies, furthermore, the individual takes an active role in generating someone or something that will potentially outlive the self. But there is more to heroism than that. "If you are going to be a hero then you must give a gift," Becker writes.[11] Becker is not glib about gift giving. We never know how our gifts will turn out. We never know how they will be accepted by the world. Working on his own cultural gift during the last years of his own life, Becker said that it is with great terror and confusion that people generate and then offer their legacies of the self:

> Who knows what form the forward momentum of life will take in the time ahead or what use it will make of our anguished searching? The most that any of us can seem to do is to fashion something—an object, or ourselves—and drop it into the confusion, making an offering of it, so to speak, to the life force.[12]

How will it all end up? What will become of the beginnings we offer? There are no objective answers to these questions. We are storytellers who are never certain how our stories will turn out. As self-conscious adults who long to transcend the limitations of our natural lot, the best we can really do is carry on, with the hope that the gifts we offer end up justifying the substantial effort we expend to create them, care for and nurture them, and ultimately let them go.

The Gift of Generations

In order to understand how adults fashion endings and new beginnings in the making of personal myths, we need to combine Becker's concept of heroism with the idea of generativity.[13] Psychological research suggests that our concerns about death decline and our thoughts about "how much time is left" increase steadily through the middle years of adulthood.[14] As a response to this increasing concern, we are challenged in middle adulthood to fashion what I call a generativity script. The generativity script is an adult's plan for what he or she hopes to do in the future to leave a heroic gift for the next generation. We recast and revise our own life stories so that the past is seen as giving birth to the present and the future, and so that beginning, middle, and end make sense in terms of each other. A legacy of the self is generated and offered up to others as the middle-aged adult comes to realize, in the words of Erik Erikson, that "I am what survives me."[15]

Erik Erikson was the first psychologist to consider the idea of generativity. He defined it as "primarily the concern in establishing and guiding the next generation."[16] As Erikson conceived it, once the adult has consolidated a sense of identity and established long-term bonds of intimacy through marriage, friendship, or both, then he or she is psychosocially ready to make a commitment to society as a whole and to its continuation, even improvement, through the next generation. The generative adult nurtures, teaches, leads, and promotes the next generation. He or she creates things and ideas that aim to benefit and continue the social system.

From Erikson's point of view, generativity may be expressed in bearing and raising children. But not all parents are especially generative, Erikson maintained, and generativity is by no means limited to the domain of parenthood. One may be generative in a wide variety of life pursuits and in a vast array of life settings, as in work life and professional activities, volunteer endeavors, participation in religious, political, and community organizations, in friendships, and even in one's leisure activities.

Our cultural folklore is filled with stories of generativity. Think for a moment of the doting Jewish mother who devotes her energies to coddling, feeding, and educating her "son the doctor." Think of the rags-to-riches entrepreneur who bequeaths the family business to the firstborn. Think of the stories of the first-generation immigrants to America who work in factories and clip coupons to save money for their children's education. And of course there are the scientists, artists, teachers, missionaries, nurses, and philanthropists whose gifts reach a larger audience. Many of the greatest tales in the Judeo-Christian religious heritage are stories of generativity: God promises Abraham and Sarah a son who will give rise to a nation; Isaac blesses Esau with the birthright (and Jacob swindles it away); Moses leads the Israelites out of the land of Egypt; Christ dies on a cross to save sinners; the New Testament martyrs give their lives to spread a message to the four corners of the world. And many of the commonplace tales of daily living say the same thing. In Studs Terkel's book *Working*, Mike Lefevre, a steelworker, explains what justifies his daily labors:

> This is gonna sound square, but my kid is my imprint. He's my freedom. There's a line in one of Hemingway's books. I think it's from *For Whom the Bell Tolls*. They're behind enemy lines, somewhere

in Spain, and she's pregnant. She wants to stay with him. He tells her no. He says, "If you die, I die," knowing he's gonna die. "But if you go, I go." Know what I mean? The mystics call it the brass bowl. *Continuum.* You know what I mean? This is why I work. Every time I see a young guy walk by with a shirt and tie dressed up real sharp, I'm looking at my kid, you know? That's it.[17]

Some of Erikson's most compelling examples of generativity appear in his psychobiographical studies of the lives of Martin Luther[18] and Mahatma Gandhi.[19] Both men appear to have been their most generative in the realm of public action rather than the private one of friends and family. A passage from Erikson's *Gandhi's Truth* signals the emergence of a profound commitment to generative action in the life of its middle-aged protagonist:

> From the moment in January of 1915 when Gandhi set foot on a pier reserved for important arrivals in Bombay, he behaved like a man who knew the nature and the extent of India's calamity and that of his own fundamental mission. A mature man of middle age has not only made up his mind as to what, in the various compartments of his life, he does and does not *care for*, he is also firm in his vision of what he *will* and *can* take *care of*. He takes as his baseline what he irreducibly is and reaches out for what only he can, and therefore, *must do.*[20]

As provocative as Erikson's writings are, the concept of generativity has been neglected by most psychologists until quite recently. In the last five to ten years, a handful of psychologists have begun to study generativity in detail and to provide a more sophisticated understanding of what generativity is all about. Significant contributions have been made in this regard by John Kotre in his book *Outliving the Self.* Abigail Stewart and her colleagues have undertaken important research on generativity at the University of Michigan.[21] In addition, my own students and I have been studying the concept of generativity for the past few years, focusing especially on the personal myths constructed by highly generative adults.[22] Our understanding of generativity has increased substantially, but it is still evolving as new findings accumulate. What follows is a description based on work in progress. As new studies are done, some of our ideas about generativity may change.

I view generativity as a seven-faceted dynamic pattern. The facets are desire, demand, concern, belief, commitment, action, and narration. All seven facets are linked by an overall personal and social goal of generativity. Each adult orients him or herself to the next generation in a unique way. In order to understand how generativity functions in a particular adult's life, one must examine the characteristic interrelationships developed over time among the seven facets.

Desire

Agency and communion are the two general sets of psychological desires that can be identified in human lives. Generativity seems to draw upon both of these motivational pools. To be generative one must, like Becker's hero, generate something in one's own image. This is a powerful thing to do. One must also care for the generated product, and ultimately let that product go, as is apparent in Becker's idea of the hero's gift. The care and letting go signal a more communal aspect of generativity.

In the first study that my colleagues and I conducted on the concept of generativity, we administered a set of psychological measures and an interview to fifty adults between the ages of thirty-five and fifty.[23] In the interview, each adult was asked to describe in detail his or her plans or dreams for the future. We rated each interview on a scale of high, medium, or low generativity. Those who scored high in generativity showed a strong concern for establishing and guiding the next generation either directly (caregiving, teaching, leading, mentoring, etc.) or indirectly (contributing something they had created to others). Those who scored low in generativity showed little interest in establishing or guiding the next generation through contributing something, sharing knowledge, and so on. In some of these low-generativity accounts, the adult seemed to be so preoccupied with his or her own personal concerns, he or she was unable to imagine making a significant investment of time and energy in the next generation.

Our results showed that the adults who had the strongest generative plans for the future also scored very high on both power and intimacy motivation. In other words, those adults who evidenced both a strong agentic need to have an impact on the world and a strong communal need to be close to others envisioned their future years as containing a significant investment in the next generation.

When it comes to generativity, the agentic desires that adults express may ultimately spring from what Becker describes as a desire for immortality. It is difficult to imagine a more agentic human longing than the longing to live forever, defy death, and attain the status of a god. John Kotre argues that generativity is primarily "the desire to invest one's substance in forms of life and work that will outlive the self."[24] Richard Dawkins speaks of the desire for immortality in terms of both passing one's own genes to the next generation, and passing on "memes"—things such as inventions, works of art, good ideas, skills, words of wisdom, and so on—that will continue to influence society even after the creator of the memes is gone:

> When we die there are two things we can leave behind us: genes and memes. We were built as gene machines, created to pass on our genes. But that aspect of us will be forgotten in three generations. Your child, even your grandchild, may bear a resemblance to you, perhaps in facial features, in a talent for music, in the colour of her hair. But as each generation passes, the contribution of your genes is halved. It does not take long to reach negligible proportions. Our genes may be immortal but the collection of genes which is any one of us is bound to crumble away. Elizabeth II is a direct descendant of William the Conqueror. Yet it is quite probable that she bears not a single one of the old king's genes. We should not seek immortality in reproduction. But if you contribute to the world's culture, if you have a good idea, compose a tune, invent a spark plug, write a poem, it may live on, intact, long after your genes have dissolved into the common pool. Socrates may or may not have a gene or two alive in the world today, as G. C. Williams has remarked, but who cares? The meme-complexes of Socrates, Leonardo, Copernicus, and Marconi are still going strong.[25]

There is a good deal of agentic hubris in these words from Dawkins. In brash terms, he provides the formula for human immortality. Don't expect to live forever through your children, he says, or through their children. Rather, seek immortality by doing something great. But even Leonardo and Copernicus will someday be forgotten, as will, we must concede, the entire human race. As John Maynard Keynes once said, in the long run we are all simply dead. In the very long run, the earth will be dead, and the sun will burn out. The desire for immortality is the purest form of agency, and in its purest form it becomes somewhat absurd. Agency must be mitigated, softened, humanized, by communion.

Communion is expressed in generativity through the deep desire to be needed by others. Erikson calls it "the need to be needed"—a communal desire to nurture, assist, or be of some important use to other people. The major virtue of generativity is "care," Erikson writes. Even if our genes are diluted with each passing generation, and our memes are someday forgotten by all, the adult is still motivated to contribute to the next generation in a variety of ways. By doing our part to make the world a better place for those who follow us, we contribute in positive ways to something that is bigger and more enduring than any one of us.

The most generative adults draw creatively upon both the agentic desire for symbolic immortality and the communal need to be needed. The spirit of that generative synthesis of agency and communion is captured well in these words from Daniel Webster: "Let us develop the resources of our land, call forth its powers, build up its institutions, promote all its great interests, and see whether we also, in our day and generation, may not perform something worthy to be remembered."[26]

Demand

It is a mistake to say, as does Erik Erikson, that generativity is a discrete stage in the human life cycle, a stage that follows the stages of identity and intimacy. Such a statement suggests that a person first achieves an identity in young adulthood, then establishes intimate relationships, and finally moves forward in middle adulthood to be generative. This is too neat to be true. I do not believe that identity is situated in a stage that is resolved in early adulthood. Rather, identity is an evolving personal myth that we begin to formulate in late adolescence and early adulthood and that we continue to develop through our middle-adult years and beyond. Generativity becomes part of the myth as we incorporate experiences into our identity throughout our adult years. We don't quit working on identity and then move to generativity. Instead, identity becomes more and more concerned with generativity as we mature.

One of the reasons that we become more concerned with genera-tivity as we grow older is that society demands that we do so. In our thirties and forties, we are expected to move into the generative roles of parents, grandparents, teachers, mentors, leaders, organizers, and so on. We do not have the same expectations of children, adoles-cents, or even most young adults in their early twenties. Children may be "altruistic" or act in a "prosocial" manner, but we do not generally characterize even the most giving and helpful of childhood behaviors as expressions of generativity. Children have yet to assume responsibility for the next generation. For the most part, they are the objects of generativity, not the agents. Generativity is therefore prompted by social expectations. The demand is normative and age-graded. It is considered "on time" to assume generative social roles in one's thirties, forties, and fifties. As adults move through this period, those who are unable or unwilling to contribute to and assume responsibility for the next generation, usually through family or work, are considered to be at odds with the social clock.

Concern

Motivated by internal desire and external demand, generativity may express itself through a growing conscious concern for the next generation. As people move through adulthood, they become more aware of the ways in which the younger generation requires the care and commitment of adults. They become concerned about oppor-tunities in adult life for making contributions that will have a lasting impact. Generative concern can be focused in many different ways. Some adults focus broadly on social or community issues. They may become worried about the quality of the world's environment, that pollution and the depletion of natural resources will spoil the world for generations to come. Or they may become more concerned about the national "war on drugs," the quality of neighborhood schools, the rights of children and other relatively powerless groups, and so on. Like Gandhi, their generative concern is best expressed in the big issues of the day, in a broad public arena. Other adults focus their concern narrowly, but intensely, on their own families. They commit a great deal of time and resources to raising their children desirably, assuring their education or success. They invest heavily in the family business or the family home in an effort to improve the lot of their kin.

The overall strength of generative concern may be assumed to vary from one adult to the next, and to vary over time as well. In order to assess individual differences in the concern for the next generation, my colleagues and I developed a short paper-and-pencil questionnaire called the Loyola Generativity Scale (LGS).[27] Included among the twenty items on the scale are statements such as "If I were unable to have children of my own, I would adopt children"; "I have a responsibility to improve the neighborhood in which I live"; and "I try to pass along the knowledge I have gained through my experiences." The respondent rates each item on a 4-point scale, from a rating of 3 for "the statement applies to me very often" to a rating of 0 for "the statement never applies to me." High scores on the LGS indicate a strong concern for being generative and contributing to the next generation; a low score suggests a weak generative concern.

In three recent studies examining responses on the LGS from almost five hundred American adults, we have obtained the following results:

1. Mid-life adults show a stronger concern for the next generation than do younger and older adults. LGS scores for approximately fifty men and women between the ages of thirty-seven and forty-two years (mid-life) were compared to those obtained for fifty younger adults (ages twenty-two to twenty-seven) and fifty older adults (ages sixty-seven to seventy-two). The mid-life group had the highest scores. The average scores of the younger group and the older group did not differ much from each other.

2. Women tend to have slightly stronger generative concerns than do men, especially among younger adults. There is a slight tendency for women to score higher than men on the LGS, but the difference does not appear to be very important after early adulthood. Thus, women seem to start out adulthood with stronger generative concerns, but men narrow the gap by mid-life.

3. Fathers show much stronger generative concerns than men who have never had children. In one study, LGS scores of fathers were much higher than those of men who had never been fathers. Among women, generative concern does not appear to be related to parental status. It would appear that becoming a father has a strong positive impact on developing the generative concerns of many men. Among women, no such development seems to take place as a result of becoming a mother, probably because women tend to be relatively high in generative concern to begin with.

4. Adults who show strong generative concerns tend to act on those concerns by engaging in a greater number of generative behaviors in daily life. High LGS scores are associated with more frequent reports of engaging in such behaviors as reading stories to children and teaching skills to others. However, generative adults are not more active overall. They do not engage in more behaviors of all kinds. Rather, they engage in more generative behaviors, compared to adults who show less concern for the next generation.

5. Adults who show strong generative concerns tend to be more satisfied with their lives compared to adults who are not as strongly concerned about the next generation. We find modest but significant positive correlations between LGS scores and scores on measures of life satisfaction and happiness.

6. Adults who show strong generative concerns tend to describe their autobiographical pasts in highly generative terms, underscoring such themes as creating new products, giving of the self to others, and having positive interactions with others in a younger generation. In terms of personal myth, people who score high on the LGS tend to highlight key events from the past that are laden with generative themes.

Belief

If generative concern is motivated by inner desire and social demand, it is reinforced by belief. In speculating about failure in generativity, Erikson writes:

The reasons are often to be found in early childhood impressions; in excessive self-love based on a too strenuously self-made personality; and finally (and here we return to the beginnings) in the lack of some faith, some "belief in the species," which would make a child appear to be a welcome trust of the community.[28]

What Erikson calls a "belief in the species" is a basic and general belief in the fundamental goodness of human life, specifically as envisioned for the future. To believe strongly in the species is to place hope in the advancement and betterment of human life in succeeding generations, even in the face of human destructiveness and deprivation. Therefore, the person who believes that human beings are basically evil or bad, that life on earth is nasty and brutish, and that things cannot be expected to improve in the future may find it difficult to summon up concern for the next generation.

It is important to note that a belief in the species can take strange forms, masquerading in some instances as gloomy prophecy. Growing up in the Baptist Church, the first Bible verse that I was asked to memorize as a child was Romans 3:23—"For all have sinned and come short of the glory of God." The starting point for this particular brand of Christianity is that human beings are evil to begin with. We are all sinners. Left to our own devices, we will destroy each other and the earth as well. I learned that we are all living in "the last days."

The fundamentalist beliefs I learned as a child appear to work against generative concern, for they suggest that humans are evil and that the world is not becoming a better place. It would appear that one should not waste too much time being concerned with the future generations if the world is going to end any day. However, this set of beliefs contains an interesting twist. Though human beings are evil, God is good and merciful. Human beings may be saved through belief in Jesus Christ. Therefore, human life is potentially perfectible and everlasting because of the intervention of divine forces. Belief in God may reinforce belief in the species. In fact, the invocation of the last days may work to provide greater urgency and intensity for one's generative concern. If the world is going to end soon, we learned as Baptists, then we better immediately get out there and spread the good news of Christ's salvation, to save as many people as we can before Christ returns! For the leaders in the Baptist Church of thirty years ago, and the members of the Jehovah's Witnesses who knock on doors today, "saving souls" becomes an imperative generative concern.

In her doctoral dissertation at Loyola University of Chicago, Donna Van de Water administered various measures of generativity and questionnaires designed to assess belief in the species to adults ranging in age from twenty-two to seventy-two years.[29] Her questionnaire about belief in the species contained such items as "Humans have a lot of problems but none that they won't eventually be able to solve." Van de Water found modest positive associations between generativity and belief, suggesting a tendency for those people who expressed the strongest optimism about the future of humankind to express the greatest amount of concern for the next generation. She also found positive associations between generative concerns and "belief in the self." Adults who endorsed questionnaire items indicating confidence in their own abilities—as in the item "I feel that chances are very good that I can achieve my goals in life"—also tended to report higher levels of generative concern.

Van de Water's results point to two separate areas of belief that would appear to reinforce adults' concerns for the next generation. Ideally, the generative adult manifests a strong belief in the species and a strong belief in the self. Generative concern is strengthened by a hopeful and optimistic attitude about the future of humankind, by the belief that human life in future generations is worthy of attention. It is also strengthened by a firm belief in the worthiness and effectiveness of the self as a generative agent.

Commitment

Ideally, the desire for immortality and the need to be needed, the developmental expectations concerning generativity expressed in societal demands, the growing concern for the next generation, strong beliefs in the goodness of the species and the worthiness of the self, all coalesce to produce commitment. In this fifth facet of generativity, the adult makes a decision, sets a goal, or draws up a plan to translate desires, demands, concerns, and beliefs into generative action. It is one thing to be concerned, and quite another to commit to a course of action.

The most generative adults are those who develop an implicit program of generative action, with a specific plan and set of objectives. Their life courses become guided by their commitments to the next generation, and their life stories become oriented toward anticipated generative accomplishments for the future. The generative adult expects a reciprocal commitment from society. Ideally, both the adult and the society in which he or she lives endeavor to fulfill an implicit social contract whereby the mature individual commits him or herself to generative pursuits "for the long run" and society offers a reciprocal commitment to support and augment these generative efforts.

Action

Desire, demand, concern, and belief lead to commitment. Commitment leads to action. There are three general classes of generative action. These are creating, maintaining, and offering.

One meaning of generative behavior is to generate things and people, to be creative, productive, and fruitful, to "give birth," both literally and figuratively. This is the most agentic meaning of generativity, and it ties most closely to the agentic desire for symbolic immortality. To create something in one's own image is the agentic act par excellence. Giving birth, inventing new products, writing books, making clothes—these are all creative actions and therefore manifestations of one class of generative behavior. However, even in the agentic act of creating, the creator may have the sense that not everything is under his or her total control. The late psychologist Henry Murray once described the creative person as "presiding over an interior transaction which may or may not come out with something that is worth seizing."[30] Murray suggested that the creative process may be beyond our own control. Nor can we fully control our creations, for they have a life of their own. The protagonist of Margaret Atwood's novel *Cat's Eye* laments over her inability to manage the art she creates: "I can no longer control these paintings, or tell them what to mean. Whatever energy they have came out of me. I'm what's left over."[31]

A second kind of generative behavior is to pass on something from the past and present into the future, to preserve and maintain traditions in order to improve or enhance the future. This is both an agentic and a communal generative behavior. Psychiatrist George Vaillant refers to this sense of generativity when he describes mid-life men and women as "the keepers of the meaning."[32] According to Vaillant, mid-life men and women must accept the responsibility of preserving the most important cultural traditions and symbol systems, keeping them safe for posterity. In his book *Generative Man,* Daniel Browning extends this idea to the entire global environment.[33] In Browning's view, the most generative adults are those who commit themselves to preserving the goodness of the earth. They are "creative ritualizers" who are able to draw upon traditions from the past in creative new ways in order to meet the challenges of the future. In this capacity, generative men and women act as guardians, trustees, or stewards of the world and of humankind.

Generative preservation can be expressed in many poignant ways. Perhaps the most dramatic and basic form is in the literal saving of lives. In an unforgettable passage from Studs Terkel's *Working,* a Brooklyn firefighter named Tom Patrick describes his perspective on generative action:

> The fuckin' world's so fucked up; the country's fucked up. But the fireman, you actually see them produce. You see them put out a fire. You see them come out with babies in their hands. You see them give mouth-to-mouth when a guy's dying. You can't get around that shit. That's real. To me, that's what I want to be. . . .
>
> I worked in a bank. You know, it's just paper. It's not real. Nine to five and it's shit. You're looking at the numbers. But I can look back and say, "I helped put out a fire. I helped save somebody." It shows something I did on this earth.[34]

The third category for generative action involves the idea of giving gifts, of making offerings to the next generation, of letting go of one's own creations so that they may eventually bear their own fruit. This is the most communal meaning of generative action, and it ties up thematically with the communal need to be needed. It also exists in direct tension with the more agentic aspects of generative behavior, as in creating. Offering up one's own creations, setting them free, is perhaps the greatest challenge in generativity. The truly generative father is both a self-aggrandizing creator and a self-sacrificing giver. Biologically and socially, he creates a child in his own image, working hard and long to promote the child's development and to nurture all that is good and desirable in that child. But he must eventually grant the child her own autonomy, letting go when the time is right, letting the child develop her own identity, make her own decisions and commitments, and ultimately create those offerings of generativity that will distinguish that child as someone who was given birth to in order to give birth in turn.

From the standpoint of society and of the individual, the most meaningful and beneficial adult generative commitments are to programs of action that blend creating, maintaining, and offering into one. The most generative adults are those men and women who are strong enough to create legacies in their own image, wise enough to preserve the best from the past and carry it forward, and loving enough to offer that which they have created or maintained to the care of posterity.

Narration

The last facet of generativity is narration. In the context of an evolving personal myth, an adult constructs and seeks to live out a generativity script, specifying what he or she plans to do in the future in order to leave a legacy of the self. The generativity script is an inner narration of the adult's own awareness of where efforts to be generative fit into his or her own personal story, into contemporary society and the social world he or she inhabits. The generativity script functions to address the narrative need for a sense of an ending, a satisfying vision or plan concerning how, even though one's life will eventually end, some aspect of the self will live on.

There are countless narrative models for generativity. But each of us must find or create the form that works best for us. There are many ways to be generative, especially in one's occupational life, creative activities, and community involvements. And there are many ways to make sense of these activities—and of their attendant desires, demands, concerns, beliefs, and commitments—in terms of a self-defining personal myth. Let us consider one particular way—how one especially generative man understands the story of his own life.

What Can I Build to Institute the Values I Have?

Daniel Kessinger is a forty-eight-year-old community organizer and executive director of a mental-health agency. He has been married for twenty-five years. His wife, Lynette, is a social worker. They have a daughter who is in the second grade. The family lives in a modest house in an inner-Chicago neighborhood that has recently undergone substantial gentrification, with a consequent increase in property values. Daniel and Lynette bought their house in 1978, long before the influx of young professionals transformed the neighborhood into one of the trendier and more desirable locations for young Chicago adults. Daniel describes his home purchase as a "defensive gesture." Before becoming homeowners, he and his wife had rented apartments, but in each case the landlords lost money and the buildings were eventually sold or abandoned. As Daniel saw it then, the only way they could continue to live in the neighborhood was to buy a house.

Despite the gentrification, Daniel's neighborhood is still home to a substantial working-class constituency, very poor families, drug addicts, and a rapidly expanding population of street people. It is to these groups that Daniel and Lynette have dedicated much of their lives. From his early involvement in the American civil rights movement, through his two-year stint with the Peace Corps, and to his current work as a builder of organizations that "institute the values I have," Daniel has constructed a personal identity that is dominated by a generativity script. A disarmingly unassuming man in public, he is not modest in private about his achievements, commitments, and aspirations. He believes that much of what he has accomplished he has done on his own. He sees himself as being similar in ways to Martin Luther King, Jr., but King is not a hero for him. "Um, to me he's more of a colleague," Daniel remarks. "My life theme is creating a better world."

The narrative tone of Daniel's personal myth blends ironic and mildly romantic elements. A bookish and lonely child, Daniel learned early on "to rely on myself, to take care of myself, and to make my own life." Born in Austria, his father emigrated to the United States in 1939 on the eve of World War II. He was a nuclear physicist who held a series of faculty and research positions at a number of major American universities. The family moved around from one university town to another through the late 1940s and 1950s. Daniel states, "We were an Adlai Stevenson type of family, shaped by liberal democratic values." His parents instilled in Daniel an appreciation for American history and a belief in the nation's destiny as the promised land of liberty and freedom, despite a troubled relationship with their son.

Through the childhood and adolescent chapters of Daniel's story, the central thematic line is agency. Daniel was hardworking, self-sufficient, and something of a loner. Even in early childhood, he seemed to have strong convictions about right and wrong, liberty and justice. It seems that the rudiments of a very strong and sophisticated ideological setting were in place even before his adolescent years. In sixth grade, he decided that he would not attend the local junior high school with the children he already knew because there were too many children there from rich families, and "this seemed immoral in some way." Instead, he attended a school where he knew nobody but where the children were from a broader mix of social classes. In high school, he protested the exclusive use of New Testament readings in mandatory morning prayer. He believed this was offensive to the school's many Jewish students. Daniel was active in the Unitarian Church at the time, and he had a strong interest in Eastern religions:

> I raised a big stink about it. I kind of said I refused to do this. My position was that I thought it was neat to do something religious first thing in the morning, and I didn't really have any objection to that. I just felt that if somebody wanted to read from the Koran they should be able to read from the Koran. Well, my homeroom teacher said basically, look, I just need a note from my mother to be excused from the activity. So I went home and I talked to my mom about it, and she said no. "You have to do what they tell you to do at school." So she wouldn't support me. This was a huge rift between my mother and myself. My dad died that year, too.

This is the low point in Daniel's life story. His mother urged him to compromise his beliefs and to conform to the school authorities. He refused and felt disillusioned and cut off from his family. Shortly before or after this incident—Daniel cannot recall precisely—his father suffered a heart attack. Daniel woke up in the middle of the night to see the paramedics rush his dad out of the house on a stretcher. The evening before, Daniel had had a big argument with his father. Their relationship had never been very smooth. Now his father was dead, and Daniel lost the chance to resolve their dispute.

Alienation and loneliness gave way to excitement and an exhilarating sense of being involved when Daniel went to Amherst College in 1960. From an early age, Daniel had believed that he would be a college professor. The professors he met in college were inspiring models for an emerging agentic imago of the sage. Amherst stressed critical thinking. "It was like there was no truth," Daniel remarks. "Everything was interpretation; the whole thrust of everything was to teach critical thinking and how to think, so your freshman physics course was not designed to teach you physics but to teach you how a physicist thinks."

As Daniel became more immersed in the intellectual life of the campus, he also became increasingly active in campus politics and social issues. John F. Kennedy was the new American president, and Amherst was awash with the excitement of his youthful administration. These were halcyon days for the kind of young, white, liberal intellectuals with whom Daniel identified. Such intellectuals were inspired by the Kennedy Peace Corps and the brewing social ferment to push for greater social equality and justice. The times were right for the articulation of a generativity script, even though Daniel was still a teenager. Bright and idealistic young people were supposed to create a better world—this was the message of the day. Accordingly, Daniel became involved with a group called Students for Racial Equality. He worked with college administrators to develop recruitment programs for black youth. He organized tutorial projects for minority kids in Philadelphia. He stood face-to-face against white-hooded Klansmen in a small southern town. As the Vietnam War heated up, Daniel moved from Amherst to Yale to pursue graduate work in East Asian studies. He became involved early on in the antiwar movement. In 1966, he married Lynette.

The year 1966 marks the turning point in Daniel's life story. With the war in Vietnam moving toward a disastrous crescendo, Daniel looked to international service as a way of avoiding the war and of pushing ahead his project to create a better world. Though morally opposed to the war, Daniel felt he could not become a conscientious objector. As he saw it then, in order to be a CO, one had to profess a religiously anchored pacifism. Such a religion would be "tied to the notion of there being a God-the-creator type of thing," and Daniel rejected that. Furthermore, while he considered himself a pacifist in his personal life, he was not philosophically opposed to all wars. "I believe in the American Revolution and the Chinese Revolution—people pick up guns, and that's how they won the liberation and independence of their countries." The American Friends Service Committee rejected his application for foreign service because he could not, in good faith, declare himself a CO. So he and Lynette joined the Peace Corps and were assigned to work with a small group of other Americans in India for a family planning operation:

> My wife and I spent almost two years in India basically going up to the villages with Indian coworkers and talking about birth control and so on. We were working for the Indian government. We distributed condoms. And I worked in the vasectomy program, which meant that we were doing education in vasectomy, recruiting people for what they called "the operation." And Lynette was basically working with the women, and they were using something like an early IUD. It turned out to have a lot of problems. So she ended up doing much more maternal education things, smallpox and infant health, all that kind of stuff, along with the birth control.

Daniel deems his time in India with Lynette to be "the two most important years in our lives in basically shaping where we were gonna go in the future." The two years mark a major leap forward with respect to the development of his identity. From childhood on, he had cultivated an image of himself for the future as a liberal, intellectual, college professor, personified in the agentic imago of the sage. In India, the sage began to share the stage with new characters who personified Daniel's growing talents and interests in health and in community organization. The sage gave way to the healer and the humanist, imagoes that are more in keeping with the liberal and humanistic ideology he had already formed. The healer and the humanist introduced communion into what had been a predominantly agentic myth. Lynette, too, brought communion to the story. Although self-sufficient and fiercely independent, Daniel began to merge his life course with another.

In his mid twenties, Daniel was going through certain changes in his life and life story that are typically reserved for mid-life. The fiery passion he displayed in a wide variety of social protests in the early 1960s now was channeled into sustained and productive work on a smaller but more intense scale, a move reminiscent of the sublimation of passion associated with mid-life. The movement from the sage to the more refined imagoes of the healer and the humanist signals a more contextualized kind of thinking. Daniel was still moved by the great abstractions of liberal democracy, but he learned in India that concrete and realistic solutions to social problems require thinking that is less absolute and more situationally determined. With the emergence of the new imagoes, Daniel confronted stark oppositions in his own personal myth, probably for the first time. Was he a thinker or a doer? An intellectual or an activist? Should he strive for agency or communion?

Daniel and Lynette returned to the United States in 1968 to find a nation dramatically polarized by the Vietnam War. The alliance between liberal whites and blacks of the early 1960s had begun to dissolve with the emergence of a more militant black consciousness. College campuses had been radicalized. Inner cities had erupted in violence. A new counterculture preached the virtues of free love and free drugs. Still firm in his humanistic and liberal values, Daniel felt increasingly uncomfortable with the radicalization of certain segments of American society, and he feared the growing backlash of the conservative white majority. Emotions ran high on both the left and the right. Daniel's was a voice of reason and tolerance, as he describes it. As much as ever, he wanted to work for a better world. He believed in radical change. But he did not expect such change to occur easily, nor with great speed:

> I had come back from India in some ways, eh, I'll call it conservative. I mean when you spend two years trying to change people's attitudes and stuff in a country like India, I mean one thing you come away with is a profound sense of how slow social change is. I mean the farthest thing from my mind was anything that was apocalyptic or immediate. I had a vision of social change taking place over a thousand years, with a lot of, eh, pain, and false starts. Step by step.

Daniel and Lynette moved to Chicago. She was employed as a social worker while he held a number of part-time and volunteer positions. He also earned a second master's degree in social-service administration. The couple earned very little income and lived very modestly for years. Daniel began organizing various community groups around issues of health, housing, and jobs. For a while, he worked with handicapped children:

> In India I got used to working with people who were, like, physically weird. You know, in the villages in India you had these lepers coming up to you and kind of sticking these stumps in your face, you know, asking for money. It was pretty gruesome at times. And somehow, looking at these multiply handicapped kids was real easy for me. You know, 'cause I was bright, I mean, I read four books and I took over the school for multiply handicapped kids and I ran it—and did a good job of it.

After years of volunteer work with children, families, and the disadvantaged, Daniel had his first full-time job at age thirty-three. He was named executive director of a neighborhood mental-health council. He started with a budget of sixty-two thousand dollars and four employees. Fifteen years later, the budget is over two million dollars, with fifty-five full-time people and twelve part-time psychiatrists. As the country moved politically to the right with the election of Ronald Reagan in 1980, Daniel pushed boldly in the other direction. In recent years, he has worked hard for liberal progressive candidates in local elections, and has become active in protests over American involvement in Central America. He is the principal architect and organizer of a local food pantry that distributes free food to needy families. He remains committed to a vision of a more tolerant and compassionate American society.

With the birth of his daughter Samantha in 1983, Daniel's story warms up and becomes more communal. As a man whose life may be seen as a series of overlapping generative projects, Daniel remarks, "My historical project right now is Samantha." In mid-life, Daniel does not appear to be moving away from the major projects he has initiated to create a better world. But there is a noticeable mellowing. "I have tried to reorganize my life with much more emphasis on being around the house and being with the family." He spends more time now "just having fun." Ice skating with his daughter, playing the piano, enjoying Indian music, going to the zoo— these activities stem from the emergence of a new imago at mid-life, "the good father to Samantha." The good father is an altogether more communal character in his personal myth, a light and refreshing contrast to the sage, the healer, and the humanist. Still generative, but in a softer way.

We may identify four general features that Daniel Kessinger's myth seems to share with those of other especially generative adults. In the research that my colleagues and I have conducted in the past two years, we tend to see at least two or three of these features in life stories of extremely generative adults, whereas the personal myths constructed by less generative adults typically show none of them or only one.

The first feature is what I call a childhood sense of being chosen. Especially generative adults like Daniel Kessinger often remember their childhood years as a time in which they experienced especially positive treatment or exposure from their social environments. As they reconstruct it mythically, either an extremely warm and supportive family or a powerful system of beliefs and values provides them with a secure base upon which they can build their identities. In Daniel's case, an "Adlai Stevenson type" household was the determining factor. As his example shows, the first chapter of the myth does not have to be emotionally positive. Daniel was often lonely, and he lacked social skills. But in the life stories of especially generative people like Daniel there appears to be a positive force of some kind—a person, a relationship, a value system—that seems to single out the child and say to him or her, "You are different and special. There is something uniquely good about you."

A second feature is unwavering conviction. I have found that especially generative adults rarely describe periods in their life in which they doubted what they were doing. They rarely appear to struggle with the ambiguities of right and wrong. By the time he reached college, Daniel had formulated an articulate and compelling ideological setting for his life story, and though he has changed in many ways since then, he has never doubted his most fundamental beliefs. Daniel is open to many different ideologies, life-styles, and cultural traditions. He is accepting of many alternative points of view. But he knows he is right in what he is doing with his life, and he holds firmly to the beliefs that support his actions.

The unwavering conviction described by especially generative adults follows naturally in some stories from the sense of being chosen as a child. Through both of these narrative features, the generative adult seems to be saying that his or her destiny is guided, supported, or even directed by something larger or deeper than the self. "Why do I do what I do?" an especially generative teacher asks. "Because it is what I have been chosen to do. It is me. I can't explain it any further." In his interview, Daniel Kessinger struggles with the same question. He concludes that ultimately he does not know why he does what he does. "I'm not exactly sure where all this came from," he says.

Daniel Kessinger's personal myth provides numerous examples of turning bad things into good, a third feature we have noticed in life stories of especially generative adults. Being lonely as a child is bad, but learning self-sufficiency as a result is good. Daniel believes that he had a bad relationship with his own father, and as a result he has invested greatly in the project of being a good father for Samantha. Because of a bad war, Daniel went to India and discovered his life calling. From the standpoint of a liberal Democrat like Daniel, the election of Ronald Reagan was very bad. But Daniel turned it into a good thing in his personal myth. Because of the rise of American conservatism in the 1980s, Daniel redoubled his efforts to get liberal candidates elected at the local level. As the Reagan administration slashed funding for the programs Daniel initiated, he worked harder to get money from private foundations. As more and more Americans sank beneath the poverty line in the 1980s, Daniel built a food pantry. It is because there are such vexing problems facing humankind that Daniel is able to build organizations that institute his values.

Like many generative adults, Daniel must confront in his personal myth the inevitable conflict between agency and communion. In Daniel's case, this conflict is deep and especially complex, and its origins may be traced back at least to the Peace Corps years in India. Overall, Daniel's is an agentic life story that grows more communal over time. As the sage gives way to the healer, the humanist, and the good father, Daniel's story becomes thematically more complex, and agency and communion confront each other in intriguing ways. The conflict is perhaps most apparent in Daniel's current role as caregiver to Samantha. He describes Samantha as bright and very talented, but not as disciplined as Daniel would like. She does not work at things as hard as he did when he was a child. "I have known kids who have a lot less ability than she has but who will ultimately do more with what they have, just because they work at it." As the good father, what should he do? How hard should he push her to achieve?

> Well, I kind of get caught between one end of the scale and the other. One end is having real high standards about everything, and on the other end is, well, you know, being almost an anarchist, antiestablishment, letting her do what she wants to do.

The parenting conflict is doubly significant in Daniel's personal myth. The conflict reveals a common problem in generativity: the problem of letting the creation go. A man who builds things that institute his own values has a hard time making of those creations what Becker calls a heroic "offering." The agentic mode of generativity conflicts with the communal mode. When does the creator ease up? When does he cut back on his efforts to control? A seven-year-old daughter needs guidance and direction, certainly. But how much? It is hard to know, as Daniel will tell you.

The conflict between agency and communion also connects to values and life-style. Daniel says that he has always been politically very liberal but personally very conservative. He believes strongly in both approaches. Both are right for him. But in Daniel's personal myth, political liberalism is tied up with social activism, community organizing, healing the sick, representing the poor. It connects to rebelling against the establishment in high school, to facing down the Ku Klux Klan in that small southern town, to rational problem solving in India, to critical thinking at Amherst. Daniel's political liberalism is therefore expressed in the public actions of a boldly independent man, a powerful agent who has found his own way in the world, who has chosen his own path. The agentic quality of political liberalism is reinforced for Daniel in the Unitarian Church:

> The Unitarians basically believe that each individual works out their own religious posture and their own path and their own way. And there's a side of me which obviously sees a lot of merit to that. On the other hand, I don't think that when everything in the whole religion brings it back to the individual you have a very good thing. This doesn't bring out the best in human beings. I could never be a

249

Christian because I don't believe the myth. But there are some elements in Christianity that help people go beyond the individual. They bring out a collective commitment. The individual doesn't just stand alone. Part of me likes that a lot.

The part that likes it is the conservative, communal part. Unlike the hippies and the anarchists of the late 1960s, Daniel was never comfortable with the unbridled expression of human individuality. After all, he has been married to the same woman for twenty-five years. He owns a home; he is raising a family; he is saving money for Samantha's college education. He wants her to have all the opportunities that the American middle class can provide. He sees communal merit in traditional Christianity, even though he can't accept it for himself. In Daniel's personal myth, the split between agency and communion subsumes what Daniel perceives to be his dual nature as a liberal at work and a conservative at home.

Agency or communion? Liberalism or conservatism? Work or home? The opposition is always there. In Daniel Kessinger's personal myth, the tension between agency and communion pushes the plot forward. As his identity becomes richer and more integrated over time, Daniel finds that agency and communion confront each other again and again, at increasingly complex levels. Very generative people often seem to face this confrontation, each in his or her own unique way. It is perhaps among those who fashion the best and most enduring gifts for the next generation that we witness the most momentous conflicts between creating and giving, between controlling and letting go, between standing alone and being with others. But it is in these heroic life stories that adults best justify their time on this earth, as mature men and women who can see past their own ends to the beginnings of a better world.

CHAPTER 10

Exploring
Your Myth

After she had interviewed a number of people about their personal myths, one of my graduate students told me that I had to see the movie *sex, lies, and videotape.* As an interviewer, she found striking parallels between her own experience and that of the movie's chief protagonist, a young man who videotapes women as they tell him about their sexual fantasies. I found this an odd comment because I don't believe that an interviewee has ever told us about a sexual fantasy. The topic is not part of the standard interview we use.

After seeing the movie, however, I had to agree with my student's observation. In the film, the protagonist encourages women to describe their most desirable sexual imaginings in as much detail as they wish. Should they want to, they may remove some or all of their clothing during the process. The protagonist simply listens and asks an occasional question to help the women along. But he never interferes with the telling. He passes no judgment. He gives no advice. He affirms, but never threatens. What develops is a strange and intensely intimate relationship whose life is no longer than the running of the videotape. Most likely, he will never see the woman again. But for those moments while she is on tape, he listens intently as she discloses things that she has never said before. To be listened to with such intensity, to be accepted unconditionally as the center of another person's consciousness, even but for a few moments in time—this is what is so appealing to the women on tape. This seems to be what motivates them to tell their stories, to share that which is most private with a man who is a virtual stranger.

And what about the motivations of the protagonist? He wants the intimacy, too. As the women open up, he experiences deep feelings of care and affection. In addition, the tapes are fuel for his own sexual fantasies, as he replays them for his private viewing long after the women have gone home. Until he falls in love with the heroine in the film, the videotapes serve as a substitute for sexual intercourse with women. Indeed, it is tempting to conclude that the videotapes are but a tawdry imitation of life, a technological tool for masturbation keeping the protagonist from relating to others in genuine and healthy ways. But I think that this conclusion is too simple and misses a key point about the quality of experience on tape. The women are not acting; they are being as real as they can be. Their genuine self-disclosures create an emotionally riveting bond between the listener and the teller. It may be a sad commentary on modern life that such moments of sincere disclosure seem so rare, so strange. But here we have them—on videotape. Real people telling the truth through stories as a sympathetic listener takes it in.

As an interviewer leading people through a series of questions about their life stories, I am like the movie's sympathetic listener. I do not pass judgment. I do not offer advice, therapy, or counsel. I try to affirm as much as I can, to help the person clarify and articulate in ways that enable the true myth to be revealed, on tape. Of course, my motivations are different from those in the movie. I interview people to collect data on personal myths. It's all in the name of science, objective inquiry, gaining knowledge about real people's real lives. When I play the tapes back, I am listening with an analytic ear, discerning themes, images, symbols, and so on so that I might construct a portrait of the myth and the mythmaking that characterizes the life.

Yet my students and I cannot help but develop strong feelings of affection and intimacy for the people we interview, and it seems that they form strong feelings for us, as well. At the end of the interview, most people report that the experience of telling their stories was profoundly satisfying and enjoyable, even if they shed tears in the telling. They often ask not to receive payment for the interview, for they feel that they have already been rewarded by the experience itself. They seem puzzled at times that I, the interviewer, should be so thankful for their participation. They end up thanking me for taking the time to listen. They hope dearly that they did not bore me. The truth is I am never bored, nor are my students. Instead, we feel privileged and a little embarrassed to be given such a sincere self-disclosure—such a precious gift of intimacy. I feel that my daily interactions are rarely as real and as authentic as the interviews I have on tape.

After the interview, people often remark that they found the process of telling their story to be profoundly enlightening. "I learned a lot of things about myself," they may say. "It got me thinking about things I don't usually think about." Although its intended function is to gather data on lives, our life-story interview may also serve to help people *identify* the personal myth that they have been *living* all along. Such an identification may help in the process of *changing* the myth should the person feel that change is required. In this last chapter, I will draw together my personal reflections on (1) identifying, (2) living, and (3) changing the personal myths that shape and give meaning to our lives. My goal here is not to provide you with simple recipes for human happiness and understanding, in the manner of the proverbial self-help book in popular psychology. I sincerely believe that very few people in the world are qualified to tell you (or me) how to live a life, by writing a book. But I also believe that there are useful guidelines to be considered when applying the ideas in this book to your own life, your own personal myth. You may wish to develop your own guidelines as well.

Identifying the Myth

In contemporary modern life, the two most common tools employed to promote the identification of one's personal myth are psychotherapy and autobiography. In certain forms of psychotherapy, the therapist and the client may work together to explore conscious and unconscious domains in the client's life, with the explicit goal of enhancing self-understanding and facilitating personality change.

There are many forms of psychotherapy, but those most closely identified as "talking therapies" or "depth" approaches—typically psychoanalytic, psychodynamic, or cognitive-affective in orientation—are probably best suited for the kind of personal exploration required to help identify one's personal myth. In autobiography (and in such personal memoirs as diaries and journals), a person may self-consciously seek a narrative frame for life. The process of focusing on the life and translating it into words helps the author to identify or construct a coherent view of self, as we saw in Chapter 1 in the cases of Saint Augustine and the novelist Philip Roth.

Beyond these two valuable approaches, there are simpler and less expensive methods you may employ to enhance self-understanding and promote the identification of personal myth. Some of these involve private explorations of your inner life through such methods as keeping track of your dreams, cultivating your fantasy life, thinking through central problems and conflicts, engaging in inner dialogues with your many "selves," paying close attention to your body's rhythms, and so on.[1] While these methods may be extremely useful, my own research underscores the importance of interpersonal *dialogue* in exploring the self. Like certain forms of psychotherapy, the telling of one's story to a sympathetic listener can be extremely illuminating. Unlike a psychotherapist, however, the listener need not be a trained professional. Nor should the listener adopt an advisory or judgmental role. Instead, the listener should follow the role of an interviewer in one of my life-story interviews. He or she should serve as an empathic and encouraging guide and an affirming sounding board.

Who should the listener be? Ideally, the listener should be a friend who has not been instrumentally involved in shaping your life to this point. Both you and the friend should be ready for the intensification of your relationship that such an exploration will produce. Unlike the movie and my interviews, you and the friend are likely to remain in an ongoing relationship in the weeks and years to come. Therefore, your exploration needs to be evaluated in the context of that particular friendship. What will happen to the friendship as a result of such an exploration? How will your feelings about each other change? In some cases, it may be especially enriching for your friend to explore his or her own myth as well. You may wish to switch roles at times: You become the listener as your friend takes on the role of storyteller. It may also be helpful to tape your exchanges so that you can listen to the proceedings later on and reflect upon meanings and significance. Taping is especially useful should you decide that you wish to take concerted action to change your myth in the future. It's helpful to have a record of what you wish to change before you begin to try to change it.

Other candidates for listener include spouses, siblings, lovers, parents, or even one's adult children. All of these relationships tend to be more complex than the idealized friendship I have described above. Personal exploration in these contexts may be somewhat more dangerous, in that such people are likely to have been intimately involved in the making of your identity in the past. You may be less candid in exchanges with your husband or wife than when talking with a good friend. Still, the value of personal exploration may exceed the potential liabilities in many cases. Not only may the process of exploring the self promote your own identity understanding but it may also enrich the ongoing relationship with a lover, spouse, or family member.

Therefore, in considering who the listener should be, the two most important criteria are probably (1) the nature of your relationship with the prospective listener and (2) the listener's suitability for the role. With respect to the first, you and the listener must feel that such an exploration is appropriate and comfortable for both of you at this point in your relationship. With respect to the second, the listener should be able to take on the kind of enthusiastic, affirming, and nonjudgmental perspective I have described above. In addition, the listener should be familiar with the concept of personal myth. By way of preparation, you and the listener may wish to discuss some of the central concepts I have outlined in this book. These may include the meaning of stories in literature and lives, narrative tone, archetypal story forms (e.g., comedy, tragedy, romance, irony), story imagery, themes of power and love, personal fables of adolescence, ontological strategies, ideological settings, imagoes, changes at midlife, the generativity script, and the sense of ending in stories.

What should the listener do? As the storytelling process evolves, you (the storyteller) and the listener may develop your own guidelines for dialogue and exploration. To get you started, however, I would suggest that you follow the interview protocol that I have employed in research into personal myths. The interview typically takes between one and a half and three hours to complete. It may be done in one sitting or two. You may wish to supplement the questions we use with more personally relevant probes. You may wish to skip some of our questions if they seem redundant or irrelevant in your particular case. However you use the interview, you should see it as a tool rather than an end in itself. Ideally, it should prompt you to make further explorations in future dialogues. You should plan to follow up on material that arises in the interview in subsequent discussions with your listener.

(If you prefer not to share your story with another person, you may serve as your own listener. My general experience with this approach is that it does not lead to the kind of intimate and concerted self-disclosure that typically comes out in interpersonal dialogue. But it still may be the right approach for some people—those who find it extremely difficult to talk about themselves with others, or those for whom no suitable listener seems available in their lives. If you think that you fit into one of these two categories, I would still encourage you to make every effort possible to do the exploration through interpersonal dialogue.)

The interview begins with a general question about *life chapters:*

I would like you to begin by thinking about your life as if it were a book. Each part of your life composes a chapter in the book. Certainly, the book is unfinished at this point; still, it probably already contains a few interesting and well-defined chapters. Please divide your life into its major chapters and briefly describe each chapter. You may have as many or as few chapters as you like, but I would suggest dividing it into at least two or three chapters and at most about seven or eight. Think of this as a general table of contents for your book. Give each chapter a name and describe the overall contents of each chapter. Discuss briefly what makes for a transition from one chapter to the next. This first part of the interview can expand forever, but I would urge you to keep it relatively brief, say, within thirty to forty-five minutes. Therefore, you don't want to tell me "the whole story" here. Just give me a sense of the story's outline—the major chapters in your life.

The listener may wish to ask for clarifications or elaborations at any point in this first section, though there is a significant danger of interrupting too much. The listener should be careful not to organize the table of contents for the storyteller by suggesting chapter titles and so on. The first section of the interview is the most open-ended part. Some people will talk for hours here if allowed; others will wrap it up in five minutes. We have found that the most illuminating and cogent responses can be completed between about twenty-five minutes and an hour, so we typically suggest (as you see above) a thirty- to forty-five-minute length. The storyteller's task is to provide a general context for the more particular material to come. While it may be useful to explore important themes and incidents in some detail if they arise at this point, the storyteller should be careful not to get lost in the details of the narrative.

The life-chapters question enables you, the storyteller, to provide your life with an organizing narrative framework. Most people organize their life chapters in a quasi-chronological manner, with earliest chapters linked to childhood. For others, a thematic organization seems to work better. They may have a chapter on relationships, another on school and work, and so on. You may wish to experiment with different organizational formats before settling on one that seems right for you. How you divide things up may be especially revealing of what you consider to be the major benchmarks and developmental trends in your life. In addition, the opening life-chapters question provides an opportunity for the expression of many different elements of the self-defining personal myth. Especially noticeable are narrative tone and imagery. The extent to which a person adopts an optimistic or pessimistic tone in reconstructing the past—the extent to which he or she follows comic, tragic, romantic, and/or ironic forms—begins to become manifest in the organization of life chapters. Both the listener and the storyteller should furthermore pay careful attention to the kind of language employed in this opening section, as a clue to personally meaningful images, symbols, and metaphors.

The second section of the interview moves from the general to the specific by asking the storyteller to describe in great detail eight *key events* in his or her story:

I am going to ask you about eight key events. A key event should be a specific happening, a critical incident, a significant episode in your past set in a particular time and place. It is helpful to think of such an event as constituting a specific moment in your life that stands out for some reason. Thus, a particular conversation you had with your mother when you were twelve years old or a particular decision you made one afternoon last summer might qualify as a key event in your life story. These are particular moments in a particular time and place, complete with particular characters, actions, thoughts, and feelings. An entire summer vacation—be it very happy or very sad or very important in some way—or a very difficult year in high school, on the other hand, would *not* qualify as key events, because these take place over an extended period of time. (They are more like life chapters.) For each event, describe in detail what happened, where you were, who was involved, what you did, and what you were thinking and feeling in the event. Also, try to convey the impact this key event has had in your life story and *what this event says about who you are or were as a person.* Did this event change you in any way? If so, in what way? Please be *very specific* here.

The eight key events are

1. *Peak experience:* A high point in the life story; the most wonderful moment in your life.

2. *Nadir experience:* A low point in the life story; the worst moment in your life.

3. *Turning point:* An episode wherein you underwent a significant change in your understanding of yourself. It is not necessary that you comprehended the turning point as a turning point when it in fact happened. What is important is that now, in retrospect, you see the event as a turning point, or at minimum as symbolizing a significant change in your life.

4. *Earliest memory:* One of the earliest memories you have of an event that is complete with setting, scene, characters, feelings, and thoughts. This does not have to seem like an especially important memory. Its one virtue is that it is early.

5. *An important childhood memory:* Any memory from your childhood, positive or negative, that stands out today.

6. *An important adolescent memory:* Any memory from your teenage years that stands out today. Again, it can be either positive or negative.

7. *An important adult memory:* A memory, positive or negative, that stands out from age twenty-one onward.

8. *Other important memory:* One other particular event from your past that stands out. It may be from long ago or recent times. It may be positive or negative.

I use the term *nuclear episodes* to refer to key events in a person's life story. These rich descriptive accounts provide invaluable information about dominant themes in your personal myth, as well as imagery and tone. Indeed, if I had but one question to ask a person in order to get a quick sense of who he or she is, I would probably ask the person to recall a peak experience from the past. I find that people are most articulate and insightful when talking about particular, concrete episodes in their lives. By contrast, discussions of general trends and abstract formulations are rarely as vivid or revealing of personality or identity. Therefore, you should focus considerable time and energy on each event recalled. Provide as much detail as possible. Work hard to comprehend the significance of the particular moment in the encompassing pattern of your overall life narrative. Be ready to entertain different and conflicting meanings of the same episode. The most significant nuclear episodes are implicitly endowed with the richest meaning networks.

In Chapter 3 and in Appendix 1 and 2, I talk about how the reconstruction of such key events from the past reveals the main thematic lines of agency and communion (power and love) in personal myth. In interpreting these accounts in your own life you should therefore be asking yourself what these episodes say about what you really want in your life. To what extent are you driven by power or love? More important, in what particular ways do your needs for power and love express themselves in the story? You must remember that your accounts of key events reflect autobiographical decisions that you have made. Rather than relate your story as a secretary objectively reports the minutes of a meeting, you have subjectively chosen to highlight specific events in your life as high points, low points, turning points, and so on. And you have chosen to disregard other events. Why does a teacher's simple compliment stand out so boldly in your memory of a very eventful childhood?

Why does the death of your father *not* stand out as the worst thing that ever happened in your life?

The interview moves from key events to *Significant People:*

> Every person's life story is populated by a few significant people who have a major impact on the narrative. These may include, but not be limited to, parents, children, siblings, spouses, lovers, friends, teachers, coworkers, and mentors. I want you to describe *four* of the most important people in your life story. At least one of these should be a person to whom you are not related. Please specify the kind of relationship you had or have with each person and the specific way he or she has had an impact on your life story. After describing each of these, tell me about any particular heroes or heroines you have in your life.

The third section of the interview provides an opportunity to describe in greater detail a few people in your life that you have probably already mentioned in the life-chapters and key-events sections. The significant people described may form the basis for the main characters, or imagoes, in your personal myth. Parents, friends, lovers, and so on may serve as prototypes (ideal models) of central imagoes, such as the caregiver, the healer, the warrior, and so on. Heroes and heroines are especially well suited for this narrative role. Or significant people may function to promote or hinder the development of a particular character in your life story. For example, a coach in high school may have encouraged you to work hard on your figure skating, helping you to develop an imago of the athlete. Or an older sister may have hindered the expression of your imago, the maker, through her constant criticism of your artwork as you were growing up. Again, your description of the most significant people in your life represents an autobiographical decision, indicative of the way in which you have defined who you are. You need to ask yourself why you chose the persons you chose, and why you chose to remember them in the way you have.

After spending a considerable amount of time on the past, the interview now moves to the *future script:*

> Now that you have told me a little bit about your past and present, I would like you to consider the future. As your life story extends into the future, what might be the script or plan for what is to happen next in your life? I would like you to describe your overall plan,

outline, or dream for your own future. Most of us have plans or dreams that concern what we would like to get out of life and what we would like to put into it in the future. These dreams or plans provide our lives with goals, interests, hopes, aspirations, and wishes. Furthermore, our dreams or plans may change over time, reflecting growth and changing experiences. Describe your present dream, plan, or outline for the future. Also, tell me how, if at all, your dream, plan, or outline enables you (1) to be creative in the future and (2) to make a contribution to others.

Under future script, you are given an opportunity to extend the story into the future chapters that you envision today. This part of the interview provides many different kinds of identity information. Like key events, it is especially sensitive to the revelation of motivational themes in the life story, as you are likely to fashion goals for the future that reflect your basic wants and needs in life. Future script may also provide a glimpse of the sense of an ending. Where is the story going? How will it get there from here? A good story integrates beginning, middle, and ending in terms of a plausible plot. Thus, temporal continuity is a major challenge in personal myth-making. It is at this point in the interview that you are likely to see how your vision of yourself for the future may or may not follow in a meaningful way from how you see yourself in the present and how you now see yourself in the past. Analyzed in conjunction with life chapters and key events future script therefore provides insights into your particular approach to personal historiography. Do you proceed according to a dynastic ontological strategy, with a good past giving birth to a good present and future? Do you adopt a compensatory strategy, where bad leads to good? Does the strategy work well? Does it make for a believable and vitalizing myth?

A third kind of information you may acquire from this part of the interview concerns your characteristic approach to generativity. The section asks you to consider how your plans for the future will enable you to be creative and to make contributions to others. As we saw in Chapter 9, to be generative is to generate (create or produce) a gift of the self and offer it (make a contribution) to the next generation. The best stories from our thirties and beyond incorporate generativity in explicit ways. Mature adults have specific plans about how they are going to make a creative contribution to the next generation. This is the place in the interview where these plans are typically revealed. Their failure to appear may indicate that this part of the life story requires some concerted work, that this is an area wherein the personal myth may need to be "improved" so as to enhance one's own life and the lives of others.

The fifth section pertains to stresses and problems:

> All life stories include significant conflicts, unresolved issues, problems to be solved, and periods of great stress. I would like you to consider some of these now. Please describe *two* areas in your life where at present you are experiencing at least one of the following: significant stress, a major conflict, or a difficult problem or challenge that must be addressed. For each of the two, describe the nature of the stress, problem, or conflict in some detail, outlining the source of the concern, a brief history of its development, and your plan, if you have one, for dealing with it in the future.

By the time you have reached this point in the interview, you have probably touched on one or two significant problems in your life. This section gives you an opportunity to consider two problems, stresses, or challenges in some detail and to outline strategies for addressing them. Information gleaned from this section sometimes involves internal battles between discordant characters in the life story. For example, the imago of the carefree escapist, whose origins reside in happy days of childhood, may find it difficult to flourish in the same story with the imago of the responsible caregiver. Therefore, this section may help to signal points of potential resolution in narrative for the future—issues and conflicts that need to be resolved in successive revisions of your personal myth. Be careful, however, not to overinterpret problems in terms of identity, or to inflate trivial problems into mythic proportions. Many life problems have little to do with identity per se but involve such everyday concerns as getting the car fixed, losing weight, or squabbling with one's boss. These problems may have a major impact on the quality of your everyday life—they may impact on happiness and satisfaction. But they may have little to do with your personal myth per se—that is, the meaning of your life. I will consider the distinction between happiness and meaning later in this chapter.

Moving now toward the interview's conclusion, it is time to consider *personal ideology:*

Now I will ask you a few questions about your fundamental beliefs and values. Please give some thought to each of these questions, and answer each with as much detail as you can. (1) Do you believe in the existence of some kind of God, deity, or force that reigns over or in some way influences or organizes the universe? Explain. (2) Please describe in a nutshell your religious beliefs. (3) In what ways, if any, are your beliefs different from those held by most of the people you know? (4) Please describe how your religious beliefs have changed over time. Have you experienced any periods of rapid change in your religious beliefs? Explain. (5) Do you have a particular political orientation? Explain. (6) What is the most important value in human living? Explain. (7) What else can you tell me that would help me understand your most fundamental beliefs and values about life and the world?

People vary widely in their responses to this section. For some especially philosophical people, this is their favorite part of the interview, and their responses may be quite lengthy. For people differently inclined, these questions may seem especially difficult. Their responses may be shorter and more tentative. I have found that once people realize that we are not simply talking about conventional religion and politics and that they may substitute such expressions as *spirituality, ultimate meanings, the good society,* and so on, they tend to become more comfortable, and open up more. As the storyteller in this section, you should remember that the ideological setting for your personal myth specifies how your beliefs and values are both similar to and different from those held dear by others. Many people are hesitant to talk about the "different from" part. They are too quick to suggest that what they believe is essentially the same as what they think everybody else believes. When pushed a bit, however, they often reveal understandings and perspectives in personal ideology that are quite distinctive, even unique. You should strive to articulate the distinctive characteristics of your ideological setting without losing sight of the fact that your identity is grounded in a social world wherein certain people share certain values.

The interview's last section asks you to take stock of what you have said by entertaining an overall *life theme:*

Looking back over your entire life story as a book with chapters, episodes, and characters, can you discern a central theme, message, or idea that runs throughout the text? What is the major theme of your life? Explain.

In the research interviews we have done, respondents are often quite insightful at this point in the session. After focusing unwavering attention on their life narrative for two hours or more, they are often able to capture part of the essence or central meaning of the myth in a pithy phrase or expression. In the context of our research, this is the only explicit opportunity that the respondent has to "analyze" the meaning of his or her words. The quick self-analysis at the end of the interview may serve as a springboard for the deeper psychological analyses that my associates and I will perform after we listen to the interview tape or read the transcript. For your purposes, however, the life-theme section provides an opportunity for an initial look back while prompting you to carry on your self-examination in future dialogues with the listener.

Identifying your personal myth should be seen as a life process. It cannot be fully achieved in a single interview. The questions I have posed should get you going. But don't stop with my questions. Plan to meet with your listener again. Follow up on interesting leads of the first interview. Make time to get to know yourself and to share yourself with the listener. The process is enjoyable in itself. And it promises to pay personal dividends in enhancing your understanding of the story you live by.

Living the Myth

The interview should help make conscious and explicit that which already exists implicitly, generally outside of your everyday awareness. I believe that coming to a conscious understanding of the details of your self-defining personal myth can markedly enrich your life and promote your development as a person. It is also a necessary first step in the process of changing your myth for the better. But you do not need to identify your self-defining personal myth—to bring it into full conscious awareness—in order to live according to it. Indeed, whether or not you choose to examine your myth explicitly, you have already been more or less successful in constructing a myth for yourself over the years, and shaping parts of your life around the myth you have constructed. You have already created, and continue to create, a story to live by. And you have been living by it all along.

Let us, then, consider the process of living the story from both a psychological and a social perspective. What does living the myth do for you? What does it do for society? From the standpoint of the individual's psychology, to live the myth is to provide your life with *meaning*—more so than with *happiness*. This is not to say that a personal myth exists to make you unhappy. Rather, it suggests that a personal myth functions first and foremost to provide life with meaning, unity, purpose. Happiness may follow, but in some cases it may not. From the standpoint of society, to live the myth is to connect to the grand narratives of your social world. Myths are created and lived in a social context. As a social participant, you are responsible for creating and living a personal myth in such a way as to commit your life to the generative agenda of humankind. Without this commitment, identity loses any trace of social responsibility and degenerates into trivia or narcissism.

It is common practice in popular psychology to suggest that all good things come together, in an undifferentiated gold mine of riches. From this popular point of view, to find meaning in life is to be happy, satisfied, fully functional, self-actualized, fulfilled, well-adjusted, mature, free of anxiety, liberated, enlightened, individuated, and saved. It is true that the definitions and connotations of these different terms overlap considerably. But we should also be aware of important distinctions. Indeed, empirical research reveals significant nuances in people's understandings of these terms and shows that for all the overlap, people tend to evaluate their lives on many different dimensions.[2] No single concept covers it all when you are considering the overall quality of a human life. Each concept is limited and qualified, and no psychological process or product can "do it all."

So it is with personal myths. There are two essential qualifications to underscore here. First, as important as it is, your personal myth is not implicated in everything you do. Much of your everyday behavior has little or nothing to do with your personal myth. What you wear to work, the conversation you have at breakfast, your striving to complete a project on time, an argument you have with your spouse, consuming one too many drinks at a college reunion—all of these behaviors and countless more may conceivably be irrelevant for the story you live by. To put it another way, living your story does not mean that your story is your life.

Academic psychologists make an important distinction between "personality" and "identity." Your personality is the entire motivational, attitudinal, and behavioral system that characterizes your adjustment to the world. It is made up of traits, values, motives, and many other processes and constructs. A subset of personality is the concept of identity, which (from my perspective) is the personal myth you construct to define who you are. All of your behavior connects up in one way or another to your personality as a product of traits, motives, and so on (inner personality characteristics) in interaction with your environment (outer situational characteristics). But only those behaviors and episodes in life that have significance for the question Who am I? are connected up with personal myth.

To take an example from my own life, driving to work this morning had nothing to do with my identity. It was not a self-defining act. Nor was the dinner party I attended last weekend, even though I had a very good time. But writing this book *is* implicated in my identity. It is very much a part of my personal myth, for it connects to my ideological setting, my generativity script, and an important imago of mine that we might simply call the professor. In a very real way, I am defining myself as I write this book. I am performing an act with consequences for identity and myth. The act is partly shaped by the myth I have now, and it will partly shape the myth I create for the future. I am sure that you can make the same kinds of distinctions in your own life.

People can drive themselves crazy looking for mythic meaning in everything they do. Life is too big to make everything meaningful for identity. While your unique personality traits may shape many of your daily activities, your identity becomes involved only during those moments or for those behaviors that promise further self-definition. Of course, it is sometimes difficult to know what those behaviors may be. A seemingly trivial conversation with a friend may, in retrospect, turn out to be an essential component of your personal myth, reconstructed later on as a turning point in your life story. In sum then, you should be aware that life may present many opportunities for living the personal myth, and for creating it anew. You should be ready for them; you should be open to opportunities in everyday life for personal mythmaking. But don't be overly vigilant. You can't make meaning out of everything.

A second qualification concerns the distinction between meaning and happiness. In his recent book, *Meanings of Life,* Roy Baumeister writes:

> Being happy is not the same as finding life meaningful, although there is some overlap. Perhaps the best way to state the relation is that a meaningful life seems necessary but not sufficient for happiness. It is possible for life to be meaningful but not happy. The life of a guerilla or revolutionary is often passionately meaningful but rarely a happy one. The reverse, however, is much less possible: Few people manage to be happy if their lives are empty and pointless.[3]

Research bears out Baumeister's suggestion. There is a slight tendency for people who report that they are relatively happy to say also that their lives are highly meaningful.[4] But the tendency is not a perfect relationship. Some people who feel that life is meaningful do not feel very happy. With less frequency, some people who feel happy do not report that life is very meaningful. In the latter case, it may be that some people do not feel that life *needs* to be meaningful. They may be content living in a world that provides them with creature comforts but for which no meaning can be discerned. In any case, personal mythmaking is a major mechanism for making life meaningful. Identity refers to meaning. Living the myth so that life is meaningful, unified, and purposeful may increase the chances of experiencing happiness and satisfaction in life. But it is no guarantee. Happiness is determined by many different forces and factors, some of which are within the person (personality) and some of which are in the environment.

To take it one step further, happiness is only one of many goals in human life. As Americans, we tend to see happiness as *the* ultimate life goal. After all, our nation was founded on the principles of "life, liberty, and the pursuit of happiness." Our tendency to underscore happiness runs the risk, though, of denigrating other equally worthy pursuits, like liberty for example. If it doesn't make us happy, then what good is it? we may ask. Why have a meaningful life if meaning doesn't assure happiness? One answer to these questions is to take Baumeister's point to heart: Meaning may not assure happiness, but it increases your chances of being happy. A second answer is to suggest that meaning is a good in and of itself, even if it doesn't directly contribute to your happiness. To justify everything in terms of happiness reduces human life to that of the animals. If the search for meaning is a unique feature of the human species, then it would seem advisable to consider meaning's merits on their own. Our lives are made meaningful by living our personal myths. The better our myths—the more vitalizing and meaningful our stories—the better our lives. Thus, meaning enriches and enhances our time on earth. It gives life a certain quality that happiness itself cannot assure. We should hope and strive to find happiness in the meanings we make through myth. But we would be naive to think that such strivings will always pay off.

It is common practice in popular psychology to place prime emphasis upon the self, over and against the social world. Bookstore shelves are brimming with *self*-help books. The implication is that selves need to be helped. The material and social world is too much for each of us. As individuals, we need support, inspiration, therapy, salvation, and the like. By contrast, books written to "help society" are typically considered to be "policy studies." They fall within the realms of sociology and economics. With few exceptions, they tend not to sell as well. The primacy of the self is equally apparent in the technical writings of research and academic psychology. Some critics have suggested that psychology encourages selfishness while neglecting the social good. In their influential book *Psychology's Sanction for Selfishness,* Michael and Lise Wallach identify what they call "the error of egoism" in psychological theory and therapy. They question whether it is ethical for psychologists to devote so much energy and thought to the glorification and actualization of the individual. They ask, "Should we always be looking out for Number One?"[5]

This is a book about the self, about how selves are made through narrative. A major message of the book, however, is that selves are made in a social context. The stories we live by have their sources within our own imaginations, in our personal experiences, and in the social world wherein we live and tell. Society has a stake in the stories we make. Not only does the social world contribute material for the construction of our personal myths, but the social world is also the beneficiary and the victim of the myths we live. From the standpoint of society and, indeed, the earth at large, each of us has a responsibility to live a myth that enhances the world we live in. Through our personal myths, we must make commitments to the people we know and love, to those we will never know but with whom we share today our planet's resources, and to those of future generations, the legacies of our collective generative efforts.

From the standpoint of society, then, a personal myth that promotes generative integration is a good myth. In Chapter 9, I suggested that we seek meaningful endings for our personal myths in the generativity scripts we fashion, especially at mid-life and beyond. The generativity script puts into narrative form our yearnings for agentic immortality and communal nurturance. We want to live forever, and we want to be needed. A healthy and humane society requires the enlightened translation of these internal desires into social action and commitment. People like Daniel Kessinger (the community activist), Shirley Rock (the madam turned minister), and Betty Swanson (the T-shirt lady) are living their personal myths in ways that promote the well-being of their social worlds. They have created good stories, and they are living according to them. Their personal search for unity and purpose in life is wedded to larger human struggles, for freedom and equality, for justice and enlightenment, for the progressive development of generations to come, for feeding the poor. As we face a world of shameless inequality and dwindling resources, we would do well to look to Daniel Kessinger, Shirley Rock, and Betty Swanson. Not so we can borrow their stories and make them our own. But so we can emulate their commitment to fashioning stories that bring both meaning to their own lives and hope for a troubled world.

Changing the Myth

How do people change? Literally thousands of books in psychology have been written on this central question.[6] Many of them speak directly to change in identity, which I construe as transformation in the personal myth. In presenting a theory of identity as a personal myth constructed in society, I am not aligning myself with any particular approach to psychotherapy, counseling, or any other domain within which people work to change themselves and others. I believe that therapists and counselors of many different stripes might benefit from adopting the literary metaphors and narrative perspectives I have presented in this book. I believe that people who wish to change their own lives would benefit as well, but not because I offer a particular program for change. Instead, I believe that the benefits I have to offer come mainly in self-understanding. In my own work as a researcher, I seek to identify myths rather than change them. This book should help you to identify your myth and to see more clearly how you are living the myth. Identifying your myth is an extremely valuable enterprise in and of itself. You don't need to change anything to be enriched and enlightened about yourself. But should you wish to change your myth, then identifying it is probably the necessary first step.

What is the second step? Unfortunately, neither I nor any other author can tell you this. While certain self-help books provide valuable advice for changing specific problems in your life (e.g., sexual dysfunction, alcoholism, codependency, divorce), identity is bigger, more encompassing, and somewhat more personalized than all of these things. Without knowing what your story is and how you have been living it, I cannot tell you how to change it for the better. The answer can only come from you and through your experience of your own particular world. I can, however, help you identify the kind of positive change that may be required. In general, there are two different kinds of progressive change in personal mythmaking.

The first kind of change is *developmental*. The word *development* connotes growth, fulfillment, maturation, moving ahead. Development is oriented toward the future. If you feel that your myth is stagnant, if you sense that you are not moving forward in life with purpose, if you believe that you are falling behind in some sense with respect to the growth of your personal identity, then what you are looking for is developmental change in personal myth. I have adopted an explicit developmental framework in organizing this book. Each concept in personal mythmaking is linked to a particular developmental period. For example, narrative tone has its origins in infant attachment; imagery originates in preschool play and imagination; motivational themes may be traced back to the elementary-school years; the ideological setting is laid down in adolescence; imagoes begin to form in early adulthood; the generativity script becomes more salient as we move into mid-life; narrative reconciliation is a challenge for mid-life and beyond. To discern the kinds of developmental changes that are required in your personal myth, you must first determine where you are within the developmental framework I have described.

If you are a young adult eager to fashion a niche for love and work in the world, you may need to explore the ideological setting you have consolidated to determine exactly what your most cherished beliefs and values are, so that they can be personified in the imagoes you are about to create. If you are forty-five years old and your children are about to leave home for college, then you might wish to examine the nature of your generativity script in order to explore ways in which your personal myth can enable you to generate new legacies for the future. In developmental change, you should be dealing with issues that are appropriate to your particular level of psychosocial development. You need to concentrate your identity work on that aspect of your story whose time is ripe—maybe over-ripe—for exploration and growth, so that you can move ahead in life with meaning and purpose.

Developmental change must be understood in the context of the six developmental trends in mythmaking I outlined in Chapter 4: coherence, openness, differentiation, reconciliation, generative integration, and credibility. The ideal personal myth—the good story to live by—gets high marks for all six of these criteria. But different criteria are more or less important at different stages of life.

The first two criteria—coherence and openness—form a dialectical tension in identity. If a personal myth is too coherent, then it will lack openness. If it is too open, it will be incoherent. Ideally, your personal myth should strike a balance between the two, but the balance is likely to be weighted differently at different points in development. For example, openness is generally to be valued over coherence during adolescence and very early adulthood. The consolidation of an ideological setting and the formulation of early imagoes require an openness to alternative possibilities in life. Erik Erikson has written that a major problem in identity development during this time is premature foreclosure—a tendency to cut off options in identity exploration and settle, prematurely, for an overly coherent (narrowly self-consistent) story of the self. By contrast, it would seem that the refinement and articulation of imagoes in your twenties and thirties require a good deal of coherence in one's personal mythmaking. At this time, too much openness to alternative ideological, occupational, and interpersonal possibilities may keep you from focusing on the home and work goals through which you articulate the characters in your myth. Whereas foreclosure, therefore, may be a major threat in adolescence, a chronic inability to make even provisional commitments to plans and goals in your twenties and thirties can keep you from formulating the kind of coherent personal myth that this period in the life cycle seems to call for. At mid-life, the pendulum may swing back again to openness as you seek to reconcile the conflicting imagoes that you have created with such care and conviction in your young-adult years.

A similar kind of dynamic may be identified for the criteria of differentiation and reconciliation. A mature personal myth should display many different parts and aspects. It should be richly differentiated. During your twenties and thirties, you may be focused on a number of different character lines in your personal myth. You may be articulating a host of important imagoes in your life story, providing each with greater and greater detail and characterization. During this time, you are probably not too concerned with reconciliation in your life story. In other words, it may be fine and developmentally appropriate to focus on different imagoes and pursuits that are, in some fundamental way, inconsistent with each other. Each of these requires room and freedom to express itself in the fullest manner. At mid-life, however, you may switch your attention in mythmaking from differentiation to reconciliation. Now it may be developmentally appropriate to search for unity and synthesis in the rich and conflicting imagoes you have formulated in earlier years. You may need to refashion the story in a way that brings the different characters together in some manner, or in a way that makes their oppositions even starker, so as to find unity and purpose in the dialectical contradictions of mid-life.

As you move from adolescence through young adulthood and into mid-life, generative integration becomes an increasingly important criterion in personal mythmaking. While coherence trades off with openness and differentiation trades off with reconciliation in personal mythmaking across the life cycle, generative integration has no worthy "opposite." It simply grows steadily in importance over time. It is a mild but noteworthy problem in identity if a twenty-five-year-old man has found little room in his personal myth for generativity; if he is thirty-five the problem is much more serious; if he is forty-five it is a tragic developmental failing.

Equally steady is the sixth criterion, credibility. But the importance of credibility in myth does not generally increase or decrease across the life span. In other words, whether you are a teenager or retired, the extent to which your personal myth is true to the facts of your life and your world is an important standard of its adequacy. At no point in the life span do we have the psychological or ethical license to create myths that are willful deceptions or fantastical lies. The good and mature personal myth is grounded in social and personal reality. It is what you have created from the real resources you have been given. Mature identity does not transcend its resources; it is true to its context. The myth and the mythmaker must be credible if we are to live in a credible world.

In sum, developmental change moves you forward in mythmaking as you construct, revise, and reconstruct your myth to make sense of new developmental issues and changing life circumstances. Although I have outlined some normative expectations for developmental change across the life span, you should realize that this or any other general sequence may not apply perfectly to you. Every person follows a unique path. You need to determine what is "on time" with respect to your own developmental trajectory. Some people become consumed with generativity issues in their early twenties. Others remain open to alternative ideologies throughout their adult lives. In addition, unscheduled and nonnormative life events can have a major impact on the mythmaking process. The death of a young husband will challenge a widow to remake her myth in ways that do not fit a standard developmental scheme. Winning the lottery can challenge you to change your identity, too.

The second kind of change is *personological*. I refer here to a more profound and difficult kind of identity transformation that is typically the stuff of intense, in-depth psychotherapy. This kind of change is oriented to the past rather than the future. The goal is not to move forward in development, but to go back and, in a sense, start over. The problem is not that your myth is stagnant. The problem is that your myth is no good. It doesn't work. Perhaps it never worked. Or perhaps it doesn't exist. There is no identity at all, no sense of self.

In personological change, you face the awesome task of creating yourself anew. Going back to Freud, psychoanalysts have urged their clients to explore the primitive, unconscious dynamics of the mind, rooted inexorably in early childhood experience and fantasy. Psychoanalysis aims to create a new self. From the standpoint of my theory of personal myths, the psychoanalytic exploration of the unconscious involves, among other things, the *search for new narrative material*. I have repeatedly said that even before we conceptualize our lives in terms of narrative—even as infants and young children—we are gathering material for the story we will someday construct. In psychoanalysis, the client symbolically returns to childhood in order to find new raw materials, new resources for the construction of the self. There is no buried identity, no hidden story waiting beneath the surface. We can never go back to the past to find the personal myth that has been waiting for us all along. The stories we live by are made, not found. But, with the assistance of a skilled therapist, we may be able to discover a more suitable tone, better imagery, and long-forgotten motivational themes in order to begin the arduous process of putting ourselves together again.

Let me end by saying that the changes you are seeking in your own identity are most likely developmental, rather than personological, in nature. Developmental change is less dramatic and is ushered in by problems that are somewhat less severe and less complicated than those facing the person who, in need of profound personological change, may feel completely shattered, empty, without narrative form. As in the case of personological change, psychotherapy may be helpful in promoting developmental change, too. But in many cases, it may not be necessary. Many people are able to modify, adjust, and transform their identities to meet new developmental demands and changing life circumstances in the contexts of their everyday personal and interpersonal lives. They get help in these matters from friends, lovers, spouses, parents, children, ministers, teachers, and even authors of books.

Beyond Story

Whither is fled the visionary gleam?

Where is it now, the glory and the dream?

—*William Wordsworth*

Our lives divide roughly into three phases: premythic, mythic, and postmythic. This book concerns itself with the first two. During the premythic era of infancy and childhood, we gather material for the stories we will someday construct. The origins of narrative tone, image, and theme may be traced to a time in our lives when we are not consciously concerned with finding meaning and purpose in life. It is a time before identity, in which we are unknowingly preparing for questions we cannot as yet understand. With the development of formal thought and the emergence of a historical perspective on the self, life begins to take on mythic proportions in our teenage years. In young adulthood, we consolidate an ideological setting for our personal myth, and we endeavor to fashion the right kinds of characters to play the main agentic and communal roles for the script. As we move into and through our mid-life years, we become more and more concerned with the sense of the story's ending. Through generativity, we are able to envision endings that give birth to new beginnings, extending the story line of our identity beyond the temporal confines of our stay on earth.

But what happens after that? Contemporary adults living in Western democracies can expect to live well into their seventies and eighties. For many people, these are years of good health and strong activity. What happens to personal myth and mythmaking after mid-life? Our conceptions of ourselves change across the life span, and we continue to modify how we see ourselves and our own lives even until our last days. Both positive and negative experiences, planned scenarios, and chance encounters may have a strong impact on how each of us understands who he or she is. Especially influential are changes in personal health and interpersonal losses through separation or death of loved ones. Any and all of these things may be incorporated into our personal myths, and their influences may be felt in changing tone, images, themes, setting, character, and endings. When it comes to our life stories, nothing is ever final. Things can always change.

Still, in some lives there seems to come a time when the main perspective on myth changes from "making" to "looking back on the making." The gerontologist Robert Butler speaks of a process of "life review" in later years.[1] According to Butler, a crucial psychological project for many elderly people is the concerted reflection upon the past in order to "settle accounts" one last time before death. Erik Erikson suggests that adults enter a final stage in old age wherein we look back upon our lives and confront the final psychosocial issue of "ego integrity vs. despair." For Erikson, ego integrity is the "post-narcissistic love of the human ego" and "the accrued assurance" of "order and meaning" that comes with "the acceptance of one's one and only life cycle as something that had to be and that, by necessity, permitted no substitutions."[2]

During the later years of life, our mythmaking may subside somewhat as we begin to review the myth we have made. It is now time to evaluate the story that has been produced. What Erikson describes as a "post-narcissistic" approach to life may mean, on one level at least, the attainment of a certain kind of distance from a personal myth and the process of making it. Ego integrity involves the eventual acceptance of that myth. As such, integrity stands in intriguing contrast to generativity. While in our generativity scripts we seek to create a gift to offer the next generation, the prospect of integrity in the postmythic years challenges us to receive "one's one and only" personal myth as if it were the gift. In old age, we become recipients of the myth we have generated from adolescence onward. To experience integrity is to accept the myth with grace. To experience despair is to reject the gift as unworthy.

What William Wordsworth calls the "glory and the dream" is contained in the personal myths we create to provide our lives with unity, meaning, and purpose. In his "Ode: Intimations of Immortality from Recollections of Early Childhood," Wordsworth begins by lamenting the passing of the joyous days of youth. The poem is concerned with the inevitable movement we must make out of life's prime time and into the winter of our decline. But Wordsworth ends with hope, strength, and grace. Although the past is gone for good, its goodness never leaves us:

> Though nothing can bring back the hour
> Of splendor in the grass, or glory in the flower;
> We will grieve not, rather find
> Strength in what remains behind;
> In the primal sympathy
> Which having been must ever be.[3]

For years and years, we struggle to create ourselves through myth. The struggle is necessary and good. It is the glory and the dream of human life. We are given but one opportunity to create a self and a world, and it is both our joy and our responsibility to make the most of that opportunity. Having taken up the challenge in all earnestness and vigor, we eventually let it go in our last, postmythic years. We accept in return the product of our strivings. We look back and cherish the personal myth with the faith that what we have done and what we have made are worthy gifts.

Agency and Communion

Throughout this book, I have identified agency and communion as two central themes in personal myths. In one way or another, most life stories are organized along the lines of agency and/or communion. I argued in Chapter 3 that motivational dispositions concerning agency and communion begin to coalesce in human personality around the time that elementary-school children begin to shift their attention in stories from image to theme. The origins of agentic motives for power and achievement and communal motives for intimacy may be traced back to the grade-school years. As we also saw in Chapter 3, the ideological settings we begin to construct in adolescence may be characterized in terms of the extent to which agency (power, achievement, independence, mastery, justice, etc.) or communion (love, intimacy, interdependence, responsibility, care, etc.) organize the beliefs and values a person holds dear. In Chapter 6, we took a close look at prototypes of agentic and communal imagoes as main characters in myth personifying power and love, respectively. We saw in Chapter 9 how agency and communion are both implicated in generativity, and how the personal myths of especially generative adults script a dynamic tension between these competing human desires. In what follows in Appendix 1, I supplement the discussion of agency and communion by providing some research background on these concepts as revealed in personality studies of human motivation.

Agency: The Path of Power and Achievement

While everybody desires to assert and expand the self to one extent or another, certain individuals seem to be exceptionally strongly disposed toward power, autonomy, mastery, and achievement. Some people have high levels of agentic traits. Their behavior exhibits an especially dominant and forceful style, compared to most other people. They tend to command great attention in social settings, to be "the life of the party," to exert substantial control over people and over their environments. Other people hold strong agentic values and beliefs. They cherish courage and valor as ultimate human virtues; they argue that all people should look out for themselves and act as "rugged individualists"; they tend to espouse strong beliefs in national defense, human independence, freedom over equality. Other people may express strong agency by attributing agentic qualities to themselves, articulating what some psychologists call an agentic self-schema, or self-concept. An agentic man or woman may describe himself or herself as especially dominant, assertive, achieving, independent, disciplined, and aggressive. These qualities are traditionally associated with the sex-role stereotype of masculinity.[1]

An especially agentic person is driven by recurrent desires for power and achievement. The power motive is a desire for feeling strong and having impact on the world. The achievement motive is a desire for feeling competent and doing things better than others do them. Power and achievement motives, although both agentic, differ from each other in important ways. Psychologists have developed sensitive ways of determining how "high" or "low" a person's power motive and achievement motive are. The measurement method involves analyzing the content themes in imaginative fantasies that people create when responding to ambiguous pictures, a method that goes by the name of the Thematic Apperception Test (TAT) in psychological research.[2] Over the past forty years, psychologists have conducted a large number of studies on power and achievement motivation in order to understand the manifestations, correlations, and origins of these two highly agentic dispositions in human lives.[3]

People who score high on the power motive appear to engage in behaviors that are consciously and unconsciously designed to increase their influence and impact on others and to promote their own prestige. Studies have shown that high power motivation is positively associated with (1) holding elected offices, (2) exerting oneself in an active and forceful way in small groups, (3) accumulating prestige possessions such as credit cards and sports cars, (4) taking large risks in order to gain visibility, (5) getting into arguments, (6) choosing occupations in which one strongly directs the behavior of others (such as executive, teacher, and psychologist), and among men only (7) impulsive and mildly aggressive behavior.[4]

A number of studies have shown that people who regularly adopt strong leadership roles or who rise to positions of high influence in organizations tend to score relatively high on power motivation. Some laboratory studies have looked more closely at how the person high in power motivation actually exerts impact in a leadership role. In one study, the researchers investigated how business students high in power motivation direct the behavior of others in group decision making.[5] Forty groups containing five students each met to discuss a business case study that concerned whether a company should market a new appliance. In each group, a leader was appointed. Half of the leaders had previously scored high in power motivation, as assessed on the TAT, and the other half had scored low. Observations of the group behavior indicated that students in the groups with the high-power-motive leaders tended to present fewer proposals for consideration, to discuss fewer alternative plans, and to show less moral concern about the activities of their hypothetical company, compared to students in groups with low-power-motive leaders. The researchers interpreted these findings to mean that leaders high in power motivation encourage "groupthink"—a form of hasty decision making characterized by diffusion of responsibility, failure to consider long-term ramifications, and domination by a single leader whose opinion goes unchallenged.

What about the personal lives of people high in power motivation? On this topic, intriguing sex differences have been found. Perhaps surprisingly, men do not consistently score higher than women on power motivation. However, high power motivation seems to be related to different patterns of love relationships for men and women.

In the case of men, high power motivation has been associated with greater dissatisfaction in marriage and dating relationships, less stability in dating, more sexual partners over time, and higher levels of divorce. For women, however, none of these negative outcomes has been observed as a function of power motivation. Rather, one study suggests that power motivation in women is positively associated with marital satisfaction.[6] Further, well-educated women high in power motivation tend to marry successful men.[7] It may be that because women are socialized, from childhood onward, to accept roles of caregiving in which they are responsible for others, a woman with high power motivation is likely to express the motive in more benevolent ways than is a man high in power motivation—ways that promote rather than undermine intimate relationships.[8]

In the realm of friendship, both men and women high in power motivation tend to understand their own friendship patterns in highly agentic terms. In one study I conducted with Steven Krause and Sheila Healy, we asked college students to keep track of the "friendship episodes" they engaged in over a two-week period of time.[9] We defined a friendship episode as any interaction with a friend lasting for at least fifteen minutes. We found that students who were high in power motivation reported a greater number of friendship episodes in which they interacted with a large group of friends (five friends or more at a time) compared to students who were low in power motivation. Presumably, more friends make for a larger audience for powerful behavior and self-display. Students high in power motivation reported that they characteristically adopted an active, assertive, or controlling role in friendship episodes. When with their friends, students high in power motivation typically reported adopting these behaviors: taking charge of a situation, assuming responsibility, making a point in an argument or debate, giving advice, making plans, organizing activities, attempting to persuade others, and, quite frequently, helping others.

"Helping one's friend" is a central activity in accounts of friendship provided by people high in power motivation. In a study in which I asked students to recall in detail the "greatest friendship you ever had," men and women high in power motivation overwhelmingly described specific incidents in which they and their best friend "grew closer" through helping or being helped.[10] For power-driven people, the proof of good friendship is the ability to come to the rescue of one's friend. As strong and dominant agents in the world, friends do things for each other. They perform powerful feats that may be remembered as agentic turning points in the story of a particular friendship. Friendships tend to dissolve via inappropriate assertion of power. Students high in power motivation remark that their greatest fear in friendships is that they and their friends will come into repeated conflict with each other. Consequently, they are careful to avoid conflicts, lest their own agentic strivings undermine the friendship.[11]

Whereas power suggests impact and prestige, achievement focuses more on competence, mastery, and "doing better." A large body of psychological research shows that people high in achievement motivation are especially concerned with effective performance in instrumental tasks—that is, tasks having to do with "things" rather than with "people." People high in achievement motivation tend to prefer and show high performance in tasks of moderate challenge that provide immediate feedback concerning success and failure; they tend to be persistent and efficient in many kinds of performance, sometimes cutting corners or even cheating a little in order to maximize productivity; they tend to exhibit high self-control and focus their energies on careful planning for the future; and they tend to be restless, innovative, and drawn toward change and movement.[12]

One of the most interesting lines of research on achievement motivation concerns how people who differ on this motive pursue careers and adapt to work settings. For many students, personal involvement in a career begins in college, where they take academic courses that are specially designed to prepare them for a certain career path. Research has shown that being high in achievement motivation does not necessarily guarantee high grades in college courses.[13] However, when the courses are perceived as directly relevant to their future careers, students high in achievement motivation earn higher grades than students low in achievement motivation. Furthermore, students high in achievement motivation appear to have more realistic career aspirations, adopting a levelheaded and pragmatic manner in career choice, settling on a path that is likely to offer optimal challenge and risk—not too much and not too little.[14]

A nationwide survey of American adults indicates that men high in achievement motivation report more job satisfaction, evaluate their jobs as more interesting, and prefer work to leisure, to a greater extent than do men low in achievement motivation.[15] (The same relations, however, have not been found for women.) Young men high in achievement motivation tend to be drawn to careers in business. Indeed, many domains of business are a good match for the achievement motive, in that they require that people take moderate risks, assume personal responsibility for their own performance, pay close attention to feedback in terms of costs and profits, and find new or innovative ways to make products or provide services. These hallmarks of entrepreneurship are precisely the same behavioral and attitudinal characteristics that laboratory studies have shown "belong" to persons high in achievement motivation. In this regard, studies of adult businessmen have tended to show a positive connection between achievement motivation and productivity. For instance, one study found that among small knitwear firms in England increases in investment, gross value of output, and number of workers in the firm over time were positively associated with the achievement motivation scores of the owners and top executives.[16] Following agricultural entrepreneurs over seven years, another study found that those with high achievement motivation showed greater gains in productivity over time than did those farmers scoring low on achievement motivation.[17]

In general, men and women do not differ in overall levels of achievement motivation.[18] Only a few studies, however, have examined the relation between achievement motivation and career striving in women. The results obtained are modestly consistent with the findings for men. For instance, college women scoring high in achievement motivation tend to pursue more challenging careers than do college women scoring low in achievement motivation.[19] Adolescent girls who plan to combine career and family tend to be higher in achievement motivation than girls who do not plan to pursue a career.[20] There is very little research, however, on the topic of entrepreneurship and achievement motivation among women in the business world.

Communion: The Path of Love and Intimacy

Like agency, communion may express itself in many different ways. Some people have high levels of communal traits. Their behavior exhibits an especially warm and friendly style, compared to most other people. They tend to be especially valued as friends, caregivers, and people who are able and willing to listen carefully and to offer gentle counsel. Other people hold very strong communal values and beliefs. They cherish love and compassion as ultimate human virtues; they argue that people should be responsible for each other and committed to expressing categorical love and affection; they tend to espouse strong beliefs in world peace, human interdependence, equality over freedom. Other people attribute communal qualities to themselves, articulating a communal self-schema or self-concept. A communal man or woman may describe himself or herself as especially warm, compassionate, responsible, loving, gentle, and nurturant. These qualities are traditionally associated with the sex-role stereotype of femininity.[21]

The most detailed scientific exploration of the communal side of human motivation in individual lives is my own work on intimacy motivation, described in my book *Intimacy: The Need to Be Close*. The intimacy motive is a recurrent desire for warm, close, and sharing interaction with other human beings. Like power and achievement motivation, individual differences in intimacy motivation may be assessed through analysis of imaginative fantasies that people compose in response to the TAT. Over the past thirteen years, my colleagues and I have conducted a number of studies examining the manifestations and correlations of intimacy motivation in human lives. The research supports the general proposition that people who score high in intimacy motivation are strongly oriented, in their behavior and their experience, to interpersonal communion.

People high in intimacy motivation are described by their friends and acquaintances as especially "loving," "sincere," "natural," and "appreciative," and are rated especially low on adjectives such as "self-centered" and "dominant."[22] In small groups, they tend to promote friendly relations and build group solidarity, sometimes at the expense of their own prestige and status.[23] Rather than dominate others, they prefer to surrender control in many interpersonal situations, adopting the role of the listener or the person who works behind the scenes to promote interpersonal harmony and goodwill. Over the course of a normal day, people high in intimacy motivation tend to spend more time thinking about other people and their relationships with them, to engage in more conversations with other people, and to experience high levels of joy and happiness in the presence of other people, compared to people low in intimacy motivation.[24] In conversations with others, they tend to show high levels of laughter, smiling, and eye contact—nonverbal behaviors indicative of positive sentiment and warm relationships with others.[25]

Intimacy motivation is associated with an especially communal friendship style.[26] Students high in intimacy motivation report many one-on-one kinds of friendship episodes in which they and one other friend spent time together, talking and sharing stories. They tend not to engage in many large-group friendship episodes. Students high in intimacy motivation tend to describe their friendship episodes as involving intensive sharing of personal information. Their descriptions of their "greatest friendship" underscore this idea. The high point of such a friendship usually involves a scene of intimate self-disclosure in which one friend shared a secret about him or herself that he or she had rarely told anybody before. In the eyes of the person high in intimacy motivation, the ideal friend is the person with whom you can share the most personal information, knowing that the friend will listen, accept, and never betray your confidence. Consequently, friendships fall apart when one friend betrays a trust, in breaking a promise, disclosing a secret to a third party, or failing to show the expected warmth and understanding to the other. Rather than conflict, high-intimacy people fear separation in their friendships. When people grow apart, they are no longer able to connect in warm and reciprocal ways. In their minds, friendship cannot survive a deterioration in intimacy.

Some recent research suggests that intimacy motivation may be implicated in health and psychological well-being. Many theories of personality and psychotherapy suggest that the capacity for intimacy is a hallmark of adjustment and maturity in life. In keeping with these theories, a study conducted by George Vaillant and myself shows a strong link between intimacy motivation, as assessed at around age thirty, and overall psychosocial adjustment determined seventeen years later, when the subjects were middle-aged.[27] In this study of men who graduated from Harvard College in the early 1940s, having high intimacy motivation ten years after graduation predicted later marital enjoyment and occupational satisfaction. In other words, those men who showed a strong concern, in their TAT fantasies, with warm and close relationships tended to adapt more successfully and happily to challenges faced in their marriages and at work.

In a nationwide study of more than twelve hundred adults, social psychologist Fred Bryant and I found that women high in intimacy motivation were relatively happy with their lives and satisfied with the various roles they played, as wife, mother, professional, etc., compared to women low in intimacy motivation. Men high in intimacy motivation reported less stress in their lives and less concern about ambiguities and uncertainties about the future.[28]

Research on intimacy motivation has shown fairly consistent sex differences, unlike studies of power and achievement. In general, women and girls tend to score slightly higher on intimacy motivation than men and boys.[29] While the difference is not overwhelming, it is rather consistent. Therefore, while there are many highly intimate men, and many women with low scores in intimacy motivation, in the average scores of men and women as groups women tend to have higher scores. While we do not know precisely why this difference appears, many reasonable explanations can be offered, ranging from possible biological differences between the sexes to pervasive cultural differences concerning how we expect men and women to act, think, and feel.[30]

What is the relation between intimacy and love? While both of these concepts may be seen as facets of human communion, the two are not exactly the same. Intimacy refers mainly to the sharing aspects of human relationships. To be intimate is to share one's inner self with another. Through sharing, people come to know each other better, and to care for each other. The ideal model of intimacy is what the philosopher Martin Buber has described as the "I-Thou" relation. In an I-Thou experience, two people focus intensively and unswervingly on each other, sharing their innermost thoughts and feelings but remaining separate beings in the process. We do not "merge" or "unite" with other people in intimacy. Rather, the "I" confronts the "Thou," and in the confrontation each becomes enriched through relation. Buber describes the experience well:

> When I confront a human being as my Thou and speak the basic word I-Thou to him, then he is no thing among things nor does he consist of things. He is no longer He or She, a dot in the world grid of space and time, nor a condition to be experienced and described, a loose bundle of named qualities. Neighborless and seamless, he is Thou and fills the firmament. Not as if there were nothing but he; but everything else lives in his light.[31]

Intimacy improves love, but it is not the same thing as love. Love appears to be more complex than intimacy. For one thing, there appear to be many different kinds of love, whereas intimacy seems to have rather a singular quality. For another, experiences of love appear to involve many different elements, some of which may contradict each other. Intimacy often is one of those elements. In other words, a loving relationship should be one in which partners are able to share their innermost selves with each other. But there is likely to be more to love than that. In erotic love, for instance, lovers desire to merge into each other as one ("fusion"), to view each other as perfect and their relationship as romantically heroic ("idealization"), and to possess the other as one's own ("jealousy").

Intimacy, fusion, idealization, and jealousy are four important components in erotic love. Yet the four may sometimes work at cross purposes as well. Lovers want to possess each other (jealousy), but they also want to open up to each other and share their innermost selves (intimacy). Yet how can they do both to the fullest? To own the other is to treat the other like an object, which will likely ruin intimacy; one cannot share equally with an owned object. To idealize the other is to overlook many less-than-perfect qualities that are part of the other's essence, again undermining intimacy. And how can one lover worship the other and fuse with the other at the same time? If two lovers "become one," then worshiping the other becomes a form of narcissism. Erotic love is driven by many masters. No wonder poets have looked upon it as a "divine madness" that is out of our control.

Beyond erotic love, we may identify at least three other kinds of love, each of which may involve intimacy in one way or another.[32] The humblest and most widely diffused form of love is affection, or what the ancient Greeks called *storge*. Affection is the form of love parents show their children and all of us show to people with whom and to things with which we are very familiar. Affection is an especially gentle, natural, and unassuming form of love that grows stronger over time. While intimacy may be an important part of affection, it does not appear to be essential to the experience. One can feel great affection for another and yet not need to share the self with that object of affection. A parent can feel tremendous affection for a newborn infant, but little by way of intimacy would be expected while the infant is very young.

A second form of love is friendship, or what the ancient Greeks called *philia*. Ideally, this is a rational and tranquil form of love between equals. Two friends are united by a shared truth or common interest. Intimacy would appear to be especially instrumental in enriching bonds of friendship as friends come to know each other better and to care for each other more strongly through the I-Thou kinds of sharing described by Buber. Philia also involves admiration for the friend. Good friends admire qualities in each other, sometimes seeing themselves, or what they would like themselves to be, in their friends.

Finally, love may come in the form of charity, or what the ancient Greeks termed *agape*. Agape is unconditional and selfless love for all humanity. It is the least conditional, selective, and natural of the four loves. But it is also the form of love that some theologians and poets have described as ideal and divine. Selfless love for all humankind is, in theory, an ultimate form of communion. In agape, the self becomes one with all others, and the welfare of all becomes the welfare of the one. Agency is dashed, for the self no longer needs to assert, protect, and expand itself over and against the other. In a sense, the self has become identified with the other.

Nuclear
Episodes

The remembrance of things past is highly selective, and it involves substantial reconstruction. There is no objective way of recording human lives. Experience is inherently subjective. As adults, exactly what we remember from a given chunk of our childhood years is a complex product of actual events, our state of mind at the time the events occurred, our state of mind at the time we come to remember the events, and the particular meaning we have chosen to ascribe to the childhood events in the context of our own adult lives.[1]

For example, consider one particular event that you are likely to remember quite clearly if you are over the age of thirty-five. Most people who were of school age or older in the early 1960s remember something of the afternoon of November 22, 1963.[2] As I recall it, the day began as might any gray and chilly weekday in late autumn, for the boys and girls in the fourth grade of Pittman Square Elementary School. The morning was uneventful. We said the Pledge of Allegiance and sang "My Country, 'Tis of Thee." Sometime around noon, we started our artwork with Miss Porter. In the middle of our lesson, I clearly remember that Mr. Damascos, the school principal, walked into the classroom and turned on a radio. Class stopped, and we all listened to the report from Dallas that President John F. Kennedy had been shot. We sat in silence, knowing that something big was happening. The principal had never before interrupted class in such a sudden fashion.

With class effectively suspended, we were free to sit in our seats and talk with our neighbors. We chattered excitedly about who might have shot the president. We wondered aloud what the term *critical condition* meant; it did not sound hopeful. A couple of kids were certain the president would die and asked the teacher what would happen. She told us that the vice president would assume office. We did not know who the vice president was. Some kids thought it was probably Richard Nixon, since he had finished second in the 1960 election. Failing to understand the gravity of the situation, most of us were mildly confused and excited. Only later did many of us feel pain, anger, and the despair of loss. But a few children seemed genuinely sad at the time, even before we learned that John Kennedy had died. Mary Lee Walters sat two rows to my left. She put her head down on her desk and cried bitterly. She kept saying that she wished she had been shot instead.

Why is this memory so vivid in my mind? Cognitive psychologists Roger Brown and James Kulik asked the same question in research they conducted in the mid-1970s.[3] Brown and Kulik asked eighty American men and women, ranging in age from twenty to fifty-four, to describe their memories of certain key events in recent American history. All but one of the respondents reported a "flashbulb memory" of the moment they learned of the assassination of John F. Kennedy. The researchers defined a flashbulb memory as an especially vivid and detailed recollection of a particular event in one's life. Like a photograph, the memory captures forever the concrete experience of the happening, and what he or she was doing, thinking, and feeling at the moment the flash went off. Unlike a photograph, however, the flashbulb memory is selective. I remember Miss Porter, the principal, and Mary Lee Walters most clearly; I cannot remember who was sitting right next to me in class, what I was wearing, or how much time elapsed between learning of the shooting and the death.

Another psychologist offers a different interpretation of the memory. According to Ulric Neisser, the Kennedy assassination is not akin to a flashbulb picture but is rather a "life-history benchmark."[4] Over the years, I and others of my generation have come to understand the momentous nature of November 22, 1963, argues Neisser. We have rehearsed and replayed the event in our minds. Over time, the event has become etched in memory as one of "the places where we line up our lives with the course of history itself and say, 'I was there.' "[5]

I think that Neisser is right. Certain events from our past take on extraordinary meaning over time as their significance in the overall story of our lives and times comes to be known. In a sense, then, our current situation in life and our anticipation of what the future will bring partly determine what we remember and how we remember it. Therefore, the flashbulb metaphor is all wrong. The past is not recorded in objective detail. It is constructed by subjective human beings. And human beings may indeed get some of the facts "wrong." For instance, although I remember Mr. Damascos breaking into the classroom, Mr. Damascos could not have done so—he was the principal at Kuny School, where I attended the second and third grade, and not Pittman Square, where I was the day of the assassination. I don't remember who the principal of the latter school was. In some of the details of the day, my memory is inaccurate. No flashbulb went off at the time. But in retrospect, the event has assumed great prominence. In response, I have unconsciously put together pieces of autobiographical material into a vivid scene that is probably more or less accurate in its global and emotional contours but with some errors in fact.

In my own life story, I believe that the Kennedy assassination has the added significance of symbolizing a loss of innocence and a growing awareness of the complexities of the world. Kennedy's administration has been characterized as a Camelot by some. For me, the first few years of grade school also had a Camelot quality. It was not until fourth grade that I began to fear the foul-mouthed bullies in the classroom, and that I became painfully self-conscious of my gift for getting good grades, which was just then beginning to cause peer resentment. It was in fourth grade that a girl first said I was conceited. It seems as if it was around this time that I began to make my first enemies, as well as my first close friends. As I remember it, my world was just beginning to encompass things that were big and dangerous—gallant presidents being gunned down, schoolboys being beaten up, big people, as well as little kids, hating each other.

It is probably fair to say that November 22, 1963, didn't directly change me. But I believe that the event has come to symbolize changes that were occurring in my own life. At least that is how I see it now. That is how this part of my story reads, for the time being.

As we begin to adopt a historical perspective on the self in adolescence and young adulthood, we select and reconstruct those scenes from our past that are the climaxes of different acts of the life story. I call these scenes *nuclear episodes*.[6] These past episodes represent our subjective memories of particular events, in particular times and places, which have assumed especially prominent positions in our understanding of who we were and, indeed, who we are. Nuclear episodes may include, but are not limited to, high points, low points, and turning points in our narrative accounts of the past.

Some nuclear episodes suggest continuity in the self, whereas others suggest change. A nuclear episode of continuity might illustrate within a narrow narrative compass a consistent trait or characteristic. A woman who sees herself as a faithful friend to people throughout her life may remember any number of incidents in which she provided good counsel. Particularly vivid incidents become nuclear episodes in her personal myth. Thus, a nuclear episode may serve as narrative proof that "I am what I am." Or it may provide a narrative explanation for how a personal characteristic began to express itself. For example, a nursing student traces her ambivalent fascination with medical settings to a frightening childhood experience:

> My earliest memory involves a feeling of panic. I was playing in the living room of our old house and I overheard my mother on the telephone scheduling a doctor's appointment for me. I can remember trying to figure out when the date was and plotting how to avoid going. (I was going to hide in the closet.) I remember starting to cry when my mother came out of the kitchen and refusing to tell her what was wrong. I don't remember why I was so terrified of going to the doctor, but I always have been. What's funny about the whole thing is that I'm in nursing now. Someday some little kid will be scared of me.[7]

Other kinds of nuclear episodes symbolize personal change, or transformation. Many people describe dramatic turning points in which they came to a new understanding of self, or experienced a major change in their lives. The following is the answer a forty-three-year-old woman provided when asked to describe in written form a major turning point in her life:

> A New Year's Eve several years ago, my husband and I were at home with our two daughters and a friend/coworker's daughter. We adults had been invited to a party. Sam and Barbara left Amanda with us. My husband didn't want to go to the party, but he wanted me to go. I was tired, lonely, scared; I needed to feel wanted, needed, loved. He became angrier with me. We waited for Sam and Barbara to come for Amanda. They arrived around four A.M. My husband was so cold, so angry and distant. He wouldn't talk to me, be in the same room with me. I felt so defeated, abandoned, rejected. I felt that I had to do something, talk to someone because this was a horrible, horrible way to live. This was when I decided to go for help—wherever, anywhere, but professional help because I knew life could be better. The next day I talked to two women friends who urged me to seek out counseling, with or without my husband. With this vote of confidence I did. It was one of the healthiest moves I ever made. It's been several years now. Things are better, but the future is still a bit of a mystery. I feel worlds better; able to live life in a healthier, happier way.

Nuclear episodes often reveal central thematic lines in identity. The superordinate themes of agency and communion run through many accounts of nuclear episodes of continuity and of change. Therefore, narrative accounts of nuclear episodes are windows into the organization of human desire. Agentic needs for power and achievement and communal needs for love and intimacy are expressed clearly in many accounts of life-story high points, low points, and turning points. And as might be expected, research that I and my colleagues have conducted over the past ten years suggests that people who have a strong need for power tend to construct life stories in which themes of agency predominate, whereas those high in intimacy motivation underscore themes of communion.[8]

People with strong power motivation tend to remember key events from their past in which the following four agentic story motifs frequently appear:

1. *Strength/Impact:* A character strives to be a powerful agent by either (a) attaining or trying to attain a sense of enhanced

297

physical, mental, emotional, or moral strength; or (b) having or trying to have a strong impact on other people.

2. *Status/Recognition:* A character strives to attain a high status or position, seeks to be praised or granted recognition, acts in order to become prestigious or to be considered central or important.

3. *Autonomy/Independence:* A character strives for a sense of autonomy, independence, self-sufficiency, separation, freedom, emancipation, or self-control.

4. *Competence/Accomplishment:* A character strives for success in achieving goals, meeting standards of excellence, performing in a competent manner, and in being efficient, productive, and effective.

People with a strong need for intimacy tend to recall nuclear episodes characterized by these four communal motifs:

1. *Love/Friendship:* A character experiences positive emotions (love, liking, happiness, excitement, peace, etc.) as the result of an interpersonal relationship.

2. *Dialogue/Sharing:* A character experiences mutual communication with another person, as in a good conversation.

3. *Care/Support:* A character cares for or is cared for by another character, involving the providing or receiving of aid, assistance, help, comfort, support, or therapy.

4. *Unity/Togetherness:* A character experiences a sense of unity, harmony, synchrony, togetherness, or solidarity with other people or, indeed, with the world as a whole.[9]

In addition to providing clues about recurrent themes in personal myths, certain nuclear episodes may also signal the emergence or development of a particular life-story character. A man high in power motivation may relate a series of nuclear episodes starring the warrior. In each of these events, he figuratively (or in some cases literally) goes to war. He repeatedly battles various forces and foes. He describes his actions in martial terms. There are battles, skirmishes, weapons, assaults, alliances, crusades, peace treaties, demilitarized zones, truces, prisoners, campaigns, tactics, defenses, fronts, winners, and losers. The rhetoric, the action, and the characterization in each of the episodes suggest that in these events the man acted, thought, and felt in the guise of the warrior. The man need not claim to actually be a warrior. His "warrior" is simply one imago among many others. Therefore, the warrior is one of the things the man is, or has been, in his life story. It is one of the central characters in his personal myth. His story likely has other central characters, as well.

Introduction

1. The sharing of the self with another is the hallmark of interpersonal intimacy. To be intimate with another means to share one's innermost self. The desire for intimacy with another is a universal human need, though people differ markedly with respect to how salient or strong this particular need is for them at any given point in life. Indeed, the relative strength of a person's need for intimacy can be measured through analyzing the person's imaginative fantasies, a method I have developed and refined in my own psychological research. I will talk briefly about my own empirical work on the need for intimacy, or what I have called the "intimacy motive," later in this book. A full treatment of this work appears in McAdams, D.P. (1989). *Intimacy: The need to be close.* New York: Doubleday.

2. For example, see Bolen, J.S. (1984). *Goddesses in everywoman: A new psychology of women.* New York: Harper & Row, & Bolen, J.S. (1989). *Gods in everyman: A new psychology of men's lives and loves.* New York: Harper & Row.

3. Pearson, C.S. (1989) *The hero within: Six archetypes we live by.* New York: Harper & Row, p. 24.

4. Erikson, E.H. (1982). *The life cycle completed.* New York: W.W. Norton. See also Erikson, E.H. (1963). *Childhood and society* (2nd Ed.). New York: W.W. Norton.

5. Most relevant articles and chapters: McAdams, D.P. (1982) Experiences of intimacy and power: Relationships between social motives and autobiographical memory. *Journal of Personality and Social Psychology,* 42, 292–302. McAdams, D.P. (1984) Love, power, and images of the self. In C.Z. Malatesta and C.E. Izard (Eds.), *Emotion in adult development* (pp. 159–174). Beverly Hills, CA: Sage Publications. McAdams, D.P. (1985). The "imago": A key narrative component of identity. In P. Shaver (Ed.), *Self, situations, and behavior: Review of personality and social psychology* (Vol. 6, pp. 115–141). Beverly Hills, CA: Sage Publications. McAdams, D.P. (1987)

A life-story model of identity. In R. Hogan and W.H. Jones (Eds.), *Perspectives in personality* (Vol. 2, pp. 15–50) Greenwich, CT: JAI Press. McAdams, D.P. (1989). The development of a narrative identity. In D. Buss and N. Cantor (Eds.), *Personality psychology: Recent trends and emerging directions* (pp. 160–174). New York: Springer-Verlag. McAdams, D.P. (1990). Unity and purpose in human lives: The emergence of identity as a life story. In A.I. Rabin, R.A. Zucker, R.A. Emmons, and S. Frank (Eds.), *Studying persons and lives* (pp. 148–200) New York: Springer. McAdams, D.P. (1991). Self and story. In R. Hogan (Ed.), *Perspectives in personality* (Vol. 3A, pp. 133–159). London: Jessica Kingsley. McAdams, D.P., Ruetzel, K., & Foley, J.M. (1986) Complexity and generativity at midlife: A study of biographical scripts for the future. *Journal of Personality and Social Psychology*, 50, 800–807. Van de Water, D., & McAdams, D.P. (1989). Generativity and Erikson's "belief in the species." *Journal of Research in Personality*, 23, 435–449.

6. McAdams, D.P. (1985). *Power, intimacy, and the life story: Personological inquiries into identity*. New York: The Guilford Press.

Chapter 1

1. The name Margaret Sands is a pseudonym. In order to assure anonymity, I have made up all of the names used in this book for subjects who participated in research studies. In addition, particular details of the subjects' lives, such as birthplaces and other identifying information, have been altered somewhat in some cases, again in order to assure anonymity.

2. Social scientists have written at length about the strengths and weaknesses of the one-on-one interview as a research strategy. While the interview enables the researcher to gain a great deal of open-ended information that cannot be obtained in any other way, one must remember that the quality of that information is a function of the kind of human relationship that the subject and interviewer have established. Personal information is divulged and received as part of a complex human interaction; the interviewer can in no way be seen as a passive "tape recorder" of objective reality. Rather, knowledge is collected in a context of interpersonal subjectivity, even under the most standardized interview conditions. Knowing this, the interviewer is still committed to discovering as much as he or she can about who the person is outside of the given interview itself. We assume that there is valid and important information to be gleaned from the interview, despite its subjective nature. A less sanguine and more skeptical perspective on life-history interviewing is offered in Wiersma, J. (1988). The press release: Symbolic communication in life-history interviewing. In D.P. McAdams and R.L. Ochberg (Eds.), *Psychobiography and life narratives* (pp. 205–238). Durham, NC: Duke University Press.

3. We employed a popular self-report measure called the Bem Sex Role Inventory (BSRI). This inventory contains sixty adjectives and adjective phrases, and for each the subject is asked to rate the item on a 7-point scale, ranging from a rating of 1 ("never or almost never true") to 7 ("always or almost always true"). One third of the items refer to attributes commonly associated with masculinity (e.g., "self-reliant," "assertive," "aggressive," "dominant"), another third refer to attributes commonly associated with femininity (e.g., "affectionate," "yielding," "warm," "loves children"), and the final third refer to generally desirable attributes that are

not typically associated with either masculinity or femininity (e.g., "helpful," "happy," "adaptable," "truthful"). While men typically score higher in "masculinity" and women in "femininity," many people give high ratings to adjectives of the opposite gender. The masculinity and femininity scales of the BSRI are independent. Therefore, a person may score high on both, indicating a position of what Bem and others have called "psychological androgyny." There is some research evidence to suggest that seeing oneself as highly psychologically androgynous can be adaptive in certain situations and can make for more flexible styles of interacting with others and solving life's problems. Sources: Bem, S.L. (1974). The measurement of psychological androgyny. *Journal of Consulting and Clinical Psychology*, 42, 155–162. Bem, S.L. (1987). Gender schema theory and the romantic tradition. In P. Shaver and C. Hendrick (Eds.), *Sex and gender: Review of personality and social psychology* (Vol. 7, pp. 251–271). Beverly Hills, CA: Sage Publications. Cook, E.P. (1985). *Psychological androgyny.* New York: Pergamon Press.

4. The measure employed is the Thematic Apperception Test (TAT), a standard procedure in personality research in which a subject is asked to tell or write a short imaginative story in response to each of a small set of ambiguous pictures. The measure has been used in many scientific studies of individual differences in human motivation. Stories are subjected to rigorous content-analysis procedures in order to arrive at scores on such personality constructs as "achievement motivation," "intimacy motivation," and "power motivation." Some of this research is described in Chapter 3 and Appendix 1. Major sources: Atkinson, J.W. (Ed.) (1958). *Motives in fantasy, action, and society.* Princeton, NJ: D. Van Nostrand. McAdams, D.P. (1980). A thematic coding system for the intimacy motive. *Journal of Research in Personality*, 14, 413–432. McAdams, *Power, intimacy, and the life story.* McAdams, *Intimacy: The need to be close.* McClelland, D.C. (1985). *Human motivation.* Glenview, IL: Scott, Foresman. Murray, H.A. (1943). *The Thematic Apperception Test: Manual.* Cambridge, MA: Harvard University Press. Stewart, A.J. (Ed.) (1982). *Motivation and society: Essays in honor of David C. McClelland.* San Francisco: Jossey-Bass. Winter, D.G. (1973). *The power motive.* New York: The Free Press.

5. A "story grammar" is the implicit set of rules determining what a story is and how it works. A "story schema" is a particular person's implicit understanding of what a story grammar is. Research on children's understanding of stories suggests that by the time a child is six years of age, he or she has a very well developed story schema. Thus, from an early age onward we expect stories to follow certain conventional rules. When stories violate these conventions, they may seem odd or confusing, or not even stories at all. A number of studies have shown that adults and children more easily remember stories that have canonical form (that is, contain the appropriate story-grammar constituents in the correct order) than those missing a constituent or those in which constituents are mixed up. When recalling stories originally presented in noncanonical form, adults and children frequently convert them to canonical form by rearranging elements that were mixed up, and/or inventing new elements as substitutes for those that were missing in the original story. Sources: Applebee, D.N. (1978). *The child's concept of story.* Chicago: University of Chicago Press. Mandler, J.M. (1984). *Stories, scripts, and scenes: Aspects of schema theory.* Hillsdale, NJ: Lawrence Erlbaum.

6. Mandler, Stories, scripts, and scenes. See also Trabasso, T., Secco, T., & Van Den Broek, P. (1984). Causal cohesion and story coherence. In H. Mandl, N.L.

Stein, and T. Trabasso (Eds.), *Learning and comprehension of text*. Hillsdale, NJ: Lawrence Erlbaum.

7. Some scholars insist that the essence of a story is not so much its "grammar" or internal structure but the extent to which it is able to evoke a particular emotional reaction in the person who reads, hears, or sees the story. Three emotions that are commonly evoked by stories are suspense, surprise, and curiosity. Source: Brewer, W.F., & Lichtenstein, E.H. (1982). Stories are to entertain: A structural-affect theory of stories. *Journal of Pragmatics*, 6, 473–486.

8. Bird, S.E., & Dardenne, R.W. (1988). Myth, chronicle, and story: Exploring the narrative qualities of news. In J.W. Carey (Ed.), *Media, myths, and narratives: Television and the press* (pp. 67–86). Newbury Park, CA: Sage Publications.

9. Sources on the primacy of story in human experience: Howard, G.S. (1989). *A tale of two stories: Excursions into a narrative psychology*. Notre Dame, IN: University of Notre Dame Press. Landau, M. (1984). Human evolution as narrative. *American Scientist*, 72, 262–268. Sarbin, T.R. (Ed.). (1986). *Narrative psychology: The storied nature of human conduct*. New York: Praeger.

10. Forster, E.M. (1954). *Aspects of the novel*. San Diego, CA: Harcourt Brace Jovanovich.

11. Rouse, J. (1978). *The completed gesture: Myth, character, and education*. New Jersey: Skyline Books.

12. Jerome Bruner (1990). *Acts of meaning*. Cambridge, MA: Harvard University Press.

13. Ibid.

14. Ibid.

15. Ricoeur, P. (1984). *Time and narrative* (Vol. 1). Chicago: University of Chicago Press, p. 3. (Translated by K. McLaughlin and D. Pellauer.)

16. Robert Coles has written eloquently of the use of stories in college teaching. Students are drawn to stories, Coles argues, because it is through stories that they are enlightened as well as entertained. Stories are the main vehicles by which we learn the important lessons in life. In ways that a teacher's lecture on criminal law or a diagram of the human digestive system can never approach, stories may become central parts of our lives, as we hear in this striking excerpt from one of Coles's classes: " 'Who is this Stecher?' a student of mine at Harvard Business School asked, referring to the central figure in William Carlos Williams' trilogy, an immigrant who eventually rises high socially and economically. The student— to our fascination in that class—was intent not only on an intellectual summary. 'He's a mass of words, I suppose—what we read in a novelist's book. But to me Stecher is—oh, now, part of me! What do I mean? I mean that he's someone; he's a guy I think of. I picture him and can hear him talking. And he looks different to each of us, and the way he talks is different for each one of us, because each of us has our own accent. He's inside us, and so is Gurlie his wife. I can see him walking, or working, or climbing those stairs to his apartment, or eating—and listening to his wife, as she pushes him to get out there and climb the ladder. Williams' words have become my images and sounds, parts of me. You don't do that with theories. You don't do that with a system of ideas. You do it with a story, because in a story—oh, like it says in the Bible, the word becomes flesh.' " From Coles, R. (1989). *The call of stories: Teaching and the moral imagination*. Boston: Houghton Mifflin, p. 128.

17. Bettelheim, B. (1976). *The uses of enchantment: The meaning and importance of fairy tales.* New York: Alfred A. Knopf.

18. Kushner, H. (1981). *When bad things happen to good people.* New York: Avon.

19. Jay, P. (1984). *Being in the text: Self-representation from Wordsworth to Barthes.* Ithaca, NY: Cornell University Press.

20. Roth, P. (1988). *The facts: A novelist's autobiography.* London: Penguin.

21. Ibid, pp. 184–185.

22. Shafer, R. (1981). Narration in the psychoanalytic dialogue. In W.J.T. Mitchell (Ed.), *On narrative* (pp. 25–49). Chicago: University of Chicago Press. Spence, D.P. (1982). *Narrative truth and historical truth: Meaning and interpretation in psychoanalysis.* New York: W.W. Norton.

23. Marcus, S. (1974). Freud and Dora: Story, history, and case history. *Partisan Review,* 41, 12–23, 89–108.

24. Bascom, W. (1984). The forms of folklore: Prose narratives. In A. Dundes (Ed.), *Sacred narrative: Readings in the theory of myth* (pp. 5–29). Berkeley, CA: University of California Press.

25. Simonson, H.P. (1971). *Strategies in criticism.* New York: Holt, Rinehart and Winston.

26. Levi-Strauss, C. (1969). *The raw and the cooked: Introduction to a science of mythology* (Vol. 1). New York: Harper & Row.

27. This argument has also been made by David Feinstein in his interesting work on personal mythologies in psychotherapy, dream interpretation, and actualization of human potential: Feinstein, D. (1979). Personal mythology as a paradigm for a holistic public psychology. *American Journal of Orthopsychiatry,* 49, 198–217. Feinstein, D., & Krippner, S. (1988). *Personal mythology: The psychology of your evolving self.* Los Angeles, CA: Jeremy P. Tarcher.

28. Campbell, J. (1949). *The hero with a thousand faces.* Princeton, NJ: Princeton University Press, p. 11.

Chapter 2

1. Bowlby, J. (1969). *Attachment and loss.* Vol. 1. Attachment. New York: Basic Books.

2. Svejda, M.J., Pannabecker, B.J., & Emde, R.N. (1982). Parent-to-infant attachment: A critique of the early "bonding" model. In R.N. Emde and R.J. Harmon (Eds.), *The development of attachment and affiliative systems* (pp. 83–94). New York: Plenum Press.

3. The literature on mother-infant attachment is voluminous. Here are a few of the more noteworthy references: Ainsworth, M.D.S., Blehar, M.C., Waters, E., & Wall, S. (1978). *Patterns of attachment.* Hillsdale, NJ: Lawrence Erlbaum. Bowlby, *Attachment.* Egeland, B., & Sroufe, L.A. (1981). Attachment and early maltreatment. *Child Development,* 52, 44–52. LaFraniere, P.J., & Sroufe, L.A. (1985). Profiles of peer competence in the preschool: Interrelations between measures, influence of social ecology, and relation to attachment history. *Developmental Psychology,* 21, 56–69. Mahler, M.S., Pine, F., & Bergman, A. (1975). *The psychological birth of the human infant.* New York: Basic Books. Slade, A. (1987). Quality of attachment and early symbolic play. *Developmental Psychology,* 23, 78–85. Spitz, R. (1965). *The first year of life.* New York: International Universities Press. Sroufe, L.A. (1979). The coher-

ence of individual development: Early care, attachment, and subsequent developmental issues. *American Psychologist,* 34, 834–841. A very nice overview of the history of attachment research written for the layperson is: Karen, R. (1990). Becoming attached. *Atlantic Monthly,* February, 35–70.

4. Bowlby, *Attachment.*

5. Ainsworth et al., *Patterns of attachment.* Slade, "Quality of attachment and early symbolic play." Sroufe, "The coherence of individual development: Early care, attachment, and subsequent developmental issues."

6. Carlson, V., Cicchetti, D., Barnett, D., & Braunwald, K. (1989). Disorganized disoriented attachment behaviors in maltreated infants. *Developmental Psychology,* 25, 525–531.

7. Main, M. (1981). Avoidance in the service of attachment: A working paper. In K. Immelmann, G. Barlow, L. Petrinovich, and M. Main (Eds.), *Behavioral development: The Bielefeld interdisciplinary project.* New York: Cambridge University Press.

8. Ainsworth et al., *Patterns of attachment.* Egeland, B., & Farber, E.A. (1984). Infant-mother attachment: Factors related to its development and change over time. *Child Development,* 55, 753–771. Sroufe, L.A. (1985). Attachment classification from the perspective of infant-caregiver relationships and infant temperament. *Child Development,* 58, 1–14.

9. Matas, L., Arend, R., & Sroufe, L.A. (1978). Continuity of adaptation in the second year: The relationship between quality of attachment and later competence. *Child Development,* 49, 547–556.

10. Bowlby, *Attachment.* Erikson, *Childhood and society.* Mahler et al., *The psychological birth of the human infant.*

11. Stern, D.N. (1985). *The interpersonal world of the infant: A view from psychoanalysis and developmental psychology.* New York: Basic Books.

12. Kohut, H. (1977). *The restoration of the self.* New York: International Universities Press.

13. Harter, S. (1983). Developmental perspectives on the self-system. In P.H. Mussen (Ed.), *Handbook of child psychology,* 4th edition. Vol. 4: *Socialization, personality, and social development* (pp. 275–386). New York: John Wiley & Sons.

14. Erikson, *Childhood and society,* p. 118.

15. Cousins, N. (1977, May 28). Anatomy of an illness (as perceived by the patient). *Saturday Review,* pp. 4–6, 48–51. Peale, N.V. (1956). *The power of positive thinking.* Englewood Cliffs, NJ: Prentice-Hall.

16. In one study of middle-aged men undergoing coronary artery bypass surgery, researchers found that men who expressed high levels of optimism before the surgery showed more effective coping strategies after the surgery and physically recovered more quickly than men who were low in optimism. Scheier, M.F., Magovern, G.J., Abbott, R.A., Matthews, K.A., Owens, J.F., Lefebvre, R.C., & Carver, C.S. (1989). Dispositional optimism and recovery from coronary artery bypass surgery: The beneficial effects on physical and psychological well-being. *Journal of Personality and Social Psychology,* 57, 1024–1040.

17. Taylor, S.E. (1989). *Positive illusions: Creative self-deception and the healthy mind.* New York: Basic Books.

18. Taylor, S.E. (1983). Adjusting to threatening events: A theory of cognitive adaptation. *American Psychologist,* 38, 1161–1173.

19. See also Greenwald, A.G. (1980). The totalitarian ego: Fabrication and revision of personal history. *American Psychologist, 35,* 603–618.

20. From the realm of literary criticism, the key source on mythic forms, or "mythic archetypes," is Frye, N. (1957). *Anatomy of criticism.* Princeton, NJ: Princeton University Press. One psychologist who has examined Frye's concept of mythic archetypes is Kevin Murray: Murray, K. (1989). The construction of identity in the narratives of romance and comedy. In J. Shotter and K.J. Gergen (Eds.), *Texts of identity* (pp. 176–205). London: Sage Publications.

21. Krauss, R. (1952/1984). A hole is to dig: A first book of first defnitions. In C. Fadiman (Ed.), *The world treasury of children's literature,* Book 1, pp. 123–128. Boston: Little, Brown.

22. Piaget, J. (1970). Piaget's theory. In P.H. Mussen (Ed.), *Carmichael's manual of child psychology,* Vol. 1. New York: John Wiley & Sons.

23. The research literature on cognitive development in preschoolers does not fully support Piaget's claims concerning the child's egocentrism. It does seem to be true that children are often egocentric in their thinking patterns, but they are often able to show surprisingly sophisticated role-taking abilities, too. Young children are able to take into consideration the points of view of certain other people and to adjust their behavior accordingly. Still, preoperational thinking tends to be dominated by the child's personal perspective. Thus, while Piaget may have overstated the case concerning egocentrism, there appears still to be a kernel of truth in the idea that young children find it difficult to "decenter" themselves in their cognitive processes. Three very interesting and solid sources are: Gelman, R. (1981). Preschool thought. In E.M. Hetherington and R.D. Parke (Eds.), *Contemporary readings in child psychology* (2nd Ed.) (pp. 159–164). New York: McGraw-Hill. Kegan, *The evolving self.* Cambridge, MA: Harvard University Press. Miller, P.H. (1989). *Theories of developmental psychology* (2nd Ed.). San Francisco: Freeman.

24. Singer, J. (1973). *The child's world of make-believe.* New York: Academic Press.

25. Garvey, C. (1977). *Play.* Cambridge, MA: Harvard University Press.

26. Ibid, p. 5.

27. Ibid, p. 6.

28. See, for instance, Kohut, *The restoration of the self.* Mahler, Pine, & Bergman, *The psychological birth of the human infant.*

29. See, for instance, Fairbairn, W.R.D. (1952). *Psychoanalytic studies of the personality.* London: Routledge & Kegan Paul. Guntrip, H. (1973). *Psychoanalytic theory, therapy, and the self.*

30. Fowler, J. (1981). *Stages of faith: The psychology of human development and the quest for meaning.* New York: Harper & Row.

31. Ibid, p. 128.

32. Ibid, pp. 126–128.

33. Ibid, p. 129.

34. Of most concern here for many parents, educators, and psychologists is the relationship between exposure to images of violence on television and the development of aggressive tendencies in children. There is a large and complex empirical literature on this topic. The bulk of findings suggests a positive link between the excessive viewing of television violence and engaging in aggressive behaviors, in both boys and girls. Laboratory studies have consistently documented short-term increases in aggressive behavior following the viewing of violent films and

television shows. In one important study, after viewing segments of such shows as *The Untouchables,* children were more willing to hurt others than after viewing a neutral program about a race track. Similarly, after watching cartoon characters clobber each other for some time, children engaged in greater levels of aggressive behavior than did their peers who viewed nonviolent cartoons. Viewing erotic films laced with images of aggression—such as sadomasochism and rape—is especially likely to stimulate aggression in males and to result in greater acceptance of sexual violence directed against females. Viewing erotic films that do not portray violence, however, has not consistently been shown to have an effect on subsequent violent behavior. The most impressive longitudinal study of aggression and television viewing has been in progress for over twenty-five years now, originally conceived by Leonard D. Eron and his colleagues at the University of Illinois at Chicago. In this study, one of the best predictors of how aggressive a young man would be at age nineteen was the violence of the television programs he preferred to watch when he was eight years old. Television viewing habits in third grade also predicted criminal activity at age thirty. Essentially, the more frequently children watched violent television at age eight, the more serious were the crimes for which they were convicted by age thirty. The relationship between viewing violence on television and crime holds up for both men and women, though men show much higher levels of criminal activity overall. But does television viewing actually cause aggressive behavior? The results of empirical studies like Eron's suggest that a simple cause-and-effect interpretation cannot justifiably be made. A number of other factors appear to be involved as determinants and correlates of aggressive behavior, including low levels of intelligence, poor grades in school, harsh physical punishment from parents, parents' antisocial values, and beliefs that the violence portrayed on television provides a realistic picture of how the world works. Furthermore, studies have suggested that while viewing television violence may lead to higher levels of aggressiveness, higher levels of aggressiveness may also lead to increased viewing of television violence. Individuals who are more aggressive to begin with tend to expose themselves more often to violent imagery on television, which in turn may increase their characteristic aggressiveness, and so on. In other words, violent television imagery and aggression appear to be related to each other in a reciprocal and circular manner. Each is the cause and the effect of the other. Some sources: Eron, L.D. (1982). Parent-child interaction, television violence, and aggression in children. *American Psychologist,* 37, 197–211. Eron, L.D. (1987). The development of aggressive behavior from the perspective of a developing behaviorism. *American Psychologist,* 42, 435–442. Friedrich-Cofer, L., & Huston, A.C. (1986). Television violence and aggression: The debate continues. *Psychological Bulletin,* 100, 364–371.

35. Jean-Paul Sartre defined "the image" as a synthesis of feeling, knowledge, and inner sensation. In: Charme, S.T. (1984). *Meaning and myth in the study of lives.* Philadelphia: University of Pennsylvania Press.

Chapter 3

1. Piaget, "Piaget's theory."

2. An overview of different psychological approaches to human motivation is contained in McAdams, D.P. (1991). Motives. In V.J. Derlega, B.A. Winstead, and

W.H. Jones (Eds.), *Personality: Contemporary theory and research* (pp. 175–204). Chicago: Nelson-Hall. See also Buck, R. (1988). *Human motivation and emotion* (2nd Ed.). New York: Wiley & Sons. McClelland, D.C. (1985). *Human motivation.* New York: Cambridge University Press. Mook, D.G. (1987). *Motivation: The organization of action.* New York: W.W. Norton.

3. Aristotle. (1942). *De anima.* (On the Soul.). In R. McKeon (Ed.), *Introduction to Aristotle* (pp. 145–237). New York: Random House.

4. Jung, C.G. (1961). *Memories, dreams, reflections.* (New York: Random House). Rogers, C.R. (1951). *Client-centered therapy: Its current practice, implications, and theory.* Boston: Houghton Mifflin.

5. Plato argued, furthermore, that each of the three basic human motives would ideally be actualized by particular citizens in his utopian republic. Thus, the artisans were expected to act mainly on the spring of base appetites. Soldiers were to act according to the dictates of courage, or *thumos.* And the philosopher-kings engaged in behavior that was fundamentally guided by reason and motivated by the search for "the Good." The republic should be organized such that particular classes of people would be trained to live in accord with their corresponding motivational destinies. Thus, prospective philosopher-kings would require extensive training in the development of rational thought during their childhood and adolescent years. Soldiers would be trained to develop their courage and fortitude. Education for artisans would emphasize activities in accord with the appetites. Plato. (1956). *Great dialogues of Plato: A modern translation.* Translated by W.H.D. Rouse. New York: New American Library.

6. James, W. (1890). *Principles of psychology.* New York: Holt, Rinehart & Winston.

7. Russell, B. (1945). *A history of Western philosophy.* New York: Simon & Schuster.

8. Freud, S. (1920/1955). *Beyond the pleasure principle.* In J. Strachey (Ed.), *The standard edition of the complete psychological works of Sigmund Freud* (Vol. 18). London: Hogarth. Over the course of his career, Freud put forth three successive theories of motivation. In the first, Freud pitted the "ego instincts" against the "sexual instincts." The ego instincts were forces within the individual that assured the preservation of the self and the maintenance of daily life. For example, the hunger drive promotes survival of the individual by motivating him or her to eat. The sexual instincts assure the preservation of the species by motivating the organism to seek out love objects in the world, ultimately culminating in sexual intercourse and the generation of progeny. Freud's second theory of motivation viewed these two classes of instincts as derivatives of a common pool of energy, which he termed "primary narcissistic libido." According to this view, a finite quantum of narcissistic libido or sexual energy could be channeled into two different directions: toward the self (ego libido) or toward objects (object libido). Ego libido promotes the survival of the individual, while object libido promotes the survival of the species. The narcissist therefore invests too much libido in the self and not enough in others. Freud's third and final theory of motivation appeared in 1920, with the publication of *Beyond the pleasure principle.* In this radically transformed view, Freud argued for the existence of two discrete classes of instincts, one promoting life and the other serving death. Grouped together now under one rubric are both the ego libido (self-love) and the object libido (love of others). Ego libido and object libido are the two central components of Eros, or the sexual instincts in general. A second independent source of energy comes from the death instincts, sometimes called

Thanatos. When the death instincts are directed toward the self, we encounter inner aggression or masochism. When the death instincts are directed toward others, we encounter external aggression or sadism. For people (like myself) who appreciate symmetry in their theories, Freud's final view of motivation is a tour de force. Two perfectly opposed instincts—Eros and Thanatos—work against each other to effect opposite ends: life (union) and death (separation). Within each of the two classes, two opposite tendencies can be seen, as the "energy" of the instincts is directed either inward (self-love, self-hate) or outward (object-love, object-hate). Conflict between opposites exists throughout. Of course, both classes of instincts work behind the scenes as the forever unconscious and masterfully disguised ultimate forces in human personality. Furthermore, Freud believed that both classes of instincts are ultimately grounded in biology and evolution. He argued that both instincts are vestiges of an evolutionary past, working to "return" the organism to its past. The death instincts work to return the organism to the inert state of death that preceded the state of life. The sexual (life) instincts work to "return" the organism to an earlier stage in evolution—a kind of primal bisexuality or unity of male and female, which, Freud speculated, was the characteristic mode of existence of the primitive species who were our evolutionary forerunners millions of years ago. Both classes of instincts, therefore, are "conservative" in that they seek to "conserve" some basic aspect of the past. Freud's last theory of motivation has been strongly criticized, especially for its fanciful assertions about biology and evolution. Nonetheless, some still find the general outline of the theory quite compelling. A very fine discussion of Freud's theory of life and death instincts can be found in Monte, C.F. (1987). *Beneath the mask: An introduction to theories of personality* (3rd Ed.) (pp. 95–105). New York: Holt, Rinehart, & Winston. See also Brown, N.O. (1959). *Life against death: The psychoanalytic meaning of history.* New York: Random House. Sulloway, F.J. (1979). *Freud: Biologist of the mind.* New York: Basic Books.

9. These theories include Angyal's distinction between autonomy and surrender, Rank's fear of life (which motivates us to separate from others) versus fear of death (which motivates us to seek union), Adler's striving for superiority versus social interest, Kegan's "psychologics" of independence and inclusion, Gilligan's ethics of individuation (and pride) versus interdependence (and care), Hogan's evolutionarily adaptive tendencies toward gaining status versus acceptance in social groups, Tomkins' "psychological magnification" of excitement-interest versus joy-enjoyment, and my own distinction between power and intimacy motivation. Sources: Adler, A. (1927). *The practice and theory of individual psychology.* New York: Harcourt Brace. (Translated by P. Radin). Angyal, A. (1941). *Foundations for a science of personality.* New York: Commonwealth Fund. Gilligan, C. (1982). *In a different voice: Psychological theory and women's development.* Cambridge, MA: Harvard University Press. Hogan, R. (1982). A socioanalytic theory of personality. In M. Page (Ed.), *Nebraska symposium on motivation* (pp. 55–89). Lincoln: University of Nebraska Press. Kegan, *The evolving self.* McAdams, *Power, intimacy, and the life story.* Rank, O. (1936/1978). *Truth vs. reality.* New York: W.W. Norton. Tomkins, S.S. (1987). Script theory. In J. Aronoff, A.I. Rabin, and R.A. Zucker (Eds.), *The emergence of personality* (pp. 147–216). New York: Springer.

10. Bakan, D. (1966). *The duality of human existence: Isolation and communion in Western man.* Boston: Beacon Press.

11. Agency subsumes many different kinds of personality variables at many different levels. It cannot be identified with any particular trait, motive, schema, value, or ability. The same holds for communion. A discussion of the many faces of agency and communion can be found in McAdams, D.P. (1988). Personal needs and personal relationships. In S.W. Duck (Ed.), *Handbook of personal relationships* (pp. 7–22). New York: John Wiley & Sons.

12. Forster, E.M. (1910). *Howards end.* Hammondsworth, Middlesex: Penguin, p. 78.

13. McAdams, D.P., & Losoff, M. (1984). Friendship motivation in fourth and sixth graders: A thematic analysis. *Journal of Social and Personal Relationships,* 1, 11–27.

14. Cross-sectional data from a nationwide study suggests a slight tendency for older women to have lower intimacy motive scores than younger women. We do not know if this difference is due to development or to cohort effects. Source: McAdams, D.P. & Bryant, F.B. (1987). Intimacy motivation and subjective mental health in a nationwide sample. *Journal of Personality,* 55, 395–413.

15. On one side of the fence are psychologists of a more psychoanalytic persuasion who argue that adolescence is filled with resurgent conflicts and "storm and stress." For example, see Blos, P. (1979). *The adolescent passage.* New York: International Universities Press. On the other side are psychologists who have conducted empirical research, mostly based on self-report and questionnaires, that seems to suggest that adolescence is not an especially conflictual or turbulent time in a person's life. For example, see Offer, D., Ostrov, E., & Howard, K.I. (1981). *The adolescent: A psychological self-portrait.* New York: Basic Books. An interesting middle-ground position is staked out in this research-oriented book: Csikszentmihalyi, M., & Larson, R. (1984). *Being adolescent: Conflict and growth in the teenage years.* New York: Basic Books. A fascinating literary analysis is contained in: Spacks, P.M. (1981). *The adolescent idea: Myths of youth and the adult imagination.* New York: Basic Books. Finally, an excellent overview of research and theory in adolescence is this college textbook: Conger, J.J., & Petersen, A.C. (1984). *Adolescence and youth* (3rd Ed.). New York: Harper & Row.

16. Campbell, *The hero with a thousand faces.*

17. Blos, *The adolescent passage.*

18. Campbell, *The hero with a thousand faces,* p. 79.

19. Inhelder, B., & Piaget, J. (1958). *The growth of logical thinking from childhood to adolescence.* New York: Basic Books.

20. Elkind, D. (1981). *Children and adolescents: Interpretive essays on Jean Piaget* (3rd Ed.). New York: Oxford University Press.

21. Erikson, E.H. (1958). *Young man Luther.* New York: Norton.

22. Elkind, *Children and adolescents.*

23. Erikson, *Young man Luther,* p. 41.

24. Erikson, *Childhood and society,* p. 263.

25. For example, see Adelson, J. (1975). The development of ideology in adolescence. In S.H. Oragastin and G.H. Elder (Eds.), *Adolescence in the life cycle: Psychological change and social context.* New York: John Wiley & Sons. Marcia, J. (1980). Identity in adolescence. In J. Adelson (Ed.), *Handbook of adolescent psychology* (pp. 159–187). New York: John Wiley & Sons.

26. In its most general sense, ideology means a systematic scheme or coor-

dinated body of ideas and beliefs concerning human life and culture. The scope of the term can range from a relatively circumscribed domain such as a particular political ideology (e.g., New Deal liberalism or contemporary neoconservatism) to an all-encompassing worldview. An organized set of ideas, ideology implies an abstract and systematic outlook on the world and the human being's place in it. Thus, the formulation of ideology presupposes the ability to reason in an abstract manner so as to conceive hypothetical systems concerning what is and what ought to be. I am using the term *ideology,* as does Erik Erikson, in its most general sense as a systematic body of ideas about humankind and the world. Furthermore, like Erikson, I am focusing upon personal ideologies rather than those espoused by corporate groups, though I realize that the relationship between the two is fairly complex in some cases. Psychological research on personal ideology tends to focus most closely on religion and politics. See Marcia, "Identity in adolescence."

27. See Binswanger, L. (1963). *Being-in-the-world.* New York: Basic Books.

28. Sources: Baumeister, R. (1986). *Identity: Cultural change and the struggle for self.* New York: Oxford University Press. McAdams, D.P. (1990). *The person: An introduction to personality psychology.* San Diego: Harcourt Brace Jovanovich. Chpt. 11.

29. Langbaum, R. (1977). *The mysteries of identity: A theme in modern literature.* New York: Oxford University Press, p. 352.

30. *The Lutheran book of worship.* (1978). Minneapolis: Augsburg Publishing House, p. 65.

31. Some empirical research supports the idea that late adolescence and young adulthood are especially "impressionable" years for the development of beliefs and values. In one study of political ideology, Krosnick and Alwin (1989) found that once formed in late adolescence people's political attitudes remained relatively consistent thereafter. Krosnick, J.A., & Alwin, D.F. (1989). Aging and susceptibility to attitude change. *Journal of Personality and Social Psychology,* 57, 416–425.

32. Mill, J.S. (1859). *On liberty.* London: J.W. Parker.

33. Gilligan, *In a different voice.*

34. Brabek, M. (1983). Moral judgment: Theory and research on differences between males and females. *Developmental Review,* 3, 274–291. Ford, M.R. & Lowery, C. (1986). Gender differences in moral reasoning: A comparison of the use of justice and care orientations. *Journal of Personality and Social Psychology,* 50, 777–783.

35. McAdams, *Power, intimacy, and the life story,* Chpt. 4.

36. Kohlberg, L. (1981). *The philosophy of moral development: Moral stages and the idea of justice* (Vol. 1). *Essays on moral development.* New York: Harper & Row.

37. Damon, W. (1977). *The social world of the child.* San Francisco: Jossey-Bass.

38. Selman, R. (1980). *The growth of interpersonal understanding.* New York: Academic Press.

39. Adelson. "The development of ideology in adolescence."

40. Fowler, *Stages of faith.*

41. See, for example, Loevinger, J., Cohn, L.D., Bonneville, L.P., Redmore, C., Streich, D.D. & Sargent, M. (1985). Ego development in college. *Journal of Personality and Social Psychology,* 48, 947–962.

Notes

Chapter 4

1. Erikson, *Young man Luther*, pp. 111–112.

2. The term *psychosocial moratorium* comes from Erikson's voluminous writings on identity, especially his 1968 book, *Identity: Youth and crisis*. The term has also been profitably employed in an ambitious research program investigating "identity statuses." In this research, the term *moratorium* refers to an adolescent or young adult who has begun identity explorations—questioning past beliefs and values about ideology and occupation—but who has yet to make firm identity commitments. In this research, it is generally believed that the young person in moratorium will eventually make such commitments and thereby enter the identity status of "identity achieved." This perspective is at odds with the one employed in this book, for it is my contention that identity is never "achieved" once and for all, until, perhaps, old age. Sources: Marcia, "Identity in adolescence." McAdams, *Power, intimacy, and the life story*, chpt. 2.

3. See for instance: Coles, *The call of stories.* Kohlberg, L., & Gilligan, C. (1971). The adolescent as moral philosopher: The discovery of self in a post-conventional world. *Daedalus,* Fall, 1051–1086. Perry, W.G. (1968). *Forms of intellectual and ethical development in the college years: A scheme.* New York: Holt, Rinehart & Winston. Winter, D.G., McClelland, D.C., & Stewart, A.J. (1981). *A new case for the liberal arts: Assessing institutional goals and student development.* San Francisco: Jossey-Bass. The contrary position is adopted by Alan Bloom, who lambastes the liberal arts curriculum in American colleges for failing to ground the identities of young people in firm principles and unalienable truths. See Bloom, A. (1987). *The closing of the American mind: How education has failed democracy and impoverished the souls of today's students.* New York: Simon & Schuster.

4. The contrary position is taken by Marcia in his work on identity statuses: Marcia, "Identity in adolescence."

5. The view that we pass through repeated stages and cycles in adulthood has been popularized by many books. Most well known are Levinson, D.J. (1978). *The seasons of a man's life.* New York: Ballantine. Sheehy, G. (1976). *Passages: Predictable crises in adult life.* New York: E.P. Dutton. Empirical research, however, suggests somewhat more continuity and irregular change in adult development. See also Wrightsman, L.S. (1988). *Personality development in adulthood.* Newbury Park, CA: Sage Publications.

6. Erikson does provide a framework for understanding developmental stages of the human personality, but confines identity to the adolescent stage. See Erikson, *Childhood and society.*

7. Levinson, *Seasons of a man's life.*

8. Vaillant, G.E. (1977). *Adaptation to life.* Boston: Little, Brown.

9. Gould, R.L. (1980). Transformation during early and middle adult years. In N.J. Smelser and E.H. Erikson (Eds.), *Themes of work and love in adulthood* (pp. 213–237). Cambridge, MA: Harvard University Press.

10. Gutmann, D. (1987). *Reclaimed powers: Toward a new psychology of men and women in later life.* New York: Basic Books.

11. Jung, C.G. (1936/1969). *The archetypes and the collective unconscious.* In Vol. 9

of *The collected works of C.G. Jung.* Princeton, NJ: Princeton University Press. Jung, *Memories, dreams, reflections.*

12. Frenkel, E. (1936). Studies in biographical psychology. *Character and Personality, 5,* 1–35.

13. Havighurst, R.J. (1973). *Developmental tasks and education* (3rd Ed.). New York: David McKay.

14. White, R.W. (1975). *Lives in progress* (3rd Ed.). New York: Holt, Rinehart & Winston.

15. Neugarten, B.L. (1964). *Personality in middle and late life.* New York: Atherton Press.

16. See, for example: McCrae, R.R., & Costa, P.T. (1990). *Personality in adulthood.* New York: Guilford Press.

17. Roberts, P., & Newton, P.M. (1987). Levinsonian studies of women's adult development. *Psychology and Aging, 2,* 154–163. Stewart, A.J., Franz, C., & Layton, L. (1988). The changing self: Using personal documents to study lives. In D.P. McAdams and R.L. Ochberg (Eds.), *Psychobiography and life narratives* (pp. 41–74). Durham, NC: Duke University Press.

18. See: Shweder, R.A., & Levine, R.A. (Eds.). (1984). *Culture theory: Essays on mind, self, and emotion.* Cambridge: Cambridge University Press.

19. Data from a number of sociological studies show that most working men change occupations at least once, that mid-life occupational change is not uncommon, and that few men remain in one occupation all of their working lives. In that women's career paths tend to be more irregular than men, job change among women in adulthood is at least as common if not more so. See Kimmel, D.C. (1990). *Adulthood and aging* (3rd. Ed.). New York: John Wiley & Sons.

20. Roberts & Newton, "Levinsonian studies of women's adult development."

21. Ibid, p. 154.

22. Ibid, p. 159.

23. Havighurst, *Developmental tasks and education.*

24. Levinson, D.J., Darrow, C.M., Klein, E.B., Levinson, M.H., & McKee, B. (1974). The psychosocial development of men in early adulthood and the mid-life transition. In D. Ricks, A. Thomas, and M. Roff (Eds.), *Life history research in psychopathology* (Vol. 3) (pp. 250–271). Minneapolis: University of Minnesota Press.

25. Hayslip, B., Jr., & Panek, P.E. (1989). *Adult development and aging.* New York: Harper & Row.

26. Source: Hankiss, A. (1981). Ontologies of the self: On the mythological rearranging of one's life history. In D. Bertaux (Ed.), *Biography and society: The life history approach in the social sciences* (pp. 203–209). Beverly Hills, CA: Sage Publications.

27. Franklin, B. (1961). *Benjamin Franklin: The autobiography and other writings.* New York: Penguin. (Written in 1771.)

28. Ibid, p. 16.

29. A number of psychologists have suggested that a hallmark of maturity in mid-life and beyond is the reconciliation of opposites in adult personality. For example, Carl Jung suggests that the "fully individuated" man or woman at mid-life must find a creative balance between the masculine and feminine sides of the psyche. Robert Kegan suggests that maturity involves a reconciliation between the "psychologics of autonomy and interdependence." Otto Rank and Ernest

Becker write of a balance between the desire to merge with others and the desire to separate from them. Sources: Becker, E. (1973). *The denial of death.* New York: The Free Press. Jung, *Memories, dreams, reflections.* Kegan, R. *The evolving self: Problem and process in human development.* Rank, *Truth and reality.*

30. A consideration of the ethical realm within which story operates is presented in this fascinating new study: Booth, W.C. (1988). *The company we keep: An ethics of fiction.* Berkeley, CA: University of California Press.

Chapter 5

1. Whitman, W. (1959). Song of myself, lines 1314–1316. In Francis Murphy (Ed.), *Whitman: The Complete Poems* (p. 737). Hammondsworth, Middlesex: Penguin, 1977. New York: Viking Press.

2. Based on a March 1990 U.S. Census Bureau study reported in "New Look to U.S. Households." *Chicago Tribune,* June 7, 1991.

3. Richard Ochberg provides an engaging analysis of the imagery of acceleration in the professional lives of men: Ochberg, R.L. (1988). Life stories and the psychosocial construction of careers. In D.P. McAdams and R.L. Ochberg (Eds.), *Psychobiography and life narratives* (pp. 173–204). Durham, NC: Duke University Press.

4. Gadlin, H. (1977). Private lives and public order: A critical review of the history of intimate relations in the United States. In G. Levinger and H.L. Rausch (Eds.), *Close relationships: Perspectives on the meaning of intimacy* (pp. 33–72). Amherst, MA: University of Massachusetts Press.

5. Ibid.

6. Gay, P. (1986). *The tender passion.* New York: Oxford University Press.

7. Baumeister, *Identity: Cultural change and the struggle for self.*

8. James, W. *Psychology: A briefer course.* New York: Fawcett World Library. p. 174.

9. The concept of imago bears some resemblance to a number of related concepts in psychoanalytic clinical psychology and in cognitive social psychology. These include such concepts as "archetypes" (Jung), "personifications" (Sullivan), "internalized objects" (Fairbairn, Guntrip, Klein), "ego states" and "scripts" (Berne), "wished-for self-images" (Jacobson), "self-schemata" and "possible selves" (Marcus), "prototypes" (Cantor & Mischel), and "subselves" (Martindale). These conceptual relations are outlined in detail in McAdams, "The 'imago': A key narrative component of identity." In addition, the above paper sets forth eight principles of the imago: (1) The self is composed of personified and idealized internalized images, or imagoes, that are laden with affect. (2) The origins of a particular imago lie in the internalization of loved (and hated) "objects" in the person's world. (3) A person's most significant interpersonal relationships are profoundly influenced by his or her imagoes. (4) Imagoes are often arranged in the self as dialectical opposites. (5) The synthesis of opposing imagoes is a hallmark of the mature self. (6) Imagoes are superordinate schemata for organizing and evaluating information about the self. (7) Imagoes specify recurrent behavioral plans. (8) Imagoes give cognitive form to personal goals, fears, and desires. Also, for an extended discussion of how the concept of imago can be operationalized in empirical research, see McAdams, *Power, intimacy, and the life story,* chpt. 6. Other sources for background concepts: Berne, E. (1972). *What do you say after you say hello?* New York: Grove Press. Cantor, N., & Mischel, W. (1979). Prototypes in person

perception. In L. Berkowitz (Ed.), *Advances in experimental social psychology* (Vol. 12, pp. 3–52). New York: Academic Press. Fairbairn, *Psychoanalytic studies of the personality.* Guntrip, *Psychoanalytic theory, therapy, and the self.* Jacobson, E. (1964). *The self and the object world.* New York: International Universities Press. Jung, C.G. (1957). *Psychology of the unconscious.* New York: Dodd, Mead. Klein, M. (1948). *Contributions to psychoanalysis: 1921–1945.* London: Hogarth. Markus, H., & Nurius, P. (1986). Possible selves. *American Psychologist,* 41, 954–969. Martindale, C. (1980). Subselves: The internal representation of situational and personal dispositions. In L. Wheeler (Ed.), *Review of personality and social psychology* (Vol. 1, pp. 193–218). Beverly Hills, CA: Sage Publications. Steiner, C.M. (1974). *Scripts people live.* New York: Grove Press. Sullivan, H.S. (1953). *The interpersonal theory of psychiatry.* New York: W.W. Norton.

10. Chapter 3 and Appendix 1 of this book examine power and love—or more generally "agency" and "communion"—as the two central themes of life stories. Chapter 6 considers in detail various imago types organized along the lines of power and love.

11. Goffman, E. (1959). *The presentation of self in everyday life.* Garden City, NY: Doubleday.

12. Lifton, R.J. (1979). *The broken connection.* New York: Simon & Schuster.

13. E. Tory Higgins distinguishes among the "actual self," "the ideal self," and the "ought self." The actual self consists of your representations of the attributes that someone (yourself or another) believes you actually possess. The ideal self consists of your representations of the attributes that someone (yourself or another) would like you, ideally, to possess—that is, a representation of hopes, aspirations, or wishes. The ought self consists of your representation of the attributes that someone (yourself or another) believes you should or ought to possess—that is, a representation of duties, obligations, or responsibilities. According to Higgins's "self-discrepancy theory," problems in life occur when various selves in different domains are inconsistent with each other. Discrepancies between actual and ideal selves often lead to experiences of sadness and other "dejection-related emotions." Discrepancies between actual and ought selves often lead to experiences of fear or guilt or other "agitation-related emotions." Daniel Ogilvie focuses on the "undesired self," which consists of attributes that the person fears, dreads, hates, and actively seeks to exclude from experience. Discrepancies between the undesired self and the actual self are strong predictors of overall life satisfaction. In other words, people who report high levels of satisfaction with their lives also report that their undesired selves and their actual selves are highly dissimilar. See: Higgins, E.T. (1987). Self-discrepancy: A theory relating self and affect. *Psychological Review,* 94, 319–340. Ogilvie, D.M. (1987). The undesired self: A neglected variable in personality research. *Journal of Personality and Social Psychology,* 52, 379–385.

14. Markus & Nurius, "Possible selves."

15. See McAdams, *The person,* chpt. 6.

16. A number of trait psychologists have recently concluded that the entire domain of personality traits can be organized according to five general dimensions: (1) extraversion-introversion, (2) neuroticism-stability, (3) openness-rigidity, (4) agreeableness-antagonism, and (5) conscientiousness-unconscientiousness. See: McCrae & Costa, *Personality in adulthood.* For a critique of this point of view, see

McAdams, D.P. (1992). The five-factor model in personality: A critical appraisal. *Journal of Personality, 60,* 329–361.

17. Bellah, R., Madsen, R., Sullivan, W.M., Swidler, A., & Tipton, S.M. (1985). *Habits of the heart: Individualism and commitment in American life.* Berkeley: University of California Press.

18. Guntrip, *Psychoanalytic theory, therapy, and the self.*

19. Watkins, M. (1986). *Invisible guests: The development of imaginal dialogues.* Hillsdale, NJ: The Analytic Press.

Chapter 6

1. For an argument that suggests the contrary, see Wilson, E.O. (1978). *On human nature.* Cambridge, MA: Harvard University Press.

2. These adjectives are drawn from: Gough, H.G. (1952). *The adjective checklist.* Palo Alto, CA: Consulting Psychologists Press.

3. Adler, J., Springen, K., Glick, D., & Gordon, J. (1991). Drums, sweat, and tears: What do men really want? *Newsweek,* June 24, pp. 46–51.

4. Bly, R. (1990). *Iron John: A book about men.* Reading, MA: Addison-Wesley.

5. Keen, S. (1991). *Fire in the belly: On being a man.* New York: Bantam.

6. The section on Tom Harvester is built around a case that appeared first in: McAdams, *Power, intimacy, and the life story,* pp. 195–196.

7. The section on Margaret Mead is built around a more extended analysis of her life that appeared first in McAdams, *The person,* pp. 8–19.

8. Mead, M. (1972). *Blackberry winter: My earlier years.* New York: Washington Square Press, p. 17.

9. Ibid, p. 74.

10. Ibid, p. 7.

11. Howard, J. (1984). *Margaret Mead: A life.* New York: Simon & Schuster, p. 13.

12. Ibid, p. 253.

13. Ibid, p. 145.

14. Mead, *Blackberry winter,* p. 143.

15. Homer. *The Homeric hymns.* Translated by C. Boer (1970). Dallas: Spring Publications, p. 89.

16. For a fascinating study of Hermes see Brown, N.O. (1947). *Hermes the thief.* See also McClelland, D.C. (1961). *The achieving society.* Chapter 8, entitled "The spirit of Hermes."

17. From Gough, *The adjective checklist.*

18. The section on the lover is based on a case that appeared first in McAdams, *Power, intimacy, and the life story,* pp. 199–200. A more extended discussion of the case of Sara appears in McAdams, *Intimacy: The need to be close,* pp. 3–8.

19. Sullivan, *The interpersonal theory of psychiatry.* The first half of the section titled "The Friend" is modeled after a similar passage in McAdams, *Intimacy: The need to be close,* pp. 87–89.

Chapter 7

1. The case of Julie McPherson comes from McAdams, *Power, intimacy, and the life story,* pp. 167–169.

2. The research has been supported by an internal grant from Northwestern University for 1989–1990 and by a major grant from The Spencer Foundation for 1990–1993.

3. Fowler, *Stages of faith.*

4. McAdams, *Power, intimacy, and the life story,* chpt. 7. McAdams, D.P., Booth, L., & Selvik, R. (1981). Religious identity among students at a private college: Social motives, ego stage, and development. *Merrill-Palmer Quarterly,* 27, 219–239. Oxenberg, J. (1990). *Religiosity, faith development, and reaction to negative life events.* Unpublished master's thesis, Loyola University of Chicago.

5. In one study of 78 college students, 41 provided responses on an open-ended questionnaire that indicated adherence to a systematic creed or dogma. In a second study of 56 students involved in religious organizations, 31 claimed that they believed strongly in the teachings of their church and either (1) they had never undergone a period of doubt or questioning with respect to those teachings or (2) they had gone through a period of rejecting religious conventions but they had eventually accepted their original beliefs. McAdams, *Power, intimacy, and the life story.*

6. Ibid, p. 25.

Chapter 8

1. Frenkel, "Studies in biographical psychology."

2. Jung, *Memories, dreams, reflections.*

3. Jaques, E. (1965). Death and the midlife crisis. *International Journal of Psychoanalysis,* 46, 502–514.

4. Levinson, *The seasons of a man's life.*

5. Sheehy, *Passages.*

6. Nock, S.L. (1982). The life-cycle approach to family analysis. In B. Wolman (Ed.), *Handbook of developmental psychology* (pp. 636–651), Englewood Cliffs, NJ: Prentice-Hall.

7. McCrae & Costa, *Personality in adulthood.*

8. Neugarten, B.L. (1968). (Ed.). *Middle age and aging.* Chicago: University of Chicago Press.

9. Simonton, D.K. (1984). Creative productivity and age. *Developmental Review,* 4, 77–111.

10. Neugarten, B.L., & Datan, N. (1974). The middle years. In S. Arieti (Ed.), *American handbook of psychiatry* (Vol. 1). New York: Basic Books.

11. Levinson, *The seasons of a man's life,* p. 199.

12. Jaques, "Death and the midlife crisis," p. 502.

13. Ibid, p. 505.

14. Gould, "Transformation during early and middle adult years."

15. Frenkel, "Studies in biographical psychology."

16. There is a controversy in the literature concerning the extent to which "postformal thinking" is really a new stage in cognitive development or simply a different style of thinking. The controversy is described in detail in this excellent source: Rybash, J.M., Hoyer, W.J., & Roodin, P.A. (1986). *Adult cognition and aging.* New York: Pergamon Press.

17. An engaging description of the paradox may be found in this source: Zukav,

G. (1979). *The dancing Wu Li masters: An overview of the new physics.* New York: William Morrow & Co.

18. Fowler on "conjunctive faith": "Stage 5 Conjunctive faith involves the integration into self and outlook of much that was suppressed or unrecognized in the interest of Stage 4's the Individuative-Reflective stage self-certainty and conscious cognitive and affective adaptation to reality.... There must be an opening to the voices of one's deeper self.... Alive to paradox and the truth in apparent contradictions, this stage strives to unify opposites in mind and experience.... The new strength of this stage is the rise of the ironic imagination—a capacity to see and be in one's or one's group's most powerful meanings, while simultaneously recognizing that they are relative, partial and inevitably distorting apprehensions of transcendent reality. Its danger lies in the direction of a paralyzing passivity or inaction, giving rise to complacency or cynical withdrawal, due to its paradoxical understanding of truth. From Fowler, *Stages of faith*, pp. 197–198.

19. Jung, *Memories, dreams, reflections.*

20. Gutmann, *Reclaimed powers.*

21. Levinson, *The seasons of a man's life.*

22. Gutmann, *Reclaimed powers.*

23. Merriam, S.B. (1980). *Coping with male mid-life: A systematic analysis using literature as a data source.* Washington, D.C.: University Press of America.

24. Ibid, pp. 63–64.

25. These adjectives come from: Gough, *The adjective checklist.*

26. This last section on Karen Horney is loosely adapted from a paper I presented at the Henry A. Murray Center for the Study of Lives, at Radcliffe College, in Cambridge, MA. The paper was part of a conference on the study of individual lives, May 11 and 12, 1990. It was entitled "Image, Theme, and Character in the Life Story of Karen Horney." Major sources for the paper were Horney, K. (1939). *New ways in psychoanalysis.* New York: Norton. Horney, K. (1945). *Our inner conflicts.* New York: Norton. Horney, K. (1980). *The adolescent diaries of Karen Horney.* New York: Basic Books. Quinn, S. (1988). *A mind of her own: The life of Karen Horney.* Reading, MA: Addison-Wesley.

27. Horney, *Diaries,* p. 63.

28. Ibid.

29. Ibid, pp. 55–57.

30. Ibid, p. 83.

31. Ibid, p. 79.

32. Ibid, p. 92.

33. Ibid, p. 167.

34. Ibid, p. 166.

35. Quinn, *A mind of her own.*

36. Ibid, p. 38.

37. Horney, *Diaries,* p. 271.

38. Ibid, p. 192.

39. Ibid, p. 104.

40. Ibid, p. 166.

41. Quinn, *A mind of her own,* p. 84.

42. Ibid, p. 418.

43. Horney, K. (1950). *Neurosis and human growth.* New York: Norton.

44. Quinn, *A mind of her own*, p. 406.
45. Ibid, p. 262.
46. Ibid, p. 172.
47. Horney, *Diaries*, p. 22.
48. Quinn, *A mind of her own*, p. 200.
49. Ibid, p. 300.

Chapter 9

1. Dawkins, R. (1981). Selfish genes and selfish memes. In D.R. Hofstadter and D.C. Dennett (Eds.), *The mind's I: Fantasies and reflections on self and soul* (pp. 124–144). New York: Basic Books.
2. The following section on Becker's work is adapted from my textbook: McAdams, *The person*, pp. 474–475.
3. Becker, *The denial of death*.
4. Ibid, p. 26.
5. deReincourt, A. (1974). *Sex and power in history*. New York: David McKay.
6. Becker, *The denial of death*, p. ix.
7. Ibid, p. 11.
8. Ibid, p. 5.
9. Ibid.
10. Lifton, *The broken connection*.
11. Becker, *The denial of death*, p. 173.
12. Ibid, p. 285.
13. The long section on generativity reports ideas and research findings that either (1) have appeared in previous scientific publications or (2) are part of work in progress. The work in progress is supported by a major grant from the Spencer Foundation to Dan P. McAdams for the project, "The Generative Adult: How Men and Women Work, Teach, and Contribute to Promote the Next Generation." Other sources: McAdams, D.P., & de St. Aubin, E. (1992). A theory of generativity and its assessment through self-report, behavioral acts, and narrative themes in autobiography. *Journal of Personality and Social Psychology*, 62, 1003–1015. McAdams, D.P. de St. Aubin, E., & Logan, R.L. (in press). Generativity among young, midlife, and older adults. *Psychology and Aging*. McAdams, Ruetzel, & Foley, "Complexity and generativity at mid-life: A study of biographical scripts for the future." Van de Water & McAdams, "Generativity and Erikson's 'belief in the species.'"
14. Marshall, V. (1975). Age and awareness of finitude in developmental gerontology. *Omega*, 6, 113–129.
15. Erikson, *Identity: Youth and crisis*, p. 141.
16. Erikson, *Childhood and society*, p. 267.
17. Terkel, S. (1972). *Working*. New York: Pantheon Books, p. 10. (Italics added.)
18. Erikson, *Young man Luther*.
19. Erikson, *Gandhi's truth*.
20. Ibid, p. 255.
21. Kotre, J. (1984). *Outliving the self: Generativity and the interpretation of lives*. Baltimore: Johns Hopkins University Press. Peterson, B.E., & Stewart, A.J. (1990). Using personal and fictional documents to assess psychosocial development: A case

study of Vera Brittain's generativity. *Psychology and Aging*, 5, 400–411. Stewart, Franz, & Layton, "The changing self: Using personal documents to study lives."

22. The students involved in this work include Ed de St. Aubin, Rodney Day, Gina Logan, Beth Mansfield, Karen Dicke, Janet Shlaes, and Carol Anne Stowe.

23. McAdams, Ruetzel, & Foley, "Complexity and generativity at mid-life: A study of biographical scripts for the future." We measured the relative strength of each person's power motivation and intimacy motivation through the Thematic Apperception Test (TAT). The TAT stories were scored for power and intimacy themes according to scientifically validated coding manuals. See McAdams, *Power, intimacy, and the life story*. Appendix C. Winter, *The power motive*. Appendix.

24. Kotre, *Outliving the self*, p. 16.

25. Dawkins, "Selfish genes and selfish memes," pp. 143–144.

26. Attributed to Daniel Webster, from an inscription on a building at the University of Minnesota.

27. McAdams & de St. Aubin, "A theory of generativity and its assessment through self-report, behavioral acts, and narrative themes in autobiography."

28. Erikson, *Childhood and society*, p. 267.

29. Van de Water, D. (1987). *Present and future in generativity*. Doctoral dissertation in developmental psychology, Loyola University of Chicago.

30. Murray, H.A. (1981). Vicissitudes of creativity. In E.S. Shneidman (Ed.), *Endeavors in psychology: Selections from the personology of Henry A. Murray* (pp. 312–330). New York: Harper & Row, p. 322.

31. Atwood, M. (1988). *Cat's eye*. New York: Doubleday, p. 43.

32. Vaillant, G.E., & Milofsky, E. (1980). The natural history of male psychological health: IX. Empirical evidence for Erikson's model of the life cycle. *American Journal of Psychiatry*, 137, 1348–1359.

33. Browning, D.S. (1975). *Generative man: Psychoanalytic perspectives*. New York: Dell.

34. Terkel, *Working*, p. xxx.

Chapter 10

1. A very useful book in this regard is Feinstein & Krippner, *Personal mythology: The psychology of your evolving self*. The book tells how you may use ritual, dreams, and imagination to discover your "inner story." Should one wish to change one's personal mythology, the authors outline five stages to follow: (1) recognizing when a guiding myth is no longer an ally; (2) bringing the roots of the mythic conflict into focus; (3) conceiving a unifying mythic vision; (4) moving from vision to commitment; and (5) weaving a renewed mythology into daily life.

2. There is a voluminous research literature concerning how people evaluate the quality of their lives. A great deal of it addresses "subjective well-being," or the personal judgment you make about how satisfied you are with your life. See, for example, Bradburn, N.M. (1969). *The structure of psychological well-being*. Chicago: Aldine. Bryant, F.B. (1989). A four-factor model of perceived control: Avoiding, coping, obtaining, and savoring. *Journal of Personality*, 57, 773–797. Veroff, J., Douvan, E., & Kulka, R. (1981). *The inner American*. New York: Basic Books. An interesting exploration of well-being among middle-aged and elderly adults is Ryff, C.D. (1989). In the eye of the beholder: Views of psychological well-being

among middle-aged and older adults. *Psychology and Aging,* 4, 195–210. A recent provocative and masterful synthesis is Baumeister, R. (1991). *Meanings of life.* New York: Guilford Press.

3. Baumeister, *Meanings of life,* p. 214.

4. Ibid, chpt. 9.

5. Wallach, M.A., & Wallach, L. (1983). *Psychology's sanction for selfishness.* San Francisco: W.H. Freeman. See also Sampson, E.E. (1989). The challenge of social change for psychology: Globalization and psychology's theory of the person. *American Psychologist,* 44, 914–921.

6. I cannot begin to list the important sources on the topic of personality change, and I cannot pretend to have read most of them. However, the two excellent works that follow are classics: Frank, J. (1961). *Persuasion and healing.* Baltimore, MD: Johns Hopkins University Press. Mahoney, M. (1988). *Human change processes.* San Francisco, CA: Jossey-Bass.

Epilogue

1. Butler, R.N. (1975). *Why survive? Being old in America.* New York: Harper & Row.

2. Erikson, *Childhood and society,* p. 268.

3. Wordsworth, W. (1807). Ode: Intimations of immortality from recollections of early childhood. In *W. Wordsworth, Poems.* London: Longman, Hurst, Rees, & Orme. X, 10–15.

Appendix 1

1. "Masculinity" is usually assessed via self-report questionnaires and checklists and is "defined in terms of an active, controlling, and instrumental approach to social interaction" (Ickes, 1981, p. 96). Both men and women, therefore, can score high on masculinity. A high scorer is a person who attributes to the self a large number of traits traditionally associated with stereotypes of masculine behavior: assertiveness, aggression, dominance, achievement orientation, etc. See Ickes, W. (1981). Sex-role influences in dyadic interaction: A theoretical model. In C. Mayo and N. Hanley (Eds.), *Gender and nonverbal behavior* (pp. 95–128). New York: Springer-Verlag.

2. Murray, *The thematic apperception test: Manual.*

3. Major sources on TAT assessments of power and achievement motivation are McClelland, D.C. (1961). *The achieving society.* New York: The Free Press. McClelland, D.C. (1975). *Power: The inner experience.* New York: Irvington. McClelland, *Human motivation.* Winter, *The power motive.* Winter, D.G., & Carlson, L. (1988). Using motive scores in the psychobiographical study of the individual: The case of Richard Nixon. In D.P. McAdams and R.L. Ochberg (Eds.), *Psychobiography and life narratives* (pp. 75–104). Durham, NC: Duke University Press. Winter, D.G., & Stewart, A.J. (1978). The power motive. In H. London and J.E. Exner, Jr. (Eds.), *Dimensions of personality* (pp. 391–448). New York: John Wiley & Sons.

4. McAdams, *Power, intimacy, and the life story.* McClelland, *Human motivation.* Stewart, A.J., & Chester, N.L. (1982). Sex differences in human social motives: Achievement, affiliation, and power. In A.J. Stewart (Ed.), *Motivation and society* (pp.

Notes

172–218). San Francisco: Jossey-Bass. Winter, *The power motive.*

5. Fodor, E.M., & Smith, T. (1982). The power motive as an influence on group decision making. *Journal of Personality and Social Psychology, 42,* 178–185.

6. McAdams, D.P. (1984). Human motives and personal relationships. In V. Derlega (Ed.), *Communication, intimacy, and close relationships* (pp. 41–70). New York: Academic Press.

7. Winter, McClelland, & Stewart, *A new case for the liberal arts: Assessing institutional goals and student development.*

8. Winter, D.G. (1988). The power motive in women—and in men. *Journal of Personality and Social Psychology, 54,* 510–519. Winter argues that women are subjected to high levels of responsibility training in childhood, which ultimately softens their expressions of power motivation. Men who are also trained in this way should likewise show socially responsible expressions of the motive. Research he reports in this article supports this idea in that it shows that men who have had younger siblings (for whom they have assumedly engaged in baby-sitting and/or other nurturant and mentoring activities) and who are high in power motivation do not show the "profligate" forms of behavior traditionally associated with high power motivation in men (e.g., aggression and impulsive behavior). High-power women who have had younger siblings also show relatively low levels of profligate behavior, whereas high-power women who have not had younger siblings tend to show somewhat elevated levels of profligate behavior.

9. McAdams, D.P., Healy, S., & Krause, S. (1984). Social motives and patterns of friendship. *Journal of Personality and Social Psychology, 47,* 828–838.

10. McAdams, "Human motives and personal relationships."

11. In fearing conflict, the high-power person expresses concern over a possible clash between active agents. For agentic relationships to work well, the friends must tolerate, even condone, each other's agentic strivings, and each other's ventures of self-expansion, self-assertion, and self-display. Conflict threatens to break down the equilibrium that has supported the agentic strivings of the friends. It is not surprising, therefore, that Winter (1973) found that high-power men carefully try to avoid the possibility of conflict in their relationships with peers. McAdams, "Human motives and personal relationships." Winter, *The power motive.*

12. McClelland, *Human motivation.* Winter & Carlson, "Using motives scores in the psychobiographical study of the individual: The case of Richard Nixon."

13. Entwisle, D.R. (1972). To dispel fantasies about fantasy-based measures of achievement motivation. *Psychological Bulletin, 77,* 377–391.

14. Mahone, C.H. (1960). Fear of failure and unrealistic vocational aspiration. *Journal of Abnormal and Social Psychology, 60,* 253–261.

15. Veroff, J. (1982). Assertive motivations: Achievement versus power. In A.J. Stewart (Ed.), *Motivation and society* (pp. 99–132). San Francisco: Jossey-Bass.

16. Kock, S.W. (1965). *Management and motivation.* English summary of a doctoral dissertation presented at the Swedish School of Economics, Helsinki, Finland.

17. Singh, S. (1978). Achievement motivation and entrepreneurial success: A follow-up study. *Journal of Research in Personality, 12,* 500–503.

18. Stewart & Chester, "Sex differences in human social motives: Achievement, affiliation, and power."

19. Baruch, R. (1967). The achievement motive in women: Implications for career development. *Journal of Personality and Social Psychology, 5,* 260–267.

20. Bloom, A.R. (1971). *Achievement motivation and occupational choice: A study of adolescent girls*. Unpublished doctoral dissertation, Bryn Mawr College.

21. Like masculinity, femininity can apply to both men and women. Ickes (1981) defines femininity as a relatively "reactive, emotionally responsive, and expressive" sex-role orientation (p. 96). A man or woman scoring high on femininity attributes to the self a number of characteristics that have traditionally been associated with the female sex role: compassionate, gentle, yielding, interpersonally oriented, etc. Ickes, "Sex-role influences in dyadic interaction: A theoretical model."

22. McAdams, "A thematic coding system for the intimacy motive."

23. McAdams, D.P., & Powers, J. (1981). Themes of intimacy in behavior and thought. *Journal of Personality and Social Psychology*, 40, 573–587.

24. McAdams, D.P., & Constantian, C.A. (1983). Intimacy and affiliation motives in daily living: An experience sampling analysis. *Journal of Personality and Social Psychology*, 45, 851–861.

25. McAdams, D.P., Jackson, R.J., & Kirshnit, C. (1984). Looking, laughing, and smiling in dyads as a function of intimacy motivation and reciprocity. *Journal of Personality*, 52, 261–273.

26. McAdams, "Human motives and personal relationships."

27. McAdams, D.P., & Vaillant, G.E. (1982). Intimacy motivation and psychosocial adjustment: A longitudinal study. *Journal of Personality Assessment*, 46, 586–593.

28. McAdams & Bryant, Intimacy motivation and subjective mental health in a nationwide sample.

29. McAdams, D.P., Lester, R., Brand, P., McNamara, W., & Lensky, D.B. (1988). Sex and the TAT: Are women more intimate than men? Do men fear intimacy? *Journal of Personality Assessment*, 52, 397–409.

30. A full discussion of this appears in my book, *Intimacy: The need to be close*, chpt. 6.

31. Buber, M. (1970). *I and thou*. New York: Charles Scribner's Sons, p. 62.

32. I rely here on C.S. Lewis and his description of four different kinds of love: storge, philia, eros, and agape. See: Lewis, C.S. (1960). *The four loves*. New York: Harcourt Brace.

Appendix 2

1. The reconstructive nature of memory has become a sine qua non of modern cognitive psychology. See Bartlett, F.C. (1932). *Remembering*. Cambridge: Cambridge University Press. Bolles, E.B. (1988). *Remembering and forgetting: Inquiries into the nature of memory*. New York: Walker & Co.

2. The following section on the John F. Kennedy assassination is adapted from my book: McAdams, *The person*, pp. 516–518.

3. Brown, R., & Kulik, J. (1977). Flashbulb memories. *Cognition*, 5, 73–99.

4. Neisser, U. (1982). *Memory observed: Remembering in natural contexts*. San Francisco: W.H. Freeman.

5. Ibid, p. 48.

6. McAdams, *Power, intimacy, and the life story*, chpt. 5.

7. Ibid, p. 143.

8. Ibid.

9. The eight categories of themes for agency and communion are derived from Chapter 5 of *Power, intimacy, and the life story*. A coding manual for using these themes in psychological research is available from the author: Dan P. McAdams, Human Development and Social Policy, Northwestern University, 2003 Sheridan Road, Evanston, IL 60208.

Index

commitment:
  to adult identity, 93–95, 97–98
  flexibility vs., 111
  generativity and, 237–238
  to work, 190–192
communion, 287–291
  agency vs., 71–73, 202, 204, 281–282
  as feminine value, 88–89, 148, 201–202, 287
  generativity and, 230–232, 239, 248–250
  ideological settings and, 87, 88–89
  imago types and, 123, 124, 133, 134, 148–161, 204, 206, 208, 281
  in life-story motifs, 259, 297, 298
  of love vs. intimacy, 72–73, 289–290
compensatory strategy, 103, 105–107
concern, generativity and, 233–235
concrete operations, 68
Confessions (St. Augustine), 32
conjunctive faith, 183–184, 201
Cosmopolitan, 125
Costa, Paul, Jr., 196
counselor (imago), 124, 208
creativity, 197, 199, 207, 209, 238, 239
cultural immortality, 226–227, 231
cynicism, 108–109, 205–206

D

Daniels, Susan (pseud.), 157–158, 167, 168
Darrow, Clarence, 206, 207
Darwin, Charles, 121
David Copperfield (Dickens), 199
Dawkins, Richard, 223, 231
death:
  heroic denial of, 224–227
  mid-life attitudes toward, 198, 202, 227
"Death and the Mid-life Crisis" (Jacques), 199
death instincts, 71
demand, generativity and, 232–233
Demeter, 124, 155
Denial of Death, The (Becker), 224
denouement, 26, 27
desire, generativity and, 230–232
de St. Aubin, Ed, 174
developmental change, personological change vs., 270–275
dialectical thinking, 201
Dickens, Charles, 199
dynastic strategy, 103–104

E

early adulthood:
  commitments begun in, 93–95, 97–98
  culmination of, 100–101
  developmental arc of, 95–102, 271
  four personal myth strategies used in, 103–109
  future dreams in, 98, 101
  mentoring relationships in, 98–99
  personal myth development in, 36–37
Earth Mother, 225
ego integrity, 12, 96, 278
ego rejuvenation, 203
Elkind, David, 80
Empedocles, 70
environmental concerns, 239
Erikson, Erik:
  on adolescent quest for ideology, 80–81
  adult perspective analyzed by, 91
  on ego integrity, 12, 96, 278
  generativity discussed by, 227–228, 229, 232, 235–236
  on hope, 47
  on identity formation as early developmental stage, 95–96, 272
erotic love, 290–291
escapist (imago), 124, 171–172
evangelism, 130
existentialism, 82, 165–166
Exodus, Book of, 128

F

Facts, The (Roth), 32–33
fairy tales, 31, 55
faith:
  as basis of identity, 174–179
  conjunctive, 183–184, 201
  developmental stages of, 179–186
  existentialist views on, 165–166
  individuative-reflective stage of, 181–182
  as knowing vs. relating, 179
  ministerial service and, 177
  postmodern spiritual quest and, 187, 192–193
  research studies on, 179
  synthetic-conventional stage of, 180–181
  see also religion; *specific religions*
family:
  career vs., 99, 101, 119, 190–192
  in childhood imagery, 60–61
  in early adulthood, 97, 98
  as feminine realm, 120
  generational transitions within, 198
  generative focus on, 233–234
  nineteenth-century industrialization and, 119–120
  parental age and, 118–119
  in two-career households, 101

Index

Houdini, Harry, 169
humanist (imago) 124, 207–208, 244–245, 247
hypnotism, 120

I

identity:
  adolescent quest for, 40, 75–80
  commitment to, 93–95
  faith as basis of, 174–179
  ideological setting developed for, 36, 80–81,
    82, 84, 86, 185–186
  personality vs., 266
  Western individualism and, 82–84
Identity (Baumeister), 83
identity development:
  change vs. continuity managed in, 95
  early experimentation and, 92–93, 271–272
  individual needs balanced with social forces
    in, 94–95
  as lifelong process, 95–102, 232
  multiple social selves and, 115, 117–118,
    125–126
  youthful experimentation and, 92–93
ideology:
  adolescent explorations of, 36, 67, 77–78,
    80–81, 84–86, 89–90, 271
  adult commitment to, 94
  agentic theme vs. communal theme for, 87–
    89, 281
  for complexity and paradox, 183–186
  content vs. structure of, 87
  faith and, 179
  life-story interview questions on, 262–263
  sex-based perspectives and, 88–89
  Western cultural changes and, 82–84
illness, optimism and, 48, 49–50
imagery:
  cultural roots of, 60–65
  familial models for, 60–61
  of personal myths, 55, 61, 64, 257, 271
  preschooler's involvement with, 35–36, 53–
    59, 61–63, 65, 271
imagoes, 122–132
  agentic, 123, 124, 133, 134–148, 204, 206,
    208, 281
  common classifications of, 123–125
  communal, 123, 124, 133, 134, 148–161, 204,
    206, 208, 281
  cultural values reflected in, 129–130
  defined, 37, 122
  Greek mythology linked to, 123–124, 136,
    140, 141–142, 144, 148–149, 155, 157,
    158, 207–208

as idealized patterns, 124
integrative, 204–211, 220–221, 272
Jungian archetypes vs., 133–134
life conflicts developed through, 37, 132,
  137
life-story illustrations of, 127, 128, 136–140,
  142–160, 167–168, 204–211, 243, 244–
  245, 247
multiple aspects of self addressed through,
  122–123, 147, 208–211
opening scenes for, 128–129
personal goals expressed by, 127–128
positive vs. negative, 125
possible selves as, 128
refinement of, 36–37, 272
self-ascribed traits personified by, 129
significant others as models for, 130–131
six basic principles of, 127–132
social roles vs., 126–127, 167–168
see also specific imagoes
immortality, 224–227, 231–232
In a Different Voice (Gilligan), 88–89
independent citizen, American cultural type as,
  129–130
individualism:
  agentic emphasis on, 87
  social responsibility vs., 87–88, 94–95, 188–
    190, 268–269
  in Western civilization, 82–84, 96
individuation, 201
industrial societies, 82, 84, 119–120,
  187
infancy:
  attachment system developed in, 40–44, 47,
    48, 271
  basic selfhood established in, 44–46
  personal myth development in, 35, 40
internalized objects, 60
interview process, 251–264
  listener selected for, 254–255
  protocol suggested for, 256–264
  psychological aspects of, 251–253
intimacy, 23, 36, 72–73, 95, 287–291,
  299
Intimacy (McAdams), 287
irony, as mythic form, 50, 52, 53
I-Thou relation, 289–290

J

"Jack and the Beanstalk," 31
James, William, 70, 115, 122
Jaques, Elliott, 195, 199, 201
Jehovah's Witnesses, 236–237

Index

Sartre, Jean-Paul, 17, 65, 165, 166
Saul, Leon, 219
Scarlet Letter, The (Hawthorne), 81, 119
Schopenhauer, Arthur, 120
Schorschi, Ernst, 214
science, 29, 181, 201
Scopes, John, 206
self, 44–47
  conscious vs. unconscious, 120–121
  distorted sense of, 44–45
  multiplicity of, 115, 117–118, 120–122, 131
  ontologies of, 103–109
  possible, 128
  society vs., 87–88, 94–95, 188–190, 268–269
  subjective, 45–46
  verbal, 46–47
self-absolutory strategy, 103, 107–109
self-actualization, 70
self-esteem, mother-infant mirroring interaction and, 46
self-help books, 268, 270
Sesame Street, 65
sex, lies, and videotape, 251–252
sex differences:
  in agency vs. communion, 88–89, 134, 148, 201–202, 282, 287
  careers and, 99, 100–101, 286–287
  in early-adult dreams of future, 98
  in generative concerns, 234–235
  identity development and, 92, 96
  imago types and, 134, 135–136
  on individual rights vs. social responsibility, 88–89
  intimacy motivation and, 289
  power motivation and, 283–284
  of work world vs. family realm, 120
sex roles:
  cultural stereotypes of, 23, 282
  mid-life reevaluation of, 201–202
sexual infidelity, 119
sexuality, adolescent, 76–77
Shakespeare, William, 128, 199
Shaver, Bob (pseud.), 173–174
Sheehy, Gail, 195
situation comedies, 27
Snow White and the Seven Dwarfs, 53–54, 69
Sobel, Sam (pseud.), 166–168
social class, identity development and, 92, 96
social clock, 197, 233
socialization, 60

social responsibility:
  generative expression of, 228, 229, 233, 239, 269
  individual priorities vs., 87–88, 94–95, 188–190, 268–269
"Song of Myself" (Whitman), 118
splitting, 131
Stages of Faith (Fowler), 179
stagnation, 166–174
Steiner, Rudolf, 192–193
Stern, Daniel, 45
Stevenson, Adlai, 242, 247
Stewart, Abigail, 229
storge, 291
stories:
  children's comprehension of, 35–36
  consistent features of, 24–26
  healing power of, 31–33
  human affinity for, 27–30
  ideological development and, 84–85, 90
  motivational themes in, 67–69
  repeating structural components of, 25–26
  on television, 27
  temporal existence reflected in, 30
  truth presented in, 28–29
story grammar, 25
Streep, Meryl, 169
Students for Racial Equality, 243
subjective self, 45–46
Sullivan, Harry Stack, 157
survivor (imago), 124, 209–211
Swanson, Betty (pseud.), 151–156, 269
Swift, Jonathan, 224
symbolic play, 59

T
TAT (Thematic Apperception Test), 282, 283, 287, 289
Taylor, Shelley, 49–50
teacher (imago), 124, 208–209, 211, 220, 221
Teenage Mutant Ninja Turtles, 65
television, 27, 64–65
Ten Commandments, 88
Terkel, Studs, 228, 239
Thematic Apperception Test (TAT), 282, 283, 287, 289
theme, 67–69
thrownness, 82
time, narrative expression of, 30
Tiresias, 142
Tolstoy, Lev, 168
tradition, preservation of, 238–239
tragedy, as mythic form, 50, 51–52, 53